Musicals

CARLTON

Musicals

THE COMPLETE ILLUSTRATED STORY
OF THE WORLD'S MOST POPULAR LIVE
ENTERTAINMENT

Kurt Gänzl

THIS IS A CARLTON BOOK

Text copyright © 1995 Kurt Gänzl
Design copyright © 1995 Carlton Books Limited

First published in 1995 by Carlton Books Limited

10 9 8 7 6 5 4 3 2 1

A CIP catalogue record for this book is available
from the British Library

ISBN 0 74752 381 9

Project Editor: Tessa Rose
Copy Editor: Caroline Richmond
Design: Alyson Kyles
Project Art Direction: Paul Messam/Fiona Knowles
Picture Research: Sharon Hutton
Production: Sarah Schuman

Printed and bound in Italy

Carlton Books Limited
20 St Anne's Court, Wardour Street
London W1V 3AW

PICTURE ACKNOWLEDGEMENTS

The publishers would like to thank the following sources for their kind permission to
reproduce the photographs in this book:

AKG London; The British Musical Theatre Collection; Camera Press/ASP, Karsh of Ottawa;
Jean-Loup Charmet; Zoe Dominic; ET Archive; The Ronald Grant Archive; The Hulton
Deutsch Collection; Peter Joslin; The Kinema Collection; The Mander & Mitchenson Theatre
Collection; Pictorial Press; Range Bettmann UPI, Springer Collection; Rex Features/Eugene
Adebari, Maria Grazia Archetti, Donald Cooper, Clive Dixon, Percy Hatchman, Nils Jorgensen,
The Times, Today, Michael Le Poer Trench, Valentin, Richard Young.

CONTENTS

PREFACE

Most of us who love musicals have a special fondness for one particular part or period of the musical theatre – whether it be the nineteenth-century pieces of such composers as Offenbach and Strauss, the tongue-in-cheek comic operas of Gilbert and Sullivan, the dance-musicked musical comedies and robustly romantic musicals of the years between the wars, the shows of the great Broadway days of the 1950s and 1960s, or the new wave of *fin de* this *siècle* mega-musicals that have been the highlights of the most recent decades on the musical stage. But most of us also know that, alongside our own favourite kind of show, all those other kinds – and a whole host of others – exist as well, and that these eras and styles of story-song-and-dance show are each just one part of the same phenomenon – the phenomenon we nowadays call the "musical".

Our perception of the musical theatre and the shows it has produced over the years has ended up a bit like an underground railway network. We know about the various stops on the system, especially the ones we use all the time, but we haven't got too much of an idea how one of them joins up with another when we're wandering around the city streets on the earth's surface. "Please, constable, how do I get from 'Beggar's Opera' to 'Lloyd Webber'?"

That's what this book is going to try to do. To mark out that broad musical-theatre road from the eighteenth century down to the present day in a very brief survey of what has gone on on the mainstream musical stages of the Western world.

You'll notice that I shy very purposefully clear of the word "development" in that sentence. That word has somehow come to imply progress or improvement (which is doubtless why property "developers" have hijacked it), and it's pretty evident that the shows of today aren't "better" than those of a hundred or a hundred and fifty years ago. Give or take the dramatic and musical ways of expression of their times, they're not even all that different. "Development" has also come to suggest a connected scheme of onward-going "influences", and it would take a

determined scholar to winkle out such a one-thing-leads-to-another scheme! The theatre has never been a logical business, or one that went in nice, tidy, straight lines.

I think – I hope – that this telling of the story of the modern musical theatre will reserve the odd surprise for you. For, over the years, that story has got a touch distorted, thanks partly to theatre publicists with a fine line in memorable blarney, partly to writers and commentators with a point to "prove" or a national flag to wave (I'm a New Zealander, and I guess that's about as unaligned as you can get), and partly through the proselytizing of folk with a royalty to earn. All that is quite natural, but not good for the what-actually-happened type of history. Which is, of course, in any case not the kind of history for which showbusiness is best known – try dipping into a few theatrical biographies!

Similarly, whilst some "names" have held their fame down the years, other theatre-people equally as worthy have been unfairly forgotten. I hope I can do just a little bit here towards putting some of those down-the-years injustices right. Sometimes, even more momentously, it seems as if a whole chunk of the musical theatre's history has been quite simply wiped out. Who, for example, remembers the French musical comedies of the 1920s? And yet they were the greatest musical comedies of their era. I hope they'll soon find their way back to their deserved spot in history.

But, most of all, I hope that reading this little history will encourage you to reach outside of your own up-to-now preferred part of the musical theatre and have a look at one or two of the other parts – or, eventually, at all of them. Because there's a wealth of wonderful musical theatre out there, demanding to be heard and seen and played, and not just to become a name in a History of the Musical Theatre.

Merry musical-theatregoing

Kurt Gänzl

May 1995

'Longjumeau-eau-eau!'

Le Postillon de Longjumeau
The tale of the top-D-singing coachman who leaves his brand-new wife to go off to the big city and become an opera star.

Early Days

Ever since the theatre itself began, somewhere back in the mists of antiquity, there has been musical theatre as well. For in spite of what some folk would have us believe, the musical – as it is now rather ungrammatically called – wasn't invented half a century back by a chap called Roger N. Hammerstein. Nor was it dreamed up by a bundle of American popular songwriters in the 1920s.

The beginnings of the history of the musical lie much, much further back in time: beyond Victorian London's famous era of musical plays, beyond the twin great ages of the Austro-Hungarian operetta, beyond the comic operas of Gilbert and Sullivan, and beyond the two magnificent flowerings of the French musical theatre, the nineteenth century opéra-bouffe and the jazz-age musical comedies of the 1920s.

If the truth were known, there was probably a thriving musical theatre in ancient Babylon, and the ancient Greeks and Romans clearly produced something quite close to what we now call a "musical" with their semi-sung dramas and tragedies and their smutty- or topical-song-studded comedies and satyr plays. Sadly, their *Mia bella matronas* and *Jupiter Pluvius Superstellas* have come down to us, when they have come down to us, mostly without their music. So we'll never know what show tunes kept Athenian toes tapping.

But this swift survey of the history of mainstream musical theatre in our Western world is really intended to look largely at more recent times. So, now that we've given Caesar his nod, let's leap forward a couple of handfuls of centuries, to at least relatively modern times, and to the theatre as we know it – for the most part – today: four walls and a roof, a proscenium arch, an orchestra pit and so forth.

In the eighteenth century, and even the earliest part of the nineteenth century, what audiences enjoyed as musical theatre fell into two fairly distinct halves. And this not just in Britain and its English-speaking colonies, but in the other two main strongholds of light musical theatre: the French and German countries. On the one hand, there were the popular entertainments – the comic and romantic-comic plays and what the French called *vaudevilles*, the fairytale or fantastical spectaculars, and the burlesques – classical, topical, whimsical and/or low comical. Shows such as these were normally accompanied by a "pasticcio" score, one made up almost entirely from borrowed tunes: popular melodies or pieces pilfered from other – again, not necessarily original – stage shows, and set with fresh words which had more or less to do with the show in progress.

The most famous early example of this kind of show in the English-language theatre was John Gay's 1728 "Newgate pastoral" *The Beggar's Opera*, a tart, lowlife tale of thieves and whores intended – like similar pieces in later days – to deliciously shock while it entertained. The score put together for this show by Dr Pepusch reused tunes ranging from such popular old melodies as "Over the Hills and Far Away" to upmarket music

The Beggar's Opera

Veluti in speculum . . . Just as in a mirror . . . folk like Hogarth enjoyed emphasizing the social-satirical side of John Gay's show, but the theatre-going public has enjoyed it down the years largely as a merry bit of lowlife musical comedy.

borrowed from the works of Purcell, Handel and the Italian opera composers, all purposefully reset with Gay's lyrics.

The second main class of musical theatre was one that was considered more artistically ambitious, mainly because it boasted music that was specially written for the show in question rather than this kind of musical scissors-and-paste score. Many of these were just little musicals with anodyne plots about marquises and milkmaids and marital high- and low-jinks, and an often equally anodyne score of half a dozen or more songs and ensembles. But others were written on a larger scale, and, at various times and in various countries, they ranged very close to romantic or grand opera in their musical and textual styles.

The descriptions "comic opera", "*opéra-comique*" or "*Singspiel*" that were applied to many of these pieces – effectively to differentiate their intentions from the more lofty Italian "opera" – were often only a shadowy guide to content. These terms – like many other musical-theatre terms – seemed to change their meaning from decade to decade, and at one stage such a title appeared only to indicate that the piece in question was made

up of music and dialogue, rather than being sung through in the operatic manner – certainly not that it was necessarily in any way funny or even light-hearted. However, there were plenty of shows – particularly those composed for the hugely productive French stage by such musicians as Philidor, Grétry, Adam, Boïeldieu or Auber – which were squarely in the manner of what we would think of as "musicals" rather than "opera".

The three parallel musical theatre traditions of the time – English-, French- and German-language – didn't each exist in isolation. They fed on one another more than happily. Many producers and writers in Britain, and in the German-speaking countries, helped themselves to the melodies of the French *opéra-comique* composers, and even to their authors' tales, and blatantly or by omission claimed them as their own work. In fact, a large part of London's musical theatre in the eighteenth century consisted of made-over versions of the great French shows of the era. On the other hand, one of the most successful musicals of the blossoming German light musical stage in these years was a piece called *Der Teufel ist los*, which was none other than a remade version of the London musical hit

The Devil to Pay. This story of a brutal working man and an imperious noblewoman, cured of their bad characters by being magically given to each other as mates, was redecorated for the German stage with a score of original music.

As the half-way mark of the nineteenth century drew near, each European tradition was well settled in its double convention. The popular and often pasticcio musical plays and burlesques that each enjoyed were mostly played only in their country of origin, and only occasionally proved the stuff of which revivals are made, but the more musically substantial "comic operas" or "romantic operas", shows normally based on more substantially dramatic plots and characters, included a number that turned out to be long surviving standards.

Britain's list of favourites was topped by two pieces by talented Irishmen – two pieces that combined sentimental stories with a score of light operatic music. One was Michael Balfe's 1843 *The Bohemian Girl*, a story of a lost aristocratic child and a bunch of gypsies, and the other was *Maritana*, Vincent Wallace's 1845 version of the already much musicalized *Don César de Bazan* story. Both shows produced enormous song hits – "I Dreamt that I Dwelt in Marble Halls", "Ah! Let Me Like a Soldier Fall" – and stayed prominent on the world's stages for more than half a century.

In France, Auber and Adam held the lion's share of the musical limelight. Adam – most famous nowadays for his ballet music to *Giselle* – scored an international hit with the tale of a singing coachman turned stage star in *Le Postillon de Longjumeau*, and with the top-D hitting solo he provided for his tenor. Auber's most enduring success was a half-dramatic, half-comic tale of bungled banditry whose hero was called *Fra Diavolo* and which helped lead a generation of musical-writers into more, or usually much less serious versions of theatrical banditland.

In Germany, the most successful single composer of *komische Oper* was Albert Lortzing, whose *Zar und Zimmermann*, a musical about Peter the Great, Tsar of the Russias, and what happens when he decides to impersonate a shipyard worker, was played all round the world.

This, then, was the position in the musical theatre when the development took place that has made so many people, myself included, use the mid-nineteenth century as the take-off point for a survey of what might be called "the modern musical theatre". I suppose the simplest way to put it – at the risk of being simplistic – is to say that the middle ground between the two existing areas of musical theatre caved in. Instead of there being just pasticcio burlesques and comic operas, we now get a sophisticated version of the subject-matter of burlesque combined with music of a substance and value previously lavished only on light opera. And from this coupling came a new genre, the *opéra-bouffe* – opera-burlesque. Not burlesque of opera: opera hyphen burlesque. From this time on, the pasticcio show became a rarity in any but the most unsophisticated circumstances, and "romantic opera" of the *Bohemian Girl* type was shunted purely into operatic regions. The crazy gaiety and laughing music turned out by the greatest masters of the *opéra-bouffe* soon swamped all but the best and best-loved shows and styles of the past centuries, pushing them half way to oblivion as this new kind of musical engulfed the world's stages in a way that no body of light musical theatre had ever done before.

Zar und Zimmermann
A contemporary folio showing the characters of Lortzing's *komische Oper*. The Tsar himself is looking very shipyard worker-ish in the top left-hand corner of the image.

'Buzz, Buzz, Ber-uzzz!'

Orphée aux enfers
The King of the Gods disguises
himself as a fly for immoral
purposes. Johann Nestroy as
Jupiter in the show's original
Vienna production.

French Fizz

The famous family of French opéras-bouffes didn't just spring fully armed out of the heads of their creators one day in the mid-nineteenth century, ready to dazzle the world. They were a good while a-borning, and in the decade before the first of the series, Orphée aux enfers, burst onto the stage, there was a whole host of less ambitious specimens of the same kind of show produced in Parisian theatres: little pieces described as opérette-bouffe, bouffonnerie musicale, folie musicale or even something a bit more extravagant: "a musical cannibal-meal" for a piece about a hungry South-Seas Queen, or "a musical piece of China" for something apparently oriental.

They were pieces that were written with a zany, Monty-Pythonesque type of burlesque humour, extravagantly – even ridiculously – funny, and each was decorated with a score of six or eight or ten songs and ensembles that were set with specially composed rather than borrowed music. Music that was willing and eager to echo the crazy flavour of the story and fit the most madcap moments of the text. But, of course, these little pieces were just that. Little. They were only one act long, and made to be played just as one part of a *spectacle coupé* – those three- or four- or even five-part programmes that were featured on many playbills of the day.

The man who usually gets the credit for "inventing" this kind of mad mini-musical is the actor, singer, playwright, musician, composer, conductor, theatre-manager and producer who called himself just Hervé. And the show that loosed this loopy theatrical genius on the Paris stage in 1848 was a far-fetched little two-hander about Don Quixote and Sancho Panza. It took five further years, however, before the *opérette-bouffe* and its rather special kind of humour got up speed. In 1853, Hervé supplied the music for a "*fantaisie bouffe*" called *Les Folies dramatiques*, produced at the Palais-Royal. It caught the royal ear, he the royal favour, and as a result Hervé was granted a licence to

Above: **Hervé**

His lyrics and libretti were as wonderfully way-out as his music was marvellously madcap (caricature of 1868 from *L'Éclipse*).

Right: ***Orphée aux enfers***

Offenbach's music for the world's first full-sized *opéra-bouffe* went round the world, both in its original form and arranged and re-arranged into endless sets of dance music.

open a theatre of his own, where he wrote, composed, produced and even appeared in a whole run of the kind of little shows in which he specialized.

Bit by bit, this kind of well-musicked *opérette-bouffe* began to catch on, and soon the first real hits in the new style began to appear. Only the name that was attached to them wasn't Hervé's. It was that of Jacques Offenbach. Offenbach was a German-Parisian who'd spent a number of frustrating years trying to break into the French musical establishment, but with little success. So, in 1855, he decided to imitate Hervé's enterprising way of getting his shows produced, and he opened his own little theatre – a little theatre where the main entertainment was, of course, his own little works.

Those works, like it or not, had to be little, because the laws that controlled commercially-run play-houses in Paris at this time were very strict. Offenbach, Hervé and their colleagues were only allowed to do shows with up to three speaking or singing characters in them. It was a law that meant there was no chance of any independent theatre mounting a challenge to the well-

protected position of the big state theatres, who thus held a monopoly on big – and even middle-sized – productions. But Offenbach – like others before and after him – proved that bigger very often isn't better, and that wit and charm can win out over brainless spectacle. The very first programme at his Théâtre des Bouffes-Parisiens included a major hit – a comical little musical about the rivalry between two not-so-blind beggars called *Les Deux Aveugles*. Before his first season was over, Offenbach's theatre was prospering merrily and he'd turned out two further contrasting hits that were small only in their cast numbers. One was the endearing little country tale of *Le Violoneux* and the other a sizzling piece of *bouffonnerie* that almost out-loopied Hervé himself – the crazy Chinoiserie *Ba-ta-clan*, with its tale of shipwrecked Parisians in oriental places.

Before too long, the restrictions that hampered independent producers and writers were eased, and, after four years in business, Offenbach was able to mount a full-length, large-cast musical in his theatre. He chose to gamble on a full-sized burlesque, an *opéra-bouffe* – a piece that sent up the sacred traditions of the serious, state-supported stage. For the first full-sized musical at the Bouffes-Parisiens was nothing less than a madcap *bouffon* version of the story operatically immortalized in one of the Paris Opéra's most revered repertoire pieces, Gluck's 1762 opera *Orphée et Eurydice*.

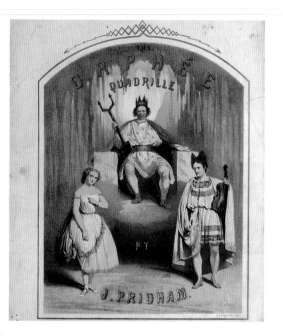

Orphée aux enfers

Very often, the first really successful example of a fresh kind of show to hit the boards remains – in spite of the subsequent arrival of more or equally well-loved successors in the same style – one of the great survivors of its genre. Orphée aux enfers is one such. Nearly a century and a half after its first showing it is still played all round the world, and is probably the most generally popular of all opéras-bouffes in the last years of the twentieth century.

What better ending for a girl like the saucy Eurydice? To the strains of the famous *Galop infernale*, she goes off to be a boozy Bacchante.

If it still makes an effect nowadays, when the Greek-mythological and operatic subjects of its burlesque mean little to the majority of theatregoers, you can imagine what hilarity and huffing it caused in 1858 Paris when it was played before a public brought up on the Classics – and ready to catch every nuance of parody – and on the venerable operas of Gluck. Some idea of the riskiness of the project can be gathered from the fact that co-librettist Ludovic Halévy refused to allow his name to be put on the programme lest it harm his advancement in the diplomatic corps.

The *opéra-bouffe* Orpheus dreamed up by Halévy and Hector Crémieux is far from the noble, lute-playing, wife-loving star of Greek legend – or the bulky contralto hero of the opera-house. He is a fairly dreary Theban music-teacher who plays a mean violin and – less successfully – the field with the local population of nymphs and shepherdesses. Eurydice, his scatty if eye- and ear-catching wife, is bored to the tip of her well-tuned tonsils with him. The lines of the old story are followed more or less faithfully to start with. Eurydice duly gets whipped off to hell for a bit of hanky-panky with Pluto, Lord of the Underworld, but in this version Orpheus definitely doesn't want her back. Then that awful busybody called Public Opinion gets in on the act, and, as a result of all her squeals and squalls about the sanctity of marriage, Orpheus and the whole population of Mount Olympus, Jupiter at their head, head for Hell to get the situation sorted out. Trouble revs up when Jupiter finally gets to see the lady in the case and his motor starts running on overdrive. Things soon turn bedroom-farcical, and Eurydice ends up the object of a four-cornered struggle amongst two Gods who want her, one husband who doesn't, and the Creature who's determined that her legitimate spouse shall take her back, like it or not. Classical legend gets a tasty twist at the end of the evening. As Orphée sulkily leads his wife out of Hell as per tradition, voluminously encouraged by Public Opinion, Jupiter flicks a

CREDITS

Orphée aux enfers

Opéra-bouffe in 2 acts by
Hector Crémieux and
Ludovic Halévy

MUSIC

by Jacques Offenbach

First produced at the Théâtre
des Bouffes-Parisiens, Paris,
21 October 1858, and in a
revised 4-act version at the
Théâtre de la Gaîté, Paris,
7 February 1874

Germany: Breslau, 17
November 1859

Austria: Carltheater, Vienna,
17 March 1860

USA: Stadttheater, New York,
March 1861

UK: Her Majesty's Theatre,
London, 26 December 1865

CAST

Jupiter	Desiré
Orphée	Tayau
Eurydice	Lise Tautin
L'Opinion Publique	
	Marguerite Macé-Montrouge
Pluto	Léonce
John Styx	Bache
Diana	Mlle Chabert

Jacques Offenbach The man
whose merry music helped carry
the sparkling, sexy *opéra-bouffe*
from one side of the world to the
other.

little thunderbolt at his rear end. The scorched tenor instinctively looks back, and Eurydice – thank goodness – is lost. But not, as per legend, to the arms of Pluto. Since the two Gods have fought out a no-score draw over her, it is decided that the lady will be handed over to Bacchus. She will be a bacchante. A very suitable ending for such a saucy soprano.

The music with which Offenbach set *Orphée aux enfers* was well in keeping with the gaiety of the libretto. There were mad moments, there were lively moments, there were moments of burlesque and even of direct parody – including a quote from Gluck – but in a manner that would characterize all of the composer's *opéras-bouffes* there were also numbers of winning lyrical beauty.

The most familiar number from *Orphée aux enfers*, a century and more down the line, is the piece of dance music that's become known as Offenbach's Can-Can. It's actually a *galop*, the *Galop infernale* to which Eurydice and the other bacchantes kick up their heels in the final act. The real gems, however, came in the sung music. Eurydice's tortured duo with her insistently violin-playing husband ("Ah! C'est ainsi"), her mock operatic prayer to death as she succumbs to a Pluto-engineered snakebite in a cornfield ("La Mort m'apparaît"), and her encounter with Jupiter who has turned himself into a fly to get through the keyhole of her bedroom and whose chatting-up routine is conducted in a series of sung buzzing noises ("Il me semble que sur mon épaule") were only the tip of a score which included numbers for Pluto, a selection of other Gods, and a lugubrious and long-dead ex-King with the hots for the heroine, as well as some glittering ensemble writing.

Orphée aux enfers ran a remarkable 228 nights in its first Paris season, and Offenbach's music sped swiftly through Europe, being quickly grabbed by the makers of pasticcio scores to illustrate their shows before the *opéra-bouffe* itself made its way out of France and into other countries and other languages. Little more than a year after its première the first foreign production was mounted in Breslau, and gradually the musical theatre capitals of the world started to pick up on this new kind of musical: first Vienna, then Berlin, then New York's German theatre and

Budapest's German and vernacular houses. The first English-language production was mounted in London in 1865. At this early stage, London didn't know quite what to do with this ever-so-Frenchified *opéra-bouffe*. So the show was tastefully rewritten and staged in the rather less sophisticated style of traditional English burlesque. Needless to say, this emasculated version didn't cause anything like the sensation the real *Orphée* had in Paris. As for America, although it saw a number of productions in the German and French languages from the 1860s onwards, it wasn't till 1883 that Broadway welcomed an English *Orpheus in the Underworld*.

In the meantime, however, Offenbach had done his show over. In 1874, having taken over the management of the big Théâtre de la Gaîté, he revived his first *opéra-bouffe* hit, remodelled to suit it to the dimensions of the Gaîté. The show was stretched to four acts, allowing the inclusion of extra scenery, ballets and new items for several artists, making the Olympus scene into something like a divine concert or variety show. The changes didn't do much for the show, but they made *Orphée* into a spectacular entertainment that pulled good houses. The gussied-up version found a number of productions overseas, but the original sparkling, pointed *opéra-bouffe* has always proved the more satisfying as the show – with intermittent fallow periods – has held its place on the international stage through the decades, even gaining ground – notably in the English-speaking theatre – on other Offenbach shows that had proven more popular than it was first time round.

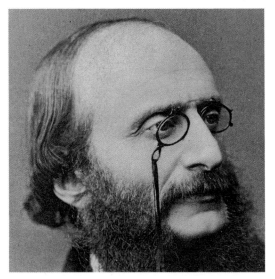

Following the triumph of *Orphée aux enfers*, Offenbach went on to turn out a whole line of musicals written on the same *opéra-bouffe* lines. After his successful revising of classical mythology he turned next to medieval legend, and presented his audiences with a marvellous burlesque perversion of the well-known Golden Legend story of the ill-used *Geneviève de Brabant*. This mighty melodrama was given the same kind of way-out treatment that Orpheus had been handed, and so poor Geneviève found herself hounded through the grotesque perils of the dark, dark forest by the evil regent of Brabant in thoroughly bouffe style, whilst her husband made merry in the south of France instead of going off to the Crusades in accordance with history. Less successful than *Orphée* in France, in spite of some hefty rewrites, *Geneviève de Brabant* nevertheless turned out to be a major hit in Britain, eclipsing in popularity not only the earlier show but almost all of Offenbach's later works.

One of the earliest rewrites put into *Geneviève* was a double-act for a couple of comics. The two of them were tacked pretty transparently into the plot, pursuing the perfectly persecuted heroine of this wonky drama deeper and deeper into the forest. Then they stopped, forgot about the plot, and went into a fall-about routine, complete with a song. That song, which became known to English-language audiences as the Gens d'armes Duo, was to be one of the composer's longest lasting song hits.

Offenbach and his writers sent up the Venice of the Doges in *Le Pont des soupirs*, and made fun of marauding, harem-seeking Turks in Russia in the less successful *Les Géorgiennes*, but they did best when they turned back to classical antiquity and produced a distinctly spicier than usual version of the much theatricalized Siege of Troy saga. This version didn't centre on Achilles or Hector or King Priam or any of those other classical worthies. Its focus was *La Belle Hélène*, otherwise Helen of Troy. This Helen isn't very classical either. She might have the time-honoured face that can launch a thousand ships, but it's the bits of her anatomy below the chin that get most of the attention in Henri Meilhac and Ludovic Halévy's remake of Homer. After all, what's a

girl to do? I mean if the Goddess of Love, no less, goes and promises this particularly handsome shepherd that he can have your body in exchange for giving her some silly old golden apple, well, what can you do? Except lie back and think of Sparta. On the other hand, since the shepherd really is particularly handsome (not to mention a Prince in disguise) and King Menelaus is played by a comedian, why not just let the Trojan War take place?

Offenbach's music for *La Belle Hélène* was in his now well-known style. The Kings of Greece marched onto the stage to the strains of a brisk burlesque march ("Voici les rois de Grèce"), Helen chided Venus for making her a Prince's plaything ("Dis-moi, Vénus") to a lovely melody, a long-legged travesty Orestes bounced out his description of a night on the town ("Au cabaret du Labyrinthe"), and Paris soared out the tenorized story of his famous Judgement ("Au mont Ida trois déesses") and brought the piece to its climax with a leaping Tyrolienne about the joys of sex ("Et tout d'abord, ô vile multitude").

The actress Hortense Schneider scored an enormous hit as *La Belle Hélène*, and whilst the newest Offenbach hit set off to conquer most of the world, the composer, his writers and their producer hurried their star into first one new show and then a second. The first was a fairytale burlesque, a *bouffe* version of the favourite tale of the legendary wife-disposer *Barbe-bleue* or Bluebeard. Mlle Schneider appeared as the murderous knight's last wife, Boulotte, a raunchy country wench who survives what is supposed to be the end of her turn as Mrs Bluebeard, and ends up dragging her legitimate spouse home by his ear to live out the rest of his existence as a hapless henpecked husband.

Although *Barbe-bleue* was an undoubted hit, and one with all the foreign future of its forebears in front of it, its success simply could not compare with that made by the next Meilhac-Halévy-Offenbach vehicle for the saucy Schneider. *La Grande-Duchesse* was a piece that had fun at the expense of persons in power in general and the military in

Geneviève de Brabant
Background: Marie Geistinger, the star and producer of many Viennese premières of Offenbach's works, is seen here in a suitably nifty pair of tights, as Drogan.
Inset: Charles Martel and his crusaders set off for the holy land . . . on the first train from the Gare du Nord.

particular, and it cast the star as a pubescent little Duchess with a suddenly discovered weakness for brawn in uniform. Male Paris – not to mention half the world's aristocracy who'd come to visit the Paris Exposition – went communally weak at the knees as Schneider cooed out her passion for soldiers in "J'aime les militaires", and the public laughed fit to bust as she guyed the military finale of opera in "Voici le sabre de mon père" and again as she flirted outrageously with a thick soldier in the third hit number of the night, "Dites-lui".

La Grande-Duchesse not only won France, and established itself there as perhaps the most enduring of all Offenbach's pieces, but also swept away London, Vienna and – in particular – New York and all the rest of America. It was the show that veritably opened the *opéra-bouffe* floodgates in the United States, and led to a craze for the French musical theatre on American stages that would last for many years.

Eventually, of course, Offenbach was joined on the fast-rolling *opéra-bouffe* bandwagon by one or two other composers, and the most effective amongst them was none other than the man who had started it all, Hervé. Hervé had been having an up and down time. He'd had to give up his theatre after only four seasons, suffering from overwork and exhaustion, and he'd since been working for other folk, as far afield as Egypt. When he finally returned, he was to find that Offenbach and his colleagues had taken the *opéra-bouffe* genre on and up to a new level, and before long he too was turning out full-sized *opéras-bouffes*. He composed a crazed Knights of the Round Table parody (*Les Chevaliers de la table ronde*) and a hugely

Chilpéric
Composer-star Hervé made his entrance astride a real, live horse – just as they do at the venerable Paris Opéra.

successful burlesque of the operas *Guillaume Tell* and *Der Freischütz* and anything else with bows and arrows in it (*L'Oeil crevé*) as well as perhaps the most splendidly preposterous of all *opéras-bouffes*, the mad Merovingian manoeuvrings of randy King *Chilpéric*. *Chilpéric* went on to score a vast hit in Britain, and it proved one of the most important elements in the success of *opéra-bouffe* in English, but at home it was Hervé's hilariously lopsided version of the story of Goethe and Gounod's *Faust* that proved his biggest winner. Hervé composed only the music of *Le Petit Faust*, but in recent years a good number of other authors had caught – and slightly tamed – his crazy style of writing, and the version of *Faust* that he set – with Méphisto a sexy soubrette in tights and Valentin done to death with a kitchen knife – was almost as loopy as if he had written it himself.

The last of the great series of *opéras-bouffes* proper of the 1860s was the Meilhac-Halévy-Offenbach *Les Brigands*, and it was a dazzling bit of comic writing. It had a plot with more disguises and identity swaps than you'd think was possible, all crammed into a piece that burlesqued operatic bandits and complex plots in general to the accompaniment of a typically bristling score. The most popular moment in the score wasn't, oddly enough, any of the tuneful *feux d'artifice* concocted for the singing stars of the piece, but a bit of the first-act finale. The bandits are deep into their wholesale impersonation of an entire Italian embassy when the local militia are heard approaching – with leaden rather than catlike tread – and, as usual, just too late to be useful. The clomp-clomp-clomping march of the carabiniers and their incompetent captain (played by the company's star comic) was the highlight of the night.

But the clomping that had caused such hilarity on the stage soon became a sound that inspired dread rather than mirth. Months after the opening of *Les Brigands*, the Prussian army marched into Paris, putting an end to the glorious days of the French Empire and everything it stood for. By the time Paris was able to raise its head again, a couple of years later, the glitter and glory of those prewar days was gone. The temper of the times was different, and the entertainments that suited the new age were less fabulously frivolous.

Opéra-bouffe still had many brilliant moments to come – beyond France. For, one by one, the main centres – with different lapses of time – began to pick up this exciting new kind of musical play, and one by one they fell hopelessly under its charms. Vienna went mad for Marie Geistinger's portrayal of *Die schöne Helena*, all of New York rushed to see Lucille Tostée's impersonation of *La Grande-Duchesse*, and London was conquered by Hervé in person as he rode onto the Lyceum Theatre stage as *Chilpéric*, and all over again by the buxom Emily Soldene as the little pastrycook hero of *Geneviève de Brabant*. One Berlin paper denounced *opéra-bouffe* as part of a Jewish plot to destabilize the country, but *Die schöne Helena* and *Blaubart* destabilized only the box-offices of Berlin's theatres. Wherever *opéra-bouffe* went, it conquered. Wherever it went, it ensured that musical theatre would never, ever be the same again.

When it went its way, after supplying little more than a decade of sophisticated, satirical, sexy entertainment to audiences who knew how to cope with sophistication, satire and sex, the *opéra-bouffe* had broken new ground in the musical theatre in no unsure way. It had laid the world's stages open to receive more light musical theatre which was neither romantic opera nor marquis-and-milkmaids stuff, nor rough-and-tumble comedy decorated with not-so-new songs. It had laid the foundations of a kind of musical theatre with a witty, comical libretto and its own original score of songs and dances and ensembles: the modern musical.

Opéra not-so-*bouffe*

Even during the heyday of the *opéra-bouffe* in France, that rather special kind of entertainment was not all that there was to see on the Parisian musical stage. A saner, less exotic, more romantic kind of musical existed hand in hand with its more extravagant and highly spiced sister.

In the early days of Offenbach's own theatre, for example, a one-act *opéra-bouffe*, all crazy action and burlesque musical fireworks, would often appear on a programme cheek by jowl with another piece that was nothing but a sweet, straightforward rustic tale, decorated with sweet, straightforward rustic numbers. No tongue in that cheek or anywhere else. And Offenbach and his writers scored as many hits with such charmful but less sophisticated little musicals as *Lischen et Fritzchen*, *Le Violoneux* or *La Rose de Saint-Flour* as they did with their *opérettes-bouffes*.

The composer also went on to score major successes with full-sized musicals that were not written in the all-conquering *bouffe* mode. There was little that was burlesque, for example, in the original version of the essentially romantic *La Périchole*, and the paper-sharp comedy of manners *La Vie parisienne* – written by the same Meilhac and Halévy who penned the burlesque scripts for Offenbach's biggest *opéra-bouffe* hits – found its fun in modern, comic situations and in comedy of character rather than in the droll extravagances of burlesque. *La Vie parisienne* followed the attempts of two young Parisian men-about-town to get their love lives into order, and homed in most particularly on the muddle that one of them gets into when he sets his sights on a Swedish Baroness and takes her and her husband to stay in his home on the pretence that it is an hotel. This show was a piece of crisp comic writing, which Offenbach decorated with crisp, comic music, and the result was a piece that – for all that its writers fashionably called it *opéra-bouffe* – belonged to a different world from *La Grande-Duchesse* or *Barbe-bleue*.

In 1870s Paris, the post-Empire Paris with its post-Empire mood and mores, it was the non-*bouffe* kind of musical play that came back into prominence. The term *opéra-bouffe* itself was soon abandoned, and once again musicals returned to calling themselves "*opéra-comique*", just as the shows from the pre-*opéra-bouffe* days had done. The new *opéras-comiques* might have seemed, on paper, to be not unlike such old ones as Boïeldieu's *Jean de Paris* or Adam's *Postillon de Longjumeau*. Their subject-matter was fairly classic: a mixture of romance and comedy,

La Grande-Duchesse de Gérolstein

"Voici le sabre de mon père" – Hortense Schneider as the loin-stirred Duchess and José Dupuis as the hastily-promoted Fritz.

La Vie parisienne
The slickly funny society situations and characters of Meilhac and Halévy's story were the stuff of real comedy rather than burlesque.

usually stiffened with a solid and well worked-out plot. But the difference could be easily heard, both in the tone of the writing and, above all, in the music. The music that decorated these new shows was light operatic music of the most bubbling, the most glittering kind. Music with a popular ring to it, an informality, a gay warmth and looseness that hadn't been there in the pre-*opéra-bouffe* days. It was almost as if the *opéra-bouffe* writers had loosened the stays of the musical theatre, allowing her now to appear before the world in all her voluptuous glory.

The postwar decade in France was one of the most richly productive eras in all the history of the musical theatre. Memorable shows poured off the Parisian stage, and were gratefully grabbed by the men who ran the rest of the international theatrical world, and whose attention had been thoroughly turned upon the French stage by the vast success of the *opéras-bouffes*. This grabbing – only sometimes a touch indiscriminate – proved to be a great idea, because the French musical stage in the 1870s produced not only more but even bigger hits than it had in the 1860s.

La Fille de Madame Angot

The biggest hit to come out of France in the 1870s was La Fille de Madame Angot. *And it had every right to be the hit that it was, for it was, and is, quite simply one of the best musical plays ever written. It has a book that is amongst the tightest, brightest, most exciting examples of its kind – lashings of politics, lashings of sex, lashings of intrigue, all of it doused in some really virile comedy.*

Plots, politics and passion. Clairette courts arrest with her pet poet's Chanson Politique, while (inset) her schoolfriend Lange goes in for a bit of dangerous double-agenting.

And as for its score, it ranges through the whole cornucopia of musical styles, from the dainty to the belting, and from solos to ensembles of all shapes and sizes. That score was the work of the young Charles Lecocq, already known to the public through his music for the successful *Fleur de thé* and *Les Cent Vierges*. Both those two internationally played shows had been broadly comical pieces, but Clairville's book for *La Fille de Madame Angot* (the other two credited librettists were "ideas men" of one kind or another) had altogether more to it than the merry sexual high-jinks that had been the heart of the matter in its predecessors.

The heroine of the piece, Clairette Angot, is an orphan who has been brought up, with all the advantages their money can buy, by the market folk of Les Halles. Now the time has come for her to be demurely wedded, and her "parents" have chosen the nice if unspectacular wigmaker Pomponnet. But Clairette isn't Mlle Angot for nothing. Her famous fishwife mother, after all, gallivanted with no less a romantic dignitary than the Grand Turk himself. A kind, unsexy wigmaker is not at all the husband material Clairette has in mind. She

CREDITS

La Fille de Madame Angot

Opéra-comique in 3 acts by Clairville, Paul Siraudin and Victor Koning

MUSIC

by Charles Lecocq

Produced at the Théâtre des Fantaisies-Parisiennes, Brussels, 4 December 1872

France: Théâtre des Folies-Dramatiques, Paris, 21 February 1873

UK: St James's Theatre, London, 17 May 1873

USA: Broadway Theater, New York, 25 August 1873

Germany: Friedrich-Wilhelmstädtisches Theater, Berlin, 20 November 1873

Austria: Carltheater, Vienna, 2 January 1874

CAST

Clairette Angot   Pauline Luigini
Mlle Lang   Marie Desclauzas
Ange Pitou   Mario Widmer
Pomponnet   Alfred Jolly
Larivaudière   Chambéry
Louchard   Ernotte
Amaranthe   Mme Delorme
Trénitz   Touzé

would prefer someone like the wild, rebellious poet Ange Pitou. So, on what should be her wedding day, Clairette stands up in the market place, sings one of Pitou's banned anti-government songs, and is whisked off to prison. She doesn't stay there for long, for one of the leading members of the Directoire government is the hyper-powerful Barras, Barras's mistress is the "merveilleuse" Lange, and Lange was Clairette's best friend at school. Lange soon has Clairette and Pitou out of jail, but then the problems really begin. Lange and Barras, it eventuates, are moles, secretly leading a plot against the ghastly government from the inside, a plot that may be on the verge of being discovered. And when Lange and Pitou meet it isn't only Lecocq's music that plays. Clairette is too smart not to notice what's going on, and both the political and the personal plots rise to dangerous peaks before the evening ends on a note more equivocal than conventionally "happy".

Lecocq's score for the show produced a dozen favourite numbers, but there were two pieces that became major hits. One of these was the Quarrelling Duet ("C'est donc toi, Madam' Barras") of the final act – a number that brought both the plot and the show to its climax. Clairette tricks Lange and the faithless Ange Pitou to an amorous rendezvous in a bushy beer garden, and then she pulls a bust. Using language that her fishwife mother would have blenched at, la fille de Madame Angot lets rip at Lange, and Lange – who hasn't been living with a politician for nothing – gives back as good as she gets.

The other big hit helped bring the second act to as effective a climax as this duo did the third. The scene is Lange's home, and when the finale begins her fellow-conspirators are on the way there for a night-time meeting, all disguised in black cloaks and white wigs, and tiptoeing thence to the tune of a droll little half-whispered chorus ("Quand on conspire"). Then, just when everyone is gathered together, a whole regiment of government troops turns up on the doorstep. The conspirators are undone. But Lange isn't fazed. She orders all the lights to be lit, the disguises are thrown away and the windows opened, and when the army blunders into her drawing room the hostess with the mostest is singing her heart out, as half the aristocracy of Paris swirls round

the room to the tune of a glorious waltz ("Tournez, tournez"). This isn't a plot, it's a party. It was a splendid curtain scene but, oddly enough, it wasn't the glorious waltz tune that became the take-home hit of the show . . . it was the funny little chorus!

If the two women dominated the evening, there were nevertheless fine rôles for the baritone playing the put-it-about Pitou, for Pomponnet (who gets his girl, perhaps a bit less than wholeheartedly, in the final reel, as well as a pretty tenor solo), and for comic actors in the parts of the snooping policeman Louchard, Lange's second-string lover – the financier Larivaudière – and above all the "incroyable" Trénitz, an aristocrat effete and foolish in speech and dress who becomes an icy hero under the threat of danger.

La Fille de Madame Angot was initially produced in Brussels, where Lecocq's previous show had first seen the light of stage, and it became a vast and instant hit that ran there for more than 500 nights. Soon the show was on the way to Paris, where its success was thoroughly repeated, and the musical went on to repeated revivals in the years and the decades that followed. The Brussels company took their production to London, and such was the reception that little more than four months later an English version had taken its place. Because of the then current copyright laws the show was up for grabs, and soon English *Angots* were everywhere. At one stage there were three different "versions" being played in three different West End houses. For many years *La Fille de Madame Angot* was probably the most ubiquitous musical on the British and colonial stages, touring in multiple companies and regularly playing metropolitan seasons, but by the time the turn of the century was reached it was seen but rarely outside France. With the removal of the remnants of the nineteenth-century operettic repertoire into the opera-houses, this show, with its exceptionally strong libretto, its two bravura prima donna rôles and its splendid music, would have seemed like a natural for a return. However, the opera-houses have tended to stick mostly to better publicized names than Lecocq's, and at the moment France is alone in regularly repeating the show that held, or at least shared, the top of the pavement, all round the world, in the 1870s and 1880s.

ecocq's show was a vast hit around the world, but almost everywhere it had to share its triumphant top spot with another French musical, Robert Planquette's *Les Cloches de Corneville*. The plot of *Les Cloches de Corneville*, initially put together by a Parisian police inspector and written up into a playable form by the same Clairville who had penned Lecocq's hit, was more than a little less sophisticated than *La Fille de Madame Angot*. In fact, it really looked all the way back to marquises-and-milkmaids days with its story of a dispossessed nobleman's son returning in disguise to reclaim his family's castle. There was even a matching search for a missing heiress who was tidily paired off with our hero at the final curtain. But the star rôle of the show was not the young marquis or the lost lassie. It was the comic-pathetic part of the miserly steward of Corneville castle. Since his master's disappearance all those years ago, Gaspard has faithfully hoarded up the estate's profits. He's hidden the money in a room in the castle, put about a rumour that the place is haunted to keep the nosy locals away, and eventually come to believe the money is his own. But then the young marquis turns up.

Les Cloches de Corneville
A jolly poster for one of the companies that took the show endlessly round Victorian Britain.

Composer Planquette, who'd never written a full-scale musical before, turned out a score that simply glistened with melody, from the ringing tones of the marquis's baritone march song ("Sous les armures") and his recounting of his wandering life at sea ("J'ai fait trois fois le tour du monde") to the heroine's famous legend of the bells, with its digue-digue-don refrain, the soubret's lilting tenor "Va petit mousse" and some splendid ensembles.

Les Cloches de Corneville ran 580 nights in its first Paris production, but it went even better in London, outpointing the rival *H. M. S. Pinafore* and anything else in sight with a record-breaking 704-performance run, before going on to decades of touring and a place, alongside *La Fille de Madame Angot*, as one of the two most internationally successful products of the French nineteenth-century stage.

Both Lecocq and Planquette went on to further successes. The composer of *La Fille de Madame Angot* turned out first an hilarious and sparkling piece of nonsense called *Giroflé-Girofla*, in which the leading lady played a twin sister, desperately trying to be both herself and her missing twin on their double wedding-night, and a delightful musical play called *Le Petit Duc*, the pretty tale of an aristocratic marriage which the families think the participants are too young to consummate. The little Duke and his little Duchess think otherwise, and by the end of the night, after having sung their way through some of the most beautiful music that Lecocq ever wrote, they have proved their point.

Le Coeur et la main, *Le Jour et la nuit* and *La Petite Mariée* were additional Lecocq hits, each of them built on rather more complex and adult sexual imbroglios than *Le Petit Duc* had been, and each both a comical joy and a musical treat. However, the Anglo-Saxon sensibilities of the age meant that these shows travelled less well than Lecocq's biggest hit had done: their libretti had to be at least partly cooled down before they could pass across the English-language stage, and they suffered from this cold shower. Planquette, in contrast, actually wrote his next biggest hit directly for the British stage. After the West End triumph of *Les Cloches de Corneville*, its producer commissioned the French composer to write the score for a London musical version of the *Rip van Winkle* story. The show was a major hit, travelled round the world, was translated back into French, and remained a standard on the French stage for half a century thereafter.

The Empire men fight back

The rise of Lecocq and Planquette, and the size of their biggest hits, didn't completely wipe the old masters of *opéra-bouffe* off the stage, even though both Offenbach and Hervé floundered a bit for a while. Finally, however, they both came back, and each made up with a vengeance for their years out of the brightest of the limelight. Offenbach found the target again first, and when he did he hit the gold twice in quick succession. Both pieces were musicals by the top-notch writing team of Henri Chivot and Alfred Duru, who had originally come into prominence as librettists to Lecocq. They provided the composer with, first, the joyously star-vehicular *Madame Favart*, a spankingly funny tale of the disguises and indignities the famous actress and her husband are put to in escaping the vengeance of a powerful man whose advances Madame Favart has spurned; and then with *La Fille du tambour-major*, a piece set in Franco-Italian wartime and flavouring the story of *opéra-comique*'s umpteenth long-lost child with a lot of farcical action, endearing characters and military displays. If the former work won hands down as a piece of theatre, Offenbach supplied some of his most charming music for the latter, and both went on to worldwide success. *Madame Favart* became one of Britain's all-time favourites, and *La Fille du tambour-major*, which is still occasionally seen in France today, produced in Australia in a vastly spectacular way, became that country's biggest hit of the 1880s.

Hervé took a little longer to reappear at the top, and when he did it was with a kind of musical in a very different vein to Chivot and Duru's ones, and also to those shows with which he had made his name in the 1860s. The manager of the Théâtre des Variétés had produced a *vaudeville* – one of those light-hearted pieces of comic theatre traditionally decorated with borrowed music – as a vehicle for his star, Anna Judic, and, to get out of a last-minute spot, had actually had it decorated with *ponts-neufs*, variations on the repertoire of old tunes musicians had always called on on such occasions. *Niniche* had been a mighty success, more plays of the same kind were ordered, and – pasticcio scores now being seriously *hors de mode* – Hervé was approached to do the music. Judic scored splendid successes in *La Femme à papa*, *La Roussotte* and above all in *Lili* and *Mam'zelle Nitouche*, and the last-named, a farcical tale of a naughty convent-schoolgirl, her *opérette*-writing music-master and a squadron of soldiers, gave the 57-year-old "crazy composer" the most enduring success of his career.

Everybody's doing it

Comedy, and particularly comedy of a sexual kind, was an essential element of the nineteenth-century *opéra-comique* libretto. Comic and/or sexual-comic action permeated each and every show – even a piece such as *La Fille de Madame Angot* with its serious political background – and sex and how to get it, or how to avoid someone else getting it, was the linchpin of a vast number of musical plots. Amongst the most blatant in this field were *La Mascotte* and *La Timbale d'argent*, a piece where – it having been discovered that sex damages your singing voice – our hero swears off it, only to find himself bound to perform conjugally. It proved impossible to disinfect the hugely successful *La Timbale d'argent* for export, and gelded versions of the piece flopped everywhere outside France, but *La Mascotte* somehow got through the moral net surprisingly intact, and went on from its Paris triumph to become a huge success in both the English and German languages (not to mention one or two others).

La Mascotte was written by Chivot and Duru, and its music was from the pen of the newly celebrated Edmond Audran, whose *Le Grand Mogol* and *Les Noces d'Olivette* had already won him international fame. It told the tale of a turkey-girl who brings good luck to whomsoever is her employer – as long as she stays a virgin. So everyone from the King down wants to hire Bettina, and the same everyone also wants to stop her getting into bed with her boyfriend and losing her gift. The evening's action centred almost entirely round this now-she-almost-does-it-now-she-doesn't theme. And there was even a song for the King describing his suitability for the post of husband to the heroine. He's impotent. Perhaps the London censor was wooed by the charm of the music, or perhaps he was swept away by the hit song of the show – because that couldn't have been more ingenuous. The Glou-glou Duo was simply a little song in which Bettina tells her Pippo she likes him better than her turkeys, and he replies that she's better value than his sheep. Like the impotence song, it simply sounded too pretty to be censorable.

Le Petit Duc
The rôle of the teenaged hero of the show was custom-made for Théâtre de la Renaissance prima donna Jeanne Granier.

Miss Helyett

Who saw little Miss Helyett hanging upside down in a bush with her nether regions bared to the breezes? The lass and her papa need to know!

But whyever, *La Mascotte* stayed reasonably intact and became a long-loved favourite.

Audran was to stay on the scene for many years, and to write many more good and successful musicals, but he never topped *La Mascotte*. And the same was true for another composer whose work the Bouffes-Parisiens had mounted shortly before its triumph with *La Mascotte*. Louis Varney's *Les Mousquetaires au couvent*, his first full-length musical, was actually based on an old *vaudeville*, but by the time it got to the stage this rather thin tale of a couple of disguised soldiers carrying off a couple of girls from a convent was in a pretty incoherent state. And, thanks to casting considerations, by the time it came off it was even more shapeless. The central romantic pair had hardly anything to do, and the best songs went to an incidental innkeeping lady and one of those irritating hero's-best-friend characters. This jolly fellow also garnered the best of the loud comedy alongside some rather more endearing stuff for a friendly clergyman. But the show had other qualities. Varney's music was lovely, the unplotworthy rôles appealed to star artists, and *Les Mousquetaires au couvent* joined *La Mascotte* on the top shelf of the French repertoire, even if it didn't export like Audran's piece.

The French musical theatre continued to flourish through the 1880s and even the 1890s, but the period in which the produce of the Paris theatres had dominated the world's musical stages was by then over, and the export rate from France to the rest of the world had slowed severely by the time the 1890s were reached. There were, however, still some pieces that went out from France to success overseas. Audran's *La Cigale et la fourmi* was one. A wholly romantic Chivot and Duru piece about a country lass who goes to the big city, becomes a singing star, gets mixed up with the aristocracy and ends up running home to her good, industrious stay-at-home sister, it was a striking contrast to the same trio's saucy *La Mascotte*, but it nevertheless found favour. So too did the same composer's *La Poupée*, a pretty piece on the ages-old theme of the doll-girl. Some piquancy was gained by making the fellow who falls for the doll-girl a novice monk, with all that signified in the way of sexual awakening, and the main story was paralleled by some lower-jinks which, with the help of Audran's attractive tunes, earned *La Poupée* an enormous success in Germany and one scarcely less in Britain. Audran's other big hit was one more in the vein of *La Mascotte* textually, and it was also – perhaps not coincidentally – a mega-hit only in France. *Miss Helyett* was about a little American Salvation

Army girl who has an accident in the mountains, is left dangling upside down over a ravine, and spends the rest of the night trying to find her rescuer and marry him, for he – alas! – had seen what only a husband may see.

Musical comedy masterpieces

Alongside such fairly traditional, if perhaps slightly decadent, musicals, the French stage of the later years of the nineteenth century also put out a series of what were often called *vaudeville-opérettes*. They were shows that rarely ran up the large runs of the biggest *opérette* hits, and most of them had chequered export careers, but they were pieces which were extremely interesting, and which have stood the test of time much better than a *La Cigale et la fourmi* or a *La Poupée*. They were finely written comic plays where the action and characters were of the kind and quality normally reserved for the straight theatre, and whose libretti were clearly as important – if not even more important – as their musical part. They were real musical comedies, with the accent firmly on the "comedy".

Paul Ferrier and Fabrice Carré's *Joséphine vendue par ses soeurs* actually called itself an *opéra-bouffe*, and that not unfairly. It was an hilariously clever piece of fun based on the biblical tale of Joseph, with the sexes reversed. Joséphine is a budding singer, the apple of her mother's eye and thoroughly jealoused by her sisters, who sell her off to what she thinks is the Cairo Opera House and turns out to be the Pasha's harem. A clever light score by Victor Roger, which included some opera parody for the heroine and her baritone and some sprightly bits for the soubrette, decorated a first-rate comedy that was wholly to Parisian tastes but, for some reason, rather less to those of other countries.

Roger was, in fact, the champion illustrator of this kind of substantial musical comedy. He was responsible for the music to Antony Mars and Maurice Desvallières's *Les Douze Femmes de Japhet*, which took the same ex-biblical line as *Joséphine* (Japhet being a Mormon, and the plot a masterpiece of complexity), to the still-popular military vaudeville *Les Vingt-huit Jours de Clairette* (by Mars and Hippolyte Raymond), which followed the farcical mishaps befalling a disguised wife in an army camp, to Maurice Ordonneau's *L'Auberge du Tohu-Bohu*, with its tale of a phoney inn, and, above all, to Mars and Maurice Hennequin's famous *Les Fêtards*, a masterly piece of comic writing which was played in umpteen versions in umpteen languages in umpteen countries – and, unlike some of its fellows, everywhere with success.

The produce of the Parisian musical stage faded thoroughly off the world scene to the strains of two last successes – two pieces that were very, very far in style from the dizzy humour of *opéra-bouffe* days, the sparkily sexy scenes and songs of the *opéra-comique*, or the skilful comedy of the *vaudeville-opérette*. Like *La Poupée*, *Les P'tites Michu* and *Véronique* were what was called "*gentille*" *opérette*: sweet, charming, pretty, inoffensive, although in no way either wan or sugary. They were musicals for a different audience to that which had enjoyed the earlier styles of show: a cooler, less demonstrative audience with less evident enjoyment of strong feelings or sounds. The pretty tale of the two little mixed-up Michu daughters who get their own identities back in time to wed the right men, and the story of the noble lassie who wins her destined husband whilst dressed up as a peasant girl, were both set to music by the most charming composer of the era, André Messager. Some pages of the score of *Les P'tites Michu* represent some of the sweetest sounds to have come from the French stage. But the *gentille* nature of Messager's music didn't just appeal to the subdued musical-theatregoers of France. Both works made a distinct hit on the English-speaking stage, and the favourite songs from *Véronique*, "Trot Here, Trot There" and the Swing Song, lasted years in the English concert repertoire.

In half a century, the French musical stage had run the gamut of musical and theatrical styles. It had gone from the lusty and the witty to the serenely pretty, with each age finding its preferred tone and level. With *opéra-bouffe* and *opéra-comique* it had led the world, but now its turn as a style-leader was over. Riding on the footplate of the authors and composers of *opéra-bouffe* and *opéra-comique*, other countries had set other traditions in musical theatre in motion, and, as the century continued, they – Vienna and London to the forefront – had caught up and overtaken the first fine founders of the modern musical.

André Messager

He produced pretty and sometimes quite simply beautiful music for pretty, well-behaved stories.

'Ja, so singt man . . .'

The Ringstrasse, which encloses
the heart of 'old' Vienna, painted
by Franz Alt in 1871. In that same
year were produced Millöcker's
Drei Paar Schuhe and Johann
Strauss's less than triumphant
Indigo und die vierzig Räuber.

Vienna's Golden Age

The Viennese theatres were the quickest out of the blocks when it came to following up their enthusiasm for French opéra-bouffe *with good, like-minded pieces of their own manufacture. The first sighting of an Offenbach musical on the Vienna stage occurred in 1856, when performances of* Le Violoneux *and* Les Deux Aveugles *were given at the Carltheater by a touring French company, playing in French.*

The first German-language version of Offenbach, an adaptation of his *Le Mariage aux lanternes*, took place there two years later, and as soon as 1859 a little Viennese *opéra-bouffe*, *Flodoardo Wuprahall*, with a score composed by Carl Friedrich Conradin, was brought out on the same stage. The "tragi-comic operetta" *Flodoardo Wuprahall* – which you can hear from its title was well and truly in the *bouffe* mode – did all right, but, perhaps because neither Conradin nor librettist Erik Nessl proved to be enduring names, it never got much credit for being in at the start of the Viennese operetta tradition. The show that normally does get that credit was one that was mounted at the Theater an der Wien the following year. *Das Pensionat* was a little Frenchified tale of high-jinks in a girls' school, and the distinctly enduring name of its composer was Franz von Suppé.

During the 1860s, Suppé, who had by this time left the Theater an der Wien to join the enterprising actor-manager-adapter Karl Treumann at his new and adventurous little Theater am Franz-Josefs-Kai, down on the banks of the Donau Canal, took the lead in providing original musicals for the Viennese stage, and he scored a number of firm successes. However, neither *Flotte Bursche*, the jolly tale of a greedy merchant tricked, nor *Zehn Mädchen und kein Mann*, a resetting of a French libretto which existed largely to give some of the ten girls of the title the chance to do a showpiece number, nor the two-act *Leichte Kavallerie*, a regulation weepie about a lost ingénue who finds her military father– all of which would be continually featured on

Franz von Suppé usually gets the credit for setting in motion the Viennese musical theatre of the modern era.

Die schöne Galathee
Hermine Meyerhoff as the statue come to life in Vienna's most enduring early musical.

European stages for many years – sported anything of the Parisian *bouffe* flavour, and Suppé's most enduring piece, *Die schöne Galathee*, although it was set in the same classical antiquity as *Orphée aux enfers*, treated antiquity in a pre-*bouffe* manner. In fact, its libretto was simply an adaptation of one set by *opéra-comique* composer Victor Massé before the onset of *opéra-bouffe* in France.

Suppé's first essays at full-length *opéra-bouffe* – burlesque versions of the popular operas *Dinorah* (*Dinorah, oder Die Turnerfahrt nach Hütteldorf*) and *Lohengrin* (*Lohengelb, oder Die Jungfrau von Dragant*) – didn't make any more of a mark than other local efforts by such writers as Julius Hopp and the Croatian composer who called himself Giovanni von Zaytz, and, just like Hervé in France, the man who had been first and foremost in getting things going found himself pipped at the post by a Johnny-come-later when the first really big hit came along.

In this case, the Johnny who came along later was no nobody. It was the famous dance-music composer Johann Strauss, who, after a quarter of a century providing waltzes and polkas to the orchestras of Vienna and the rest of the world, had been persuaded by a few friends and relatives – and a theatre-manager with an eye for a Groschen – to try his hand at writing for the stage. Strauss didn't hit the target straight away. Far from it. He made at least one false start and his first show to actually reach the stage, a piece based vaguely on the Ali Baba tale, and written to a book that seemed like chunks of *Ba-ta-clan* and several other Parisian *opéras-bouffes* all glued together, was a frank flop. The composer's name-value ensured that *Indigo und die vierzig Räuber* got productions in a number of other countries after its first appearance at the Theater an der Wien, and a thoroughly rewritten version was even given a fresh showing at the same Viennese theatre, but every time it came out the same – a flop. It wasn't until his third try – by which time the composer had abandoned the special flavour of *opéra-bouffe* for something more like the musical comedy of *La Vie parisienne* – that Strauss won the triumph hoped for and expected from him.

Die Fledermaus

The similarity between Strauss's first serious hit and Offenbach's La Vie parisienne *was no coincidence. Richard Genée's libretto for the Viennese show was quite simply an adaptation – sometimes a word-for-word one – of the Parisian play* Le Réveillon, *and the authors of the original* Le Réveillon *were none other than Messrs Meilhac and Halévy, the librettists of* La Vie parisienne.

However, if Genée followed *Le Réveillon*, and Carl Haffner's unproduced attempt to Germanize it, extremely closely – in particular in the early stages of his book – he did make one very important alteration to the story and the text, an alteration which changed the whole character of the story of a naughty husband, tricked into going out for a girlie night when he should be reporting to the police. Meilhac and Halévy's Monsieur Gaillardin once stranded his friend Duparquet, still dressed in a bluebird costume from a masked ball, and Duparquet swore to be revenged. When Gaillardin is due to report for a little prison sentence as the price of punching a policeman, Duparquet persuades him to postpone his punishment and go instead to a party. But whilst Gaillardin is having his jolly party time, flirting with a lass he thinks is an actress, he is also in jail. The police have arrested an amorous violinist who had taken advantage of his absence to play serenades at Mme Gaillardin. The imbroglios go on from there.

As far as Genée and the Theater an der Wien were concerned, this story had one very

big hole in it. It didn't have a proper leading-lady rôle for the theatre's star and co-director, Marie Geistinger, nor did it have a decent soubrette part. We saw no more of Mme Gaillardin after Act I, and the farmer's girl/actress, Métella, was seen only in the second act.

Genée changed all that. In his version, Mme Gaillardin – or Rosalinde Eisenstein, as she had become with his switching of the action from France to Austria – not only went to the ball, she did all the flirting with her misbehaving husband that had previously been the lot of the pretend actress, and the pretend actress (who was still there) was no longer an insignificant farmer's girl, but the Eisenstein's coloratura soprano soubrette of a maid, out in disguise for a lively night on the tiles.

In *Die Fledermaus*, Rosalinde Eisenstein's admirer is not a violinist but a very vocal tenor called Alfred. He has got as far in his attempt at seduction as trying on Eisenstein's dressing gown for size when the police descend and carry him off to fulfil "his" prison sentence. Then, disguised as an Hungarian countess, Rosalinde heads for the party where her

Meanwhile, back at the jail: Frank (Carl Adolf Friese) and Frosch (Alfred Schreiber) the morning after the night before.

CREDITS

Die Fledermaus

Comic *Operette* in 3 acts by
Richard Genée and Carl
Haffner based on *Le
Réveillon* by Henri Meilhac
and Ludovic Halévy

LYRICS

by Richard Genée

MUSIC

by Johann Strauss

Produced at the Theater an der
Wien, Vienna, 5 April 1874
Germany: Friedrich-
Wilhelmstädtisches
Theater, Berlin, 8 July 1874
USA: Stadt Theater, New York,
21 November 1874
UK: Alhambra Theatre, London,
18 December 1876
France: Théâtre de la
Renaissance, Paris,
30 October 1877

CAST

Gabriel Eisenstein Jani Szika
Rosalinde Eisenstein Marie
Geistinger
Adele Karoline Charles-Hirsch
Frank Carl Adolf Friese
Prince Orlofsky Irma Nittinger
Falke Ferdinand Lebrecht
Frosch Alfred Schreiber
Alfred Rüdinger

husband is having his little gallivant, and turns her heavily accented charms on to her wayward spouse. Eisenstein is actually being doubly fooled, for not only is he expending his best chatting-up routine on his own wife, he is, all unbeknown, gallivanting right alongside another gentleman who isn't admitting his real identity, the Prison Governor, Frank. Everything comes to a peak the following morning when Eisenstein turns up tardily at the prison, only to find both his jolly companion of the night before at his work, and "himself" in jail. His wife has been unfaithful! But then Rosalinde arrives, evidence of attempted adultery in hand, and friend Falke admits that he set the whole thing up. It has been his little revenge for Eisenstein's once abandoning him to the public's morning gaze dressed in a fancy-dress bat's costume.

Genée's script replaced many of the comic shades of the original play with conventional operettic tricks, but – in return – it supplied two fine rôles for the ladies of the show, and many an opportunity for Strauss to shower the stage with music. Rosalinde delivered a showy csárdás ("Klänge der Heimat") in her phoney Hungarian persona, and joined in a winning duo with her husband ("Diese Anstand") as she craftily wooed his chiming watch from him. The disguised soubrette, Adele, mocked her employer for imagining a resemblance between her and his chambermaid in a puff of coloratura ("Mein Herr Marquis") and delivered a set-piece displaying her qualifications for a career as an actress ("Spiel' ich die Unschuld vom Lande"), whilst the party's host, Prince Orlofsky, played by an actress in travesty, encouraged his guests to get up to whatever they fancied in the way of enjoyment ("Ich lade gern mir Gäste an"). Falke led the company with a mellow, loping, everybody-loving "Brüderlein und Schwesterlein", but the men's moments came more in comedy than in song, and they were topped – as in the original play – by a stand-up routine for a low comedian, in the rôle of the prison janitor, Frosch, who opened the final act with a sozzled scena.

Die Fledermaus was very much better received than Strauss's previous works had been, and it was given no less than 45 times in the Theater an der Wien's repertoire in its first few months on the stage, a total that was decidedly good if not spectacular under such circumstances. What was more spectacular was the persistence with which it stayed in a repertoire from which even some of the greatest favourites were dropped after a decade or so.

The magic name of Strauss had not been dimmed by his lacklustre stage career to date, and *Die Fledermaus* was quickly on its way to other centres. Berlin welcomed it with enormous success, but elsewhere things often went less than wonderfully. The show was mounted in London as a Christmas entertainment at the big Alhambra Theatre and did well enough through four months, but then wasn't seen again in London for thirty years. New York got its first *Fledermaus* swiftly, at the German theatre, but waited a decade to hear it in English and then without its raising any earlobes. France waited even longer, for it seemed that no one had had the politeness to ask Meilhac and Halévy for the use of their play as libretto-fodder and Genée's ripped-off version couldn't be played on its authors' home ground. Instead, Paris got a glimpse of a feeble piece called *La Tsigane* which tacked some *Fledermaus* music and some other spare Strauss onto a more conventional than conventional French tale of prince, princess and disguise. It was thirty years on before a real *La Chauve-souris* was seen in Paris.

If *Die Fledermaus* had, initially, a rather unimpressive international career, it made up for it later. As the most successful stage work attached to the well-preserved name of Strauss, it was brought back in the twentieth century to be revived, revised, readapted, souped up, horribly souped up, and even filmed, and gradually it made itself a place in the repertoire not only in the German-language countries, where it had always enjoyed a healthy life, but in those overseas areas that had, after first hearing, put it on the shelf. Nowadays – and no small thanks to the still magic name of Strauss – it has become the most played, and in some places the only played, piece from the nineteenth-century Viennese tradition, whilst shows by lesser-remembered musicians, which were better loved first time round, have now slipped from the boards.

Strauss took a while to find another hit, and during the middle and later 1870s the initiative fell instead to the versatile Genée, who composed as well as writing and adapting libretti, and to Suppé, who was encouraged by the success of *Die Fledermaus* to try his luck with a musical comedy rather than an *opéra-bouffe*. Genée and his writing partner "F. Zell" provided Suppé with a libretto that, like the *Fledermaus* one, was taken from the French. *Fatinitza* followed the adventures of a handsome army officer who – for reasons too dotty to explain – gets disguised as a girl and ends up in a Turkish harem. The idea was old, and its comic possibilities limited, but Zell and Genée remade it tidily and Suppé decorated it with some really marvellous music – from the marching strains of "Vorwärts mit frischen Mut" to the twinkling ones of "Silberglöckchen rufen Helle" and the comical ones of "Ein bisserl auffrischen", and the result was a ringing success that went round the world. In one year, Broadway was visited by no fewer than five productions of *Fatinitza*.

Suppé was altogether quicker than Strauss to confirm his first big hit. Whilst the Emperor of the Waltz turned out *Cagliostro in Wien*, *Prinz Methusalem* and the disastrous *Blindekuh*, Suppé came up with a show that topped even the triumph of *Fatinitza*. *Boccaccio* was a musical that, courtesy of Messrs Genée and Zell, simply let the unbuttoned poet of the title and a spare Prince loose amongst the women of Florence with predictable consequences – both funny and romantic – to the accompaniment of a superb score of comic opera music. Antonie Link, the young mezzo-soprano who had scored such a success in the bisexual rôle of Wladimir/ Fatinitza in Suppé's previous piece, made an even greater hit in the rôle of Boccaccio. She and the piece's ingénue shared the best of the evening's lyric music, including the waltz duo "Florenz hat schöne Frauen", but many of the highlights of the score came in its comical numbers. An about-to-be-cuckolded barrel-wright bashed away at his work to drown out his wife's chatter ("Tagtäglich zankt mein Weib"), the barber tipsily serenaded his wife whilst plonking at an umbrella ("Holde Schöne"), and three bored ladies went into raptures over an invitation to a bit of dalliance in delicious harmonies ("Wonnevolle Kunde, neu belebend").

Boccaccio became internationally the most successful musical of the nineteenth-century Austrian stage. It was produced and – unlike *Die Fledermaus* –re-produced throughout the world for two decades, making a particular success in America and in the blooming Hungarian theatre, and setting Suppé up well and truly at the head of his profession.

Six years after his *coup d'éclat* with *Die Fledermaus*, Strauss turned out a semi-success with the romantic Hispanic tale of *Das Spitzentuch der Königin*, but he topped that two years later with one of the very best *Operetten* of his career, the loopy tale of what went on in *Der lustige Krieg*. Genée and Zell were again the librettists, the text was once more a remade version of a reasonably obscure French show, and the result was a piece which eschewed the rather glutinous southern sentimentality of *Das Spitzentuch der Königin* in favour of some nicely ridiculous fun. The musical also introduced Strauss's best show song for years – a waltz song, "Nur für Natur", that had been popped into the score in rehearsals to satisfy a star who didn't think he had enough to sing.

Der lustige Krieg proved to be easily its composer's best and best-liked work since his first hit, but there was bigger and more popular yet to come. After lingering rather unsatisfactorily in the lubricious land of masked balls with the colourful if textually uninteresting story of what happened *Eine Nacht in Venedig*, Strauss turned to Hungary and set a theatricalized version

Boccaccio
Scenes from London's production of 1882 with Violet Cameron as Boccaccio and Louis Kelleher as Lotteringhi (centre) featured.

of a novel by one of that country's most admired writers, Mór Jókai. The novel was called *Sáffi*, and the musical was *Der Zigeunerbaron*, or the Gypsy Baron. The central and lushly romantic tale of an Hungarian nobleman and his gypsy bride was illustrated with some of Strauss's most appreciable romantic music – the lovers' morning-after Dompfaff Duo ("Wer uns getraut?") and the heroine's stunning Romany cry "Habet acht!" – music that was contrasted to grand effect with such pieces as the hero's insouciant entry song ("Als flotter Geist") and such comic highlights as the song of the wealthy pig farmer, who was the evening's chief comedian ("Ja, das Schreiben und das Lesen"), or the tale of a "widow" who long ago mislaid her husband during a battle ("Just sind er vierundzwanzig Jahre").

Curiously enough, although *Der Zigeunerbaron* proved enormously popular in Central Europe, and has indeed survived as number two in the Strauss-on-stage hit parade in modern times, it originally fared less well on the non-European stage than *Der lustige Krieg* or even – in America – than *Das Spitzentuch der Königin*. But at home it was one of the greatest hits of its era.

Der Zigeunerbaron was to be Strauss's last success. In the thirteen years and five shows that made up the rest of his career, he went from one flop to another, and in the end he left as his basic theatrical legacy two shows – *Die Fledermaus* and *Der Zigeunerbaron*. For, curiously, sadly, *Der lustige Krieg* has slipped away, and when the magic name of Strauss wins a showing for another of his stage works, at the dusk of the twentieth century, it is normally not the composer's third hit show we see but either the dreary scissors-and-paste *Wiener Blut* or a nastily souped-up version of *Eine Nacht in Venedig*.

Millöcker's musicals

Suppé, too, went on to write further successful musicals – *Donna Juanita*, *Die Afrikareise* and the musically splendid *Die Jagd nach dem Glück* – and, as Hervé and Offenbach had done in Paris, he and Strauss loomed large over the musical theatre scene. But, in the same way that Lecocq, Planquette and Audran had risen in France, other fine writers and composers soon came to compete with the established stars. The

Johann Strauss
A name to conjure with: the dance-music king who also scored a small but happy handful of stage hits.

first, and most important, of these was Karl Millöcker. Like Suppé, and like most of his composer contemporaries, Millöcker worked as a theatre conductor, and his compositions were often piece-work for whichever house he happened to be employed at. This meant that his earliest successes came with *Possen* – those comedies with songs that made up such an important part of the Viennese repertoire. But, again like Suppé, Millöcker was encouraged by the success of *Die Fledermaus* to try his hand at a more substantial musical. The comical *Das verwunschene Schloss*, a story about a phoney haunted castle, gave him his first big success, and the composer went on to turn out other well-liked and internationally played pieces – *Apajune der Wassermann* and *Die Jungfrau von Belleville*. Then, in 1882, he wrote the show which was both his masterpiece and his greatest success.

If *La Fille de Madame Angot* is the most complete comic opera of the nineteenth-century heyday of the French musical stage, Millöcker's *Der Bettelstudent* can fairly be said to hold the same position in the Austrian theatre. Like the French show, it is blessed with a really first-rate libretto, mixing politics, comedy and romance in expert doses, and that libretto has been illustrated by a score of quite superb light operatic music.

The story of *Der Bettelstudent* takes place in occupied Poland, and it tells how Colonel Ollendorf of the invading army took his revenge after being rebuffed by the poor but

Opposite: *Der Zigeunerbaron*
There's good money in porkers: Alexander Girardi was the creator of the part of pig-farming Zsupán.

proud Countess Laura Nowalska. Ollendorf takes a handsome beggar-student from prison, dresses him up as a nobleman, and sets him to woo and wed the finicky Laura. Politics, pretences and expediencies of all kinds intervene, but the Polish army arrives with even better timing than the US cavalry could have done, and the ending is a happy one.

Millöcker's score was dazzling. The tenor hero had a brace of soon-to-be-famous songs ("Ich hab' kein Geld", "Ich knüpfte manche zarte Band"), Laura, her soubrette sister and their boomingly ambitious mamma twinkled out a shopping trio ("Einkäufe machen") and dressed for Laura's wedding in winning harmonies ("Einen Mann hat sie gefunden"), and Ollendorf growled out the waltz-time story of the attempted kiss that had earned him a fan in the face ("Ach ich hab' sie ja nur auf die Schulter geküsst") in one of the great numbers of the Viennese *Operette* stage.

Der Bettelstudent duly went round the world, and it held its pre-eminent place in the Viennese repertoire for many years. Its super-solid book also won it repeated film exposure, but eventually it ran out of copyright and, in order to renew that copyright, a remade version of the libretto was stuck onto Millöcker's score. It was a book littered with clichés and commonplaces, one that replaced the believable ending with one worthy of a Christmas pantomime. After three-quarters of a century, the masterpiece of the "golden age" of the Vienna stage succumbed to what was no more than artistic sabotage. Today, the show that should have been the enduring glory of its era is rarely seen.

Millöcker went on to further successes – the tricksy bandit-land tale of *Gasparone*, the comic-heroic story of *Der Feldprediger* which entranced American audiences as *The Black Hussar*, and above all the comical tale of *Der arme Jonathan*, which gave its composer a second sizeable triumph on the Broadway stage – but the most winning hit of the last years of the Viennese century, and of the "golden age" of Viennese *Operette*, came from another composer, Carl Zeller.

Gold of a different colour

Zeller's *Der Vogelhändler* (1891) has a different tone and flavour to the other great musicals of its time and place. Each of the other biggest hits had a highish society or military story and music to match. The hero of *Der Vogelhändler* is a country boy, his sweetheart is the postmistress, and the story of the piece – far from the clever complexities of a *Bettelstudent* or a *Der lustige Krieg* – simply tells of a misunderstanding that arises between them for a couple of acts when Adam and his Christel get mixed up with big-city folk. Zeller gave his rustic stars winningly "rustic" music. Viennese mega-star Alexander Girardi – the same who in his rising days had introduced "Nur für Natur" in *Der lustige Krieg* – lilted onto the stage with a welcoming "Grüss enk Gott, alle miteinander", and brought the first act to its peak with a waltzing little piece that described the serious Tyrolean meaning of a gift of flowers ("Schenkt man sich Rosen in Tirol"), whilst Hungarian star Ilka Pálmay as Christel made her entrance with what would become the most popular soubrette song of the age ("Ich bin die Christel von der Post"). In contrast, there were altogether more lyrical soprano pieces for the Princess who is the cause of all the trouble – a fiendishly difficult waltz song in praise of "Fröhlich Pfalz" and a lovely "Als geblühte der Kirschenbaum" – and even a dotty duet for two comical professors.

Der Vogelhändler was another piece which prospered enormously in Central Europe but did rather less well elsewhere. However, if the rest of the world knows it little, it remains, as it has been since its production, one of the pillars of the classic Viennese repertoire. As for Zeller, he turned out another success in *Der Obersteiger*, the show that featured the famous waltz tune that's become known to English-speaking audiences as "Don't Be Cross", but he never again reached the heights of *Der Vogelhändler*.

Suppé died in 1895, Zeller passed on in 1898, and the following year Strauss and Millöcker died within months of each other. It seemed as if the Viennese tradition, which had appeared to be so thriving, had really been a tradition relying on too few writers and that it had come to an abrupt end. In a way it had. But only a few years later a new wave of Austrian, or, rather, Austro-Hungarian musicals was to spring forth, and that sparkling series of twentieth-century *Operetten* would carry Viennese music around the world with even greater success than the musicals of the nineteenth century had done.

Opposite: **Der Vogelhändler** Alexander Girardi as the birdseller, Adam, the endearing hero of Zeller's wholly endearing *Operette*.

'Well, hardly ev-er!'

H. M. S. Pinafore
The poster for D'Oyly Carte's
original West End production of
Gilbert and Sullivan's world-
wowing *opéra-bouffe*.

Merry England

British writers and producers weren't as quick to react or, at first, as effective in their reaction to the ever-growing influx of crazy cross-Channel humour and the brilliant cross-Channel music of the opéra-bouffe *years as their colleagues in Vienna had been. Old theatrical habits died hard in the musical houses of the West End and British writers stuck to familiar formats.*

Right: **John Hollingshead**
The guru at the Gaiety: the producer of some of the best Victorian English musicals.

The first attempts at turning out something more or less in the English *opéra-bouffe* line came in the mid-1860s and they were the work of the highly successful burlesque writer Frank Burnand. Burnand, who anglicized *La Belle Hélène* for its first London showing with a very traditionally British hand and with not very satisfying results, was not quite comfortable seated in the sophisticated saddle of *opéra-bouffe*. His pen ran more happily in the low-comic, word-torturing style of established British burlesque, and it was in this style that he turned out what he later claimed as "the first English *opéras-bouffes*" – less than full-length burlesques of the historical novel *Windsor Castle* and of the opera *L'Africaine*. The only feature that really differentiated these two shows from the ones that he had written before was quite simply that, like the French *opéras-bouffes*, they used original music, written in this case by the theatre's musical director, Frank Musgrave, rather than the traditional arrangement of airs and arias.

Around the same time, Burnand also put together the script for a rather more high-brow show: a burlesque-bandits comic opera called *The Contrabandista*, with music specially composed by one Arthur Sullivan. Both his burlesques and his comic opera did well enough, and the comic opera even turned in a small comic song hit ("From Rock to Rock"), but they apparently didn't encourage Burnand to continue further in the same style. He went back to writing mostly pasticcio burlesque (and, later on, forward to the editorship of *Punch*), but for the rest of his life he enjoyed telling people how he'd invented English *opéra-bouffe*.

Another burlesque writer, William Gilbert, carried on what Burnand had begun when he turned out a quaint kind of magical musical comedy called *The Gentleman in Black*, with a score by the up-and-coming composer Freddie Clay, but this show did less well than the earlier ones and it disappeared from the West End in just 26 performances.

It was John Hollingshead, the manager at the Gaiety Theatre, who really started English *opéra-bouffe* on its way to success when he commissioned a series of new musicals for his nice new theatre. The first two of these shows, however, could scarcely have been considered to be of genuinely English manufacture. Although both sported a libretto written by the Gaiety's resident dramatist and dress-designer Alfred Thompson, for each of *Aladdin II* and *Cinderella the Younger* Hollingshead commissioned a score from an established

French *opéra-bouffe* composer: Hervé and Émile Jonas, respectively. But then he went on to commission a Christmas piece from two of the few local men who'd already shown willing to dip into this new business of English *opéra-bouffe*: Mr Gilbert of *The Gentleman in Black* and Mr Sullivan of *The Contrabandista*.

Thespis, the piece that Gilbert and Sullivan wrote for Hollingshead, was based on an old German fantasy and, like the most successful of Offenbach's pieces, it burlesqued the familiar characters and tales of classical Greece. *Thespis* did well enough as a festive season entertainment and then it closed, but the partnership between its writers turned out to be – if not yet exclusive – at least a recurring one. It recurred first of all in a one-act "cantata" called *Trial by Jury*, then in a full-length English comic opera, *The Sorcerer*, and then – on their fourth time round the stage together – Messrs Gilbert and Sullivan hit gold. A dozen years and not too many more shows after Burnand's first ventures into the field, W. S. Gilbert and Arthur Sullivan turned out the first international hit musical of the modern British stage, *H. M. S. Pinafore*.

Below left: **W. S. Gilbert**
Below right: **Arthur S. Sullivan**
The writers who together helped the English musical play of the modern era to move into a new dimension.

H. M. S.
Pinafore

Like Trial by Jury *and* The Sorcerer, H. M. S. Pinafore *didn't try to copy the extravagant burlesque style of the great French opéras-bouffes. Gilbert quickly found his own equally effective, but very British, kind of cock-eyed parody humour, one that didn't echo the mannerisms of Burnandized British burlesque any more than it did the witticisms of Meilhac and Halévy, whilst Sullivan, if he did indeed mine a similar vein of light theatre music to that opened up so excitingly by Hervé and Offenbach, mined it in an equally British, and distinctly individual, fashion.*

There were no Can-Cans or Tyroliennes in praise of sex in a Gilbert and Sullivan show. In *H. M. S. Pinafore* the twinned styles of the two writers came into their fullness for the first time in what, if it wasn't actually the first *opéra-bouffe* in English, was the show that set English *opéra-bouffe* off on a career that would end up being as effective and enduring as that of their French equivalents.

H. M. S. Pinafore was a burlesque of things nautical or, more to the point, of things stage nautical: a burlesque of the *Black-Eyed Susan* kind of melodrama, of its characters and its situations. But Gilbert, in a way that would characterize his writing all through his career, used his play and his people, at the same time, to poke transparently bitter fun at anything and anyone he didn't like. Given the author's personality, the range of targets was a long one, but his hate list was topped, by miles, by anyone – just anyone – who held the inherited or aristocratic position that (it didn't need a Freud to spot it) the author so clearly and desperately longed for for himself. Lords, knights, monarchs and officialdom of every kind were mocked at every turn of a Gilbert script, both in character and in plot. In *Pinafore*, for example, the fact that an aristocratic baby and a poor child were mixed up at birth means that, when the truth comes out, their positions in adult life have to be reversed. Worth is nothing, birth is paramount. Fortunately, Gilbert coated his envious attitudes in a technicolor garb of splendidly witty words and brilliant burlesque humour, and these, combined with the apt and gay charm of Sullivan's music, ensured that the story of The Lass Who Loved a Sailor was an evening of high-class comic and musical entertainment.

Extremely Able Seaman Ralph Rackstraw is in a suicidal dilemma, for he has fallen in love with Miss Josephine Corcoran, the daughter of

Background: **A Gilbertian villain – the twisted Dick Deadeye.**

CREDITS

H. M. S. Pinafore

or The Lass That Loved a Sailor
Comic opera in 2 acts by W. S. Gilbert

MUSIC

by Arthur Sullivan

Produced at the Opera
    Comique Theatre, London,
    25 May 1878
USA: Boston Museum, 25
    November 1878
Germany: Friedrich-
    Wilhelmstädtisches
    Theater, Berlin, 1881
France: St Edmund's College,
    Douai, January 1901

CAST

Ralph Rackstraw	George Power
Josephine	Emma Howson
Captain Corcoran	Richard Temple
Sir Joseph Porter, KCB	George Grossmith
Little Buttercup	Harriet Everard
Dick Deadeye	Rutland Barrington
Hebe	Jessie Bond

his very own Captain. She, of course, given the difference in their ranks, cannot possibly conceive of loving him in return and she is, in fact, programmed to become the wife of Admiral Sir Joseph Porter KCB, a knight whose curiously liberal ideas include such unheard-ofs as "a British Sailor is any man's equal (excepting mine)" and "love levels all ranks" – including those of the Porters and the Corcorans. Miss Corcoran is encouraged by this second dictum to confess her fascination for and willingness to wed young Rackstraw, but the lovers' night-time, clergyward flight is betrayed by dastardly Dick Deadeye, and the lovers look likely to catch it in the neck until Little Buttercup, bumboat lady and former wet-nurse, comes up with a confession. In the years of their babyhood, she mixed up Josephine's father and Ralph – each is, in fact, the other! So Ralph becomes the Captain of H. M. S. *Pinafore* and weds his Josephine, for, when it comes to love levelling ranks between an Admiral and the daughter of a foremast-hand, Sir Joseph tosses his favourite maxim right out a porthole.

From the moment that the first curtain went up on Gilbert and Sulivan's theatrical tars, hymning their personal qualities in jolly tongue-in-cheek couplets, the songs of the evening scored, one after the other. Amongst the biggest popular successes were Sir Joseph's pattering curriculum vitae, describing how he rose from being the lad who "polished up the handle of the big front door" to the post of Admiral of the Fleet, in spite of never having been to sea; Captain Corcoran's modest detailing of his own character ("I am the Captain of the *Pinafore*") with its catchphrase "What Never?", "Well, Hardly Ever"; and the tripping song and dance trio ("Never Mind the Why and Wherefore"), in which Sir Joseph and the Captain try to impress the maxim of love levelling all ranks on the doubtful Josephine. Sullivan had fun at the expense of the multi-part, cabaletta-ed aria of the grand opera in Josephine's soprano scena of amorous dilemma ("The Hours Creep on Apace"), Ralph held a pistol to his head as he tenoriously threatened to end his days, and Captain Corcoran serenaded the moon ("Fair Moon, to Thee I Sing") in a slightly different tone to the conventional operatic lunar serenade. But although the whole piece was written and played in a genuine British 'bouffe' mode, with both the words and the music drawing much of their humour and appeal from the fact that they were parodies of other, more serious, genres, Gilbert and Sullivan's burlesque was never gross, either in song or in speech, the satire never stark, and there wasn't a pair of tights in sight. It was all marvellously good, clean fun.

After a slightly slow start, *H. M. S. Pinafore* caught on with a vengeance, and enormously enthusiastic audiences were soon making their way nightly to the distinctly second-class Opera Comique Theatre. So much so that, in the end, the original London production went on – in spite of management squabbles which resulted in toughs invading the stage at one performance, and even brought the show into court – to outrun all but the very biggest favourites amongst its imported competitors. But then it went further. It went on to become equally, or even more, successful not only throughout the British provinces, but in hundreds of productions – official, unofficial and pretty approximate – throughout America and the colonies, eventually, in spite of the competition from the big new hits coming hand over fist out of France, reaching every corner of the English-speaking world. At the edge of that English-speaking world, however, the show's success stopped. The musical which set the modern English-language musical theatre afloat, and which remains today a – even the – classic of its kind, made absolutely no impression in translation. Productions on the German and Hungarian stages were short-lived, and the work's only mounting in France was a brief showing in English. Was it simply that Gilbert's kind of wit did not translate? Hardly, for not too many years later Gilbert and Sullivan's *The Mikado* would become one of the most popular musicals on the German and Hungarian stages. Was it all those meaningless (to a foreigner) burlesque British sailors? But surely every country has theatrical sailors, not to mention burlesqueable statesmen and sinecured appointees. The real answer has never been found. But, whatever it was, *H. M. S. Pinafore* was never able to use up the return half of the ticket on which *La Grande-Duchesse* and *Chilpéric* had sailed so triumphantly across the English Channel.

In the later 1870s and the 1880s, Gilbert and Sullivan and their producer Richard D'Oyly Carte followed up *H. M. S. Pinafore* with a whole line of further hit shows, shows distinguished by their authors' very personal styles of plot and dialogue, of character and of music. That's not to say that what – after Carte's shift to the Savoy Theatre – became known as the Savoy operas were utterly original in every way. They weren't. It only seems that way to us now, when we no longer have the rest of nineteenth-century musical and comic theatre with which to compare them. In fact, the playwright made free with all sorts of sources – English, French and German. Gilbert's talent lay not in wholesale invention, but in doing what he did with the material he gathered together once it was gathered, and right from the start – even in his earliest days as a writer of traditional burlesque – what he wrote was recognized by the critics as being particularly classy and well written. The same praises were heaped on the music of Sullivan, who had been regarded by many, before his "descent" into writing for the musical theatre, as the white hope of the British classical music scene. The only critics who scowled at the scores for the Savoy operas were those who felt the composer was wasting his talents by writing popular theatre music.

Like *H. M. S. Pinafore*, most of the Savoy operas were, in one way or to some degree, English *opéras-bouffes* or burlesque musicals. *The Pirates of Penzance*, the show that immediately followed *H. M. S. Pinafore* into the Opera Comique, also followed the enthusiastic parody of the serious stage that had been such fun in its forebear, both in its text and in its music. The new piece told the tale of a bunch of naughty young lordlings who have organized themselves into a band of plundering pirates and, in particular, of Frederic, their handsome, tenorious apprentice who, his indentures over, is stopped from dutifully betraying the pirates to the law by means of a convenient legal anomaly. The text of *The Pirates of Penzance*, with its boozing, blood-sipping buccaneers and its Gothickally ruined chapel by moonlight, burlesqued the conventions of the popular melodrama stage, and Sullivan echoed the grotesqueries of the mock-melodramatic libretto with such musical

numbers as the heroine's uvula-in-cheek coloratura aria of "farmyard-noises" ("Poor Wandering One"), a pirate chief's number that contrasted rollicking music with snide, society-stabbing words ("I am a Pirate King"), and a chorus of policemen off to battle repeatedly insisting, in good operatic fashion, that they are going but always staying to sing another line or two.

Gilbert and Sullivan later attacked the same easily targeted area of theatrical melodrama again, and with even more sub-operatic gusto, in *Ruddigore*, one of their few works to be less than wholly and internationally successful. This time the centrepiece of the plot was an ancient curse, and the story followed the tricks employed by the unwilling new inheritor of that curse to squirm around its nasty demands. *Ruddigore* ranged into the supernatural for both its effects and its plot, into the realm of legal fictions – once again – for its dénouement, and into musical areas as far apart as operatic spoof (in such pieces as the howling "Ghost's High Noon" or a contralto Legend with *Il Trovatore*al leanings), parody of the music hall (a copy of the John Ryley/Marie Barnum Dancing Quaker Act) and a triple-tongued patter-song ("My Eyes are Fully Open").

In *Iolanthe* the partners burlesqued another theatrical genre, the Victorian féerie, that relatively grown-up fairyland for which Gilbert had always shown a particular fondness and which he had frequently visited in his plays. This story of a half-fairy shepherd sent, by wholly fairy means, into the British parliament, there to wreak havoc as a revenge for a Lord Chancerial slight on the Queen of the Fairies, also gave Gilbert one of his most straightforward opportunities to loose quiversful of sneers in the direction of the British aristocracy. The Lord Chancellor himself was the chief comic figure of the show, the defeated and indeed ridiculized suitors for the hand of the evening's ingénue were none other

Richard D'Oyly Carte
Artist and theatre-designer Faustin's sketch of Gilbert and Sullivan's producer.

than the complete House of Lords, and the text of the piece was a minefield for the peerage. But Gilbert paired his volleys of frustrated fury with a wholly romantic story, the story of the fairy Iolanthe, banished from fairyland for – like Josephine Corcoran – having dared to love beneath her station. Like Josephine, Iolanthe (and, indeed, all the rest of the cast) won a thoroughly happy ending at the final curtain of a sweet-and-sour musical of enormous charm and a little less bite, a musical which survives as one of the masterpieces of the Gilbert and Sullivan canon.

Patience, the musical with which Carte opened the Savoy Theatre in 1881, took for its butt not a theatrical convention but the "aesthetic" craze of the late nineteenth century, with its mock medievalisms and stained-glass attitudes, a craze personified to us today by Oscar Wilde but in its time taking in a much wider range of poses and personalities, many of which were by no means considered generally ridiculous. The ingenuous little

milkmaid heroine of the title has been taught – not unlike a certain number of genuine Victorian maidens – to regard love and marriage as a disagreeable duty, and she spends the course of the evening switching her "affections" back and forth between the show's two principal gentlemen, plighting herself, in turn, to whichever currently seems to be the least agreeable, and thus consistent with her idea of "duty". The "aesthetic" element of the show was not actually an integral part of this story, but was, rather, pasted – if very skilfully pasted – onto it. Each of Patience's two suitors, imitated each in his turn by most of the rest of the male cast, took on the poses and pretensions of an aesthete in order to make himself more attractive to the opposite sex.

The most widely successful of all the Gilbert and Sullivan shows was their 1885 musical *The Mikado*, a piece firmly in line of descent from such other oriental *opéras-bouffes* as the crazy *Ba-ta-clan* and Lecocq's extravagant *Fleur de thé*. By the time of *The Mikado*, English *opéra-*

Iolanthe

"Iolanthe, from thy dark exile thou art summoned" – The Fairy Queen (Alice Barnett) recalls Iolanthe (Jessie Bond) from her penitential puddle.

Opposite: **The Pirates of Penzance**

"Here's a first-rate opportunity . ." The Pirates and the extraordinarily prolific Major General Stanley's daughters pair off. The Opera Comiques's principals, headed by Richard Temple and George Grossmith, are shown in the medallions.

bouffe had moved on a mile from the colourful fooling and cheerfully minimal singing of Burnand's parody versions of *Windsor Castle* and *L'Africaine*. It had even moved on since the days of *H. M. S. Pinafore* and *The Pirates of Penzance*. The Gilbert and Sullivan English "comic opera" style had become thoroughly established in the decade that they had worked regularly together, and the *bouffe* element – that kind of humour drawn from exaggeration or parody that was at the heart of the *opéra-bouffe* – had been swallowed up into that special Savoy style. The Gilbert and Sullivan musicals had never been based on or aimed at any one show, like the old burlesques had been, but neither now did they josh any one theatrical genre or tradition, like the earliest of their own works. A piece such as *The Mikado* stood on its own, without reference to any other show or genre. It was simply written in the archly witty and curious manner Gilbert had made special to these shows, with typically amusing and characteristic rôles for the regulars of the Savoy company, characters who were put into a typically amusing and cleverly concocted plot and situations equipped with characteristic songs and ensembles, and the evening ended with the regulation "Gilbertian" twist of witty improbability which paired everyone off neatly at the final curtain.

Gilbert's plot for *The Mikado* was a fine,

funny and typically involved one. Nanki-Poo, the son of the Mikado of Japan, has run away from court rather than marry the elderly lady whom papa has designated as his bride, and whilst hiding out in the town of Titipu he falls in love with little local Yum-Yum. Yum-Yum's guardian and intended husband is the town executioner, Ko-Ko, but he – who is constitutionally unable to execute anyone, and is terrified of losing his sinecure and his head for laxism – is emphatically willing to render up Yum-Yum in exchange for Nanki-Poo's agreeing to be executed, or even pretending to be executed. Then the Mikado gets to town, and instead of being pleased that Ko-Ko has finally got down to doing some good civic work he is furious to find his heirlet has been topped. Since Nanki-Poo refuses to come back to life whilst the ghastly Katisha is still in a state of suspended spinsterhood, Ko-Ko is obliged to wed the gorgon himself in order to clear the ground for a happy (for everyone else) ending.

The characters of *The Mikado*, and their songs, were well and truly in the established Savoy mode. Little Yum-Yum, like Patience, is an ingénue more ingénue than is decent, even in comic opera, who wide-eyedly wonders in song ("The Moon and I") why she is so much prettier than anyone else in Titipu. Nanki-Poo is a concert-platform tenor with a show-off song ("A Wandering Minstrel, I"), the Mikado a roaring parody of an oriental potentate, equipped with a much wittier than usual version of the inevitable comic-opera potentate's topical song ("A More Humane Mikado"), and Pooh-Bah, the Lord-High-Everyone Else, represents the embodiment of the accepted (if not acceptable) face of political corruption. Ko-Ko is a funny little patter-singing clown who is allowed a moment of burlesque pathos ("Tit Willow") after having first reeled off a catalogue of some of his author's more amusing and distinctly un-Japanese dislikes ("I've Got a Little List"), and his Katisha is an *opéra-bouffe* dragon par excellence whose booming contralto gets to ride astride the burlesque-operatic first-act finale like a Valkyrie on a roller-coaster. That finale was the ensemble high-spot of a superb Sullivan score which also included an unaccompanied madrigal ("Brightly Dawns our Wedding Day") amongst its several other pieces of choice concerted music.

The Mikado

Below: Failed etiquette: Ko-ko (George Grossmith) and the three little maids take the oriental mickey out of Pooh Bah (Rutland Barrington).

Opposite: A splendid poster for the original road company of D'Oyly Carte's *Mikado* production.

SAVOY THEATRE

OR THE TOWN OF TITIPU

THE MIKADO

R. D'OYLY CARTE, Proprietor and Manager.

The Mikado

"Three little maids from school . . ." featured on the cover of one of the many dance-music arrangements of the show's music.

The Mikado totted up the longest first Savoy run of any of the Gilbert and Sullivan comic operas, and it went on from home base to become a classic both in its original version and, in translation, on the Continental stage. In European theatres, for more than a decade, *Der Mikado* held a position as the most successful musical ever to have been adapted from the English-language theatre.

After the orientalisms of *The Mikado*, the partners visited that other favourite holiday-home of the comic opera, the Venice of the Doges, in the tale of *The Gondoliers*. This time it was the everyone-shall-equal-be ideals of the socialists that got sideswiped by Gilbert's mockery, as he worked his way and his characters into and through a story that put an extra twist into the now rather hard-worked mixed-up babies plot. Like *The Mikado*, *The Gondoliers* didn't burlesque anything specific, but simply carried on the beloved Savoy tradition in the much-loved Savoy style, telling a comical *demi-bouffe* tale of politicians, baby-stealers and – of course – a full range of ranks and titles in the picturesque clothes and settings of Venice. Although it might, of course, have happened anywhere.

Gilbert had, over the years, reused many a plot-piece or personality from earlier shows, and most notably from his own earlier shows, as the raw material for his newer musicals. Early in his career he had even produced a whole burlesque, *The Happy Land*, which was based on his own play *The Wicked World*, and later, with *Princess Ida*, he had attempted, with rather obviously old-glued-to-new results, to remake one of his youthful pasticcio burlesques as a Savoy opera. However, never, since the days of *Thespis*, had he turned wholly to a piece by another author as the backbone for one of his musicals. In *The Yeomen of the Guard* that is exactly what he did do.

The Yeomen of the Guard, the one opera of the Savoy canon that its authors carefully did not dub a "comic opera", is based on the French play *Don César de Bazan*, the best-known version of the tale of a blindfolded lass married, for someone else's convenience, to a man who is condemned to die, but who inconveniently doesn't. Gilbert didn't treat the famous tale in the same way that Edward Fitzball had done in *Maritana*, and Sullivan did not supply it with the kind of music that Massenet had given to his operatic *Don César de Bazan*. For *The Yeomen of the Guard*, whatever its two writers' intentions may have been, was still a Savoy opera. Although its soprano heroine and its tenor hero followed through the main lines of the familiar story, singing on the way some of Sullivan's most lovely melodies ("Free from his Fetters Grim", "Is Life a Boon", "'Tis Done I am a Bride") set, for once, to words with no comic content at all, the other members of the company were provided with rôles that were anything but romantic. Onto the bones of the *Don César* tale Gilbert grafted a greedy, glum jester for Grossmith, a simple and sweet soubrette for Jessie Bond, a baritonic father-figure for Temple, a dragonistic wardress for resident contralto Rosina Brandram, and a lugubrious jailor for Bill Denny. And so, bit by bit, character by character and scene by scene, something of that very individual *demi-bouffe* flavour of the partners' previous works became mixed into what was basically an English light opera. But in spite of that flavouring, *The Yeomen of the Guard* has always stood a little apart amongst Gilbert and Sullivan's work, and it remains the favourite – in preference to the bright, burlesque works of the first years of the team's career – of many young lovers of the musical stage, as well as of those who prefer their opera to be light rather than *bouffe*.

The Gondoliers, produced in 1889, was the last of Gilbert and Sullivan's Savoy operas to be a genuine success. During its run the two men parted company, and although they later came back together and turned out two further pieces for the Savoy, after nearly 20 years at the top their time had now passed. Other musical-theatre writers and fashions had taken both their place and their patrons. They left behind them a body of work that had become an institution even during their own active years in the theatre, a series of shows that would stand up as the backbone of the English musical theatre tradition for many decades.

British bouffe and British burlesque

Of course, even though they dominated the comic opera scene of the late 1870s and the 1880s, Gilbert and Sullivan were no more alone in providing the London theatre with musical plays than Offenbach and his librettists had been in Paris. There were plenty of other theatres in the West End playing musicals in these years, and even though a lot of those musicals were adaptations of French and, less often, Austrian shows, a good number of others were home-made. And from those home-made shows came a goodly number of hits.

The success of *H. M. S. Pinafore* naturally encouraged other writers to try to write English *opéra-bouffe*, and the most successful amongst the musicians who followed where Sullivan led was Teddy Solomon, now better known for having bigamously married the American stage star Lillian Russell than for his music. Solomon's first full-length musical was a burlesque of the old nautical ballad tale of *Billee Taylor*, its libretto written by Henry Pottinger Stephens. Stephens's version of the story turned "virtuous" Billee into an altogether less than admirable character. Pressed into the navy, he turns out to be a right little opportunist and faker, and his charity-girl sweetheart who has disguised herself as a sailor and gone heroically to sea and his rescue ends up by dumping him. The show came out in the same season as *The Pirates of Penzance*, was compared favourably with Gilbert and Sullivan's show by a good number of critics, and gave Solomon the hit song of the year in the comical "All on Account of Eliza". *Billee Taylor* had a grand career on both sides of the Atlantic, and its authors went on to turn out burlesques on such other favourite ballads as *Claude Duval* and *Lord Bateman*, but it was only towards the end of his short career and life that handsome Teddy again found the success he'd known with *Billee Taylor*.

When the Gilbert and Sullivan partnership broke up, producer Carte called on Solomon to provide the replacement show for the Savoy. Solomon composed the music to a script by the young George Dance that stood up effortlessly alongside Gilbert's works, a script telling the story of *The Nautch Girl*, who recovers an Indian idol's stolen diamond eye after an evening's action containing even more than the Savoy's usual amount of complexities and legal finesses. London found, with great surprise, that their favourite comic opera writers were not irreplaceable, and *The Nautch Girl* was a fine success.

Alongside this new kind of burlesque musical, the good old-fashioned British burlesque with its heroes in tights, its old ladies played by actors in skirts, and its rhyming and pun-filled lines and popular tunes still prospered, and it prospered nowhere more thoroughly than at that same Gaiety Theatre that had been instrumental in launching the bright new English *opéra-bouffe*. For many years the pasticcio burlesque was the feature of the Gaiety's bills, played as one item on a multiple programme, but, in the final days before John Hollingshead's retirement and the arrival of a bright new manager at the helm of London's merriest musical theatre, that changed. The burlesque grew until it filled the whole evening's programme. It shed its borrowed music and instead was given specially composed tunes. The puns were slimmed and the rhymes were shunted into the lyrics, leaving the actors to speak prose dialogue. The burlesque had been given a thorough overhaul, so much so that it really needed a new brand name. And it got one. The shows that George Edwardes produced at the Gaiety were known as "new burlesques". They were also enormous hits.

A merry song and dance version of Harrison Ainsworth's old Newgate tale of Jack Sheppard, *Little Jack Sheppard*, with longtime Gaiety star Nellie Farren as Jack and comic actor Fred Leslie as Wild chasing each other over the rooftops of London, launched the series and scored a vast

PUNKA
The Rajah of
(Chutneypore)
Act I
and
PYJAMA
in Act II

Pyjamas
Turban

The Nautch Girl
The costume designs by Percy Anderson for Rutland Barrington as the Rajah of Chutneypore.

BABIL & BIJOU

How Babil and Bijou, accompanied by Auricomos, the Spirit of the Earth,
and the Spirit of the Air; start in an Aerial Ship on a voyage to the Moon.
SCENE 14. MID-AIR.

QUADRILLE

(AS PERFORMED IN THE CELEBRATED BALLET AT COVENT GARDEN)

hit. The new burlesque quickly became the hottest thing on the London musical stage. Meyer Lutz, the venerable musical director of the theatre who composed the scores, was metamorphosed into a top-of-the-pops songwriter, and as the Gaiety gave stage-space first to *Monte Cristo jr*, then to such pieces as *Miss Esmeralda, Frankenstein, Faust Up-to-Date, Ruy Blas and the Blasé Roué, Carmen Up-to-Data* and *Cinder-Ellen Up-too-Late*, and as the new kind of burlesque spread out to other theatres and other countries, Nellie and Fred became the darlings of the town. This new burlesque craze lasted only a half-dozen years, but when – perhaps coincidentally, around the time of the retirement of Farren and the death of Leslie – it went its way, it didn't just fade away.

As the Gaiety series, and such non-Gaiety shows as *Joan of Arc* or *Little Christopher Columbus* followed one another onto the stage, it became evident that the element of genuine burlesque in the shows was shrinking. These musicals were, as they had always been, a joyous series of funny scenes and lively songs and dances, but increasingly those scenes and songs had less and less – if anything – to do with the title or the nominal subject of the show. *Little Christopher Columbus*, for example, was a cabin boy who sang coon songs, fell in love with the daughter of a Chicago meat-king, and got to the shores of an already well-and-truly-discovered America in time for the World's Fair – where everyone did their song and dance number regardless. It seemed hardly worth calling the hero of such a show Christopher Columbus, except for the fact that it looked good on the bills. It was George Edwardes who ultimately decided that it wasn't worth it at all. He threw out all pretence of burlesque, popped the same kind of songs and dances that had made the success of those shows into a bright, up-to-date story and, bibbity-bobbity-boo, the Gaiety "musical comedy" was born

Spectacle and light opera

It's just a little too soon yet, however, to move on to Edwardes's bit of magic and its consequences in the world of musical theatre. For the West End 1870s and 1880s brought out a few more shows that were too famous for too long to be slipped by without mention. Amongst them there was one which survives

into productions today, one that broke the West End long-run record, and another that turned out to be the greatest comic opera hit Broadway had ever seen. Not bad references to be going on with.

The one that is still seen today was only a half-British show – one that came out whilst Britain was still groggy from the effect of all those champagne-bubbly trans-Channel musicals. The influence of France hadn't always been wholly good, and in fact London had witnessed the biggest theatrical blowout so far in its history when Dion Boucicault had attempted to ape the enormously extravagant French grand *opéra-bouffe* féerie, with a vast and sumptuous fairytale spectacular called *Babil and Bijou* at Covent Garden. *Babil and Bijou* cost a fortune. It was the most spectacular musical ever to have been seen in London. It launched a huge hit song in Jules Rivière's "Spring, Gentle Spring". And it lost a fortune. But those who saw it remembered it all their lives as a dazzling example of the scene-painters', the costumiers', the choreographer's, the machinists', and the gasman's art.

An altogether happier French influence was seen in the more modestly sized Anglo-French *opéras-bouffes* at the Gaiety, but the most successful cross-Channel collaboration was the one between London librettist H. B. Farnie and *Cloches de Corneville* composer Planquette on the London musical version of *Rip van Winkle*. *Rip van Winkle* was no *opéra-bouffe*: its characters were played for real and not for grotesque fun, and its music was as lively, bright and melodious as might have been expected from the composer of one of France's greatest *opéra-comique* hits. And its star was Fred Leslie – the same Fred Leslie who was to go on to team with Nellie Farren at the Gaiety, and whose performance as the lazy but lovable Rip helped launch the show to long-lived success.

In the history of the stage, and it seems especially the musical stage, there have been a surprising number of important hit shows that have been through anguished histories

Above: ***Faust Up-to-Date***
The Mephistopheles of this new burlesque was a jolly fellow who sang an Irish ballad. The hit of the show was a pretty *pas de quatre* danced to Meyer Lutz's version of the then novel barn dance.

Opposite: ***Babil and Bijou***
The scenery was a big feature of Boucicault's show, and a feature of the scenery was a skywards trip taken by the principals in an "aerial car".

and all kinds of remakes before scoring their hitship. One of the strangest histories of all surely belongs to the show that notched up the longest run of all on the nineteenth-century London stage. For no, it was not one of the famous Gilbert and Sullivan shows, nor even one of Paris's greatest hits, that won that distinction. It was a wholly unlikely musical called *Dorothy*. Once upon a time, H. B.

Fred Leslie as Rip van Winkle

An English producer commissioned a French composer to write a show for an English star which has endured for a century – in France.

Farnie and composer Alfred Cellier wrote a musical called *Nell Gwynne* which flopped at Manchester and was put away. But after the success of *Rip van Winkle*, Farnie took his libretto back so that his new French friend could reset it and make him a nice new hit. Cellier got a new book written around his music, and the result was *Dorothy*, an old-

fashioned "comedy opera" in which two naughty lads of the gentry court a pair of country maids who aren't, of course, country maids at all, and so forth. *Dorothy* was touted around, was finally accepted by Edwardes, and mounted at the Gaiety as a stop-gap in the new burlesque programme. When the burlesque company came back to town, the theatre's accountant bought the about-to-be abandoned production of *Dorothy*, shifted it down the road to another house, and watched this curious old-fashioned piece run on and on and on, until it had broken its record, made its main baritone song ("Queen of my Heart") into the ballad of the era, and spawned a whole brood of provincial touring versions that rolled up and down Britain for years and years. *Dorothy* was even produced in Hungary. It also, naturally given its record, got seen on Broadway, but Broadway was having no truck with this pretty but definitely olde Englishe show, and it closed quickly.

However, only a few years earlier, America had welcomed with an unprecedented enthusiasm a different English comic opera, one that had done well enough on the London stage and exceedingly well round the British country, but then proved as sensational a hit on Broadway as *Dorothy* had in England. *Erminie* was a piece based on the old French comedy-melodrama *L'Auberge des Adrets*, with its famous convict characters Robert Macaire and Jacques Strop. It had been written by the British musical-comedian Harry Paulton in order to provide himself with a fine comic rôle as Strop, and the musical part was composed by a young Londoner called Edward Jakobowski. The dapper Macaire and the low-comic Strop – called here Ravannes and Cadeau – escape from prison and attack a coach. One of the coach's noble occupants is heading for the Château Pontvert, where he is to be betrothed to the Marquis's daughter at a great ball, so Ravannes takes his place, and accompanied by Cadeau masquerading as "the Baron" they go to the château intending to rob the assembled company of their jewels during the night after the ball. There ensue more complexities and comic situations than even the suave Ravannes could have foreseen before a regulation happy ending is reached.

Jakobowski's score included a number of pieces that became popular – the topico-

Mynheer Jan

comical "What the Dicky Birds Say", the heroine's pretty dream song ("At Midnight on my Pillow Lying"), the thieves' assertion that they're "Downy Jailbirds of a Feather" – but it was a little lullaby ("Dear Mother in Dreams I See Her"), a song which had gone almost unnoticed in London, introduced on Broadway by the lovely Pauline Hall as the ingénue of the show, that became the rage and a longtime show-song standard in America. *Erminie*'s initial Broadway production was played 648 times, and the work was revived in New York on no fewer than nine occasions over the next 35 years.

Like Solomon and Stephens, the writers of *Erminie* didn't manage to repeat their big success. They put together a new show called *Mynheer Jan* that cleverly reproduced all the salient features of *Erminie* without seeming too similar, but now there was real money floating around and the authors ended up quarrelling with their young producer, Violet Melnotte, leaving the new show to fall to pieces. They didn't combine on a third.

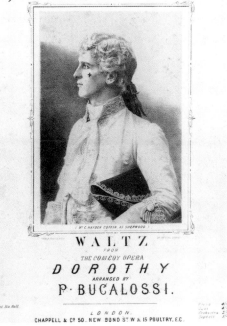

QUEEN OF MY HEART

WALTZ
FROM
THE COMEDY OPERA
DOROTHY
ARRANGED BY
P. BUCALOSSI.

LONDON.
CHAPPELL & Cº 50. NEW BOND Sᵀ W & 15 POULTRY, E.C.

Above: **Mynheer Jan**
Theatre posters of Victorian days often depicted scenes from the show, sketched from live action. So, coloured "production stills" of barely-remembered shows like this one actually survive a century later.

Left: "Queen of my Heart"
The show-song hit of the era was statuesque young Hayden Coffin's performance of Alfred Cellier's *Dorothy* serenade.

South of the Border . . .

The Toreador
A touring poster for one of the
great series of Gaiety musicals
which were played throughout
the world in the first years of the
new century.

Gaiety Days

The name of the Gaiety Theatre floats over the history of the musical theatre in Victorian Britain like that of no other – not even that of the Savoy. The image of the languorous upper-class playgoer who squeezed a glimpse at a Gaiety girl between his drinking and his dining (not uncommonly with a girl he'd been glimpsing), before rounding off his day with a bit of the other (not uncommonly with the girl he'd been dining), has bubbled down to us over the years. But so also has the Gaiety Theatre's reputation as the late century home of, and the international hub of, what became called "musical comedy".

As so often happens with long-range impressions and reputations, this one is only partly right. Certainly, the Gaiety Theatre was one of fin de siècle London's favourite places for light, bright musical entertainment (though of course not only for the toothpick-and-tails brigade), and certainly the kind of "musical comedy" that was played there in the 1890s and the 1900s became for more than a decade the latest craze in worldwide musical theatre, but the Gaiety was neither the first, nor the only, nor even in some ways the most effective of London's musical theatres in the years when it built the biggest part of its fame. What it was, was the headquarters of the producer who was indeed the first, not quite the only, but certainly the most effective of London's musical theatre producers in late Victorian and Edwardian Britain. And he was George Edwardes.

It was Edwardes who took the final steps that brought the "new burlesque" tradition to its decadent end and its logical conclusion. It was he who, realizing that there was no need for the up-to-date comedy and modern melodies of his shows to be incongruously put into the mouths of a burlesque Ali Baba or Don

Left: **The Gaiety Theatre**
From this famous theatre on London's Strand, John Hollingshead and George Edwardes sent out musicals that would entertain theatregoers all round the world.

Below: *Don Juan*
New burlesque had pretty much stopped burlesqueing anything by the time this poster was first glued to a wall.

Juan. It was he who modernized the flagging burlesque tradition, put it into modern clothes and won his tag as the inventor of the "musical comedy" – this particular kind and era of musical comedy, anyhow.

The first of Edwardes's shows to take this new turn was a piece called *In Town*, put together by house director-cum-playbuilder Jimmy Tanner and two young ex-university fellows called Adrian Ross and Frank Osmond Carr. Their piece completely dropped the trappings of burlesque, and instead simply presented two good above-the-titleable names, comic Arthur Roberts and soprano Florence St John, in a series of the same kind of comic and topical scenes and lively songs and dances as had been featured in the earlier shows. The scenes and the songs were pinned onto a loose and rather revusical framework of a plot which had Roberts, as a comically charmful man-about-town, leading a young aristocrat through the high night- and day-spots of modern London. One of those spots was the Ambiguity Theatre, where an ex-governess called Kitty (Miss St John) is the star. Disguises and mistaken identities and even a chunk of show-within-a-show burlesque took their turn between the songs and dances, and the *In Town* chorus girls got the opportunity to stroll round the stage dressed in the latest fashions, adding in their own special way an extra attraction to the entertainment.

Even though the modern chit-chat and topicalities, the modern characters and the modern little story joined up the songs and dances rather more congruously than the old burlesque texts had done, *In Town* was still far from being a finished modern musical farce. It was, as yet, still pretty much as much of a slightly shaped variety show as its predecessors had been, and that tendency was only emphasized by the way that Edwardes slipped various performers and acts in and out of the theatre scenes of the show as its run progressed. For progress it did. Edwardes's new-style show ran for 292 nights in London, and went on from there.

Fortunately for the Gaiety myth, at least some of those performances were at the Gaiety. For *In Town* was actually produced at the Prince of Wales Theatre, whilst Edwardes persisted with the last days of new burlesque at the Gaiety. When Fred Leslie's death precipitated the end of the burlesque productions, Edwardes switched *In Town* across to his flagship theatre for the important Christmas season. Its performance there encouraged him to carry on further in the same line, and though he persisted in parallel just a little longer with burlesque, Edwardes concentrated thereafter almost entirely on the kind of modern musical play of which *In Town* was the embryo.

Needless to say, the success of *In Town* quickly encouraged other writers and/or producers to leap into confecting and mounting up-to-date musical entertainments as well. Ross and Carr were snapped up to turn out a jolly piece called *Morocco Bound*, which centred round the efforts of an English squire to get himself the music-hall concessions in Morocco. This plotlet allowed a whole lot of music-hally numbers to be popped into a veritable sketch of a libretto, but most particularly it allowed virtually the whole second act of the show to be turned over to a one-number-after-another concert or music-hall programme, mooted as a kind of audition for the Bey of Morocco. The advertisedly novel music-hall element of the musical proved a big attraction, and middle-class folk who would never have dreamed of entering such an establishment crowded the Shaftesbury Theatre to splash around half-naughtily in the "dirty" stuff the other half wallowed in. They didn't pause to think that most of those theoretically dreadful, daring, down-market ditties were the work of F. Osmond Carr, Mus.Bac. (Cantab), and Arthur Ropes, alias Adrian Ross, winner of Cambridge University's most prestigious poetry prize.

Morocco Bound emphasized the variety portion of the entertainment in such a way that the kind of show that it set in fashion, the show where a reasonably coherent first act fishtailed away into a concert in the second, became known as a "variety musical". The English stage of the 1890s welcomed a good number of these pieces, but by and large their success came in the provinces, where a piece like *The Lady Slavey*, in which the bulk of the second act consisted of an after-dinner entertainment for the wealthy hero, played through more than twenty years of unbroken touring dates.

Whilst pieces such as *Morocco Bound* and *The Lady Slavey* went in one direction,

however, Edwardes went in the other. His second musical comedy production at the Prince of Wales, *A Gaiety Girl*, didn't go down-market from the first, but up. It boasted a little more of a plot (a tiny tale about a stolen comb, and a wrongly accused chorus girl) rather than less, it boasted smart, near-the-social-knuckle dialogue, concocted by the playboy lawyer who called himself Owen Hall, rather than low comedy, and it boasted songs by *In Town*'s conductor, the young Sidney Jones, a man who was soon to be firmly installed as one of the town's top musical theatre composers. *A Gaiety Girl* turned out to be even more popular than *In Town* had been, and George Edwardes and the musical theatre found themselves set in the tracks they were to roll along for the next couple of decades.

Morocco Bound

The "variety musical" could find room for almost any kind of speciality turn. Letty Lind's skirt-dance and song routine was one of the more regular.

The Shop Girl

The first new-style musical comedy to be produced at the Gaiety Theatre itself was The Shop Girl. *For some reason, Edwardes didn't choose to go again with the team that had done him so proud with* A Gaiety Girl, *but instead ordered his libretto from an American journalist, Henry Dam, and his music from the Belgian composer and conductor Ivan Caryll, who'd recently scored with the songs for* Little Christopher Columbus. *Dam did his pretty good best to imitate the newly fashionable Owen Hall style of snappily social stage dialogue, and he hung that dialogue onto a story that, if it was pretty slight, was yet a bit stiffer than that of* A Gaiety Girl *had been.*

The main plot line of Dam's libretto was about a missing baby (only missing this time, not mixed up, as in Gilbert's libretti). The now wealthy Mr Brown of Colorado has been advertising in the British papers for his long-lost daughter, and the search for the now grown-up baby has led him, and us, to Mr Hooley's London emporium. At first it seems that plump and pouting shop girl Ada Smith, an orphan from her birth, is the missing heiress. Big boss Hooley is swift off the mark with a proposal of marriage that Ada snaps up, leaving her previously promised, the little shop-walker Miggles, in the lurch. But Mr Hooley has moved too fast. It turns out that little orphan Ada really is an orphan, and the real heiress is none other than ingénue Bessie Brent, who has been breaking her heart because love

doesn't level all ranks enough to let her wed her aristocratic Charlie. Money – particularly American money – being even more of a leveller than a coronet, Bessie and Charlie can now be happily paired off whilst little Miggles consoles himself with the ravishing Miss Robinson, with whom he's been duetting since his dumping.

There had been popular songs in the other musical comedy shows already seen on the London stage – *Morocco Bound*'s "Marguerite of Monte Carlo" or *A Gaiety Girl*'s "Sunshine Above" – but *The Shop Girl* proved to be the richest show so far. Miggles and Miss Robinson sang and danced to "Love on the Japanese Plan", Brown described his rise to riches in "Brown of Colorado" and George Grossmith jr, son of the famous Gilbert and Sullivan comedian, repeated his *Morocco*

Background: Miggles (Edmund Payne) and Miss Robinson (Katie Seymour), suitably orientalled-up, describe "Love on the Japanese Plan".

Bound masher performance describing himself, to Lionel Monckton's music and his own lyrics, as "Beautiful Bountiful Bertie". However, in a manner that would characterize many a musical comedy in the turn-of-the-century years, the biggest hit of all was not part of the show's made-to-measure score, but a borrowed number that was stuck in to jolly up the rôle of one of the leading artists. In this case the artist was the determined juvenile man Seymour Hicks, later to become a considerable power in the West End musical theatre, and the song was a mildly suggestive little music-hall number written by Irishman Felix McGlennon that had been around, barely noticed, for some years. As sung by Hicks, who twinkled in all the right places, "Her Golden Hair was Hanging Down her Back" became a full-scale hit. During the run of the show, several attempts were made to interpolate other less- or more- or even previously un-used songs, including several of the fashionable coon songs of the time, but "Love on the Japanese Plan" and "Her Golden Hair" remained the star turns of the night.

The Shop Girl was an enormous hit. It filled the Gaiety for a year and a half, knocking out an innings of 546 performances and setting itself up as the model for an era not only of Gaiety Theatre musicals but of West End-wide

clones. Before long, it had been seen the length and breadth of the English-speaking world, as Edwardes himself exported companies playing the show to Broadway and to Australia as well as around the British provinces, and eager managers snapped up the rights to play the new London hit on the Pacific, the African or the oriental circuits. But *The Shop Girl* went even further than that. *La Demoiselle de magasin* was given a production at Paris's Olympia, and *Die Ladenmamsell* appeared at Vienna's Theater in der Josefstadt, as the new kind of British musical comedy went international with remarkable speed. And with remarkable staying power. For in spite of all the subsequent hit musicals that graced the Gaiety stage, only *The Shop Girl* ever won the honours of a West End revival. That revival came after Edwardes's death, in 1920, and its co-producer was none other than Seymour Hicks, the show's original *jeune premier* a quarter of a century earlier. Following the fashion that he had used to such effect in the original show, and that he had cultivated largely through the years, Hicks ladled half a scoreful of new numbers into *The Shop Girl*, but its story, its scenes and those of the old songs that remained still stood up well, and the result was another 327 performances to add to *The Shop Girl*'s West End record.

CREDITS

The Shop Girl

Musical farce in 2 acts by Henry J. W. Dam

MUSIC

by Ivan Caryll. Additional numbers by Adrian Ross and Lionel Monckton

Produced at the Gaiety Theatre, London, 24 November 1894
USA: Palmer's Theater, New York, 8 October 1895
France: L'Olympia, Paris, 4 June 1896
Austria: Theater in der Josefstadt, Vienna, 5 February 1897

CAST

Bessie Brent	Ada Reeve
Charlie	Seymour Hicks
John Brown	Colin Coop
Miggles	Edmund Payne
Miss Robinson	Katie Seymour
Ada Smith	Lillie Belmore
Mr Hooley	Arthur Williams
Dodo	Marie Halton

THE SHOP-GIRL Valse
ON Melodies by IVAN CARYLL and LIONEL MONCKTON,
ARRANGED by P. BUCALOSSI.
Copyright
LONDON.
HOPWOOD & CREW,
42 NEW BOND STREET. W.

Left: Ivan Caryll's show songs were arranged into best-selling dance-music by the composer of a hit musical of an earlier era: Procida Bucalossi.

In the years that followed, Edwardes experimented further with his Gaiety musical comedies. In *My Girl*, put together by the *In Town* team of Tanner and Carr, he went for a musical play that ventured into the world of stockbroking in a plot worthy of a straight play, but one that turned out to be rather more involved than his audiences – not to mention the critics – were willing to take. Then, with *The Circus Girl*, he got Tanner to build a piece of rather more loose-limbed musical comedy around a scene from *Eine tolle Nacht*, the hit German *Posse*. That worked much better. The audience enjoyed seeing the cast of new Gaiety favourites – little Teddy Payne, plump Connie Ediss, ingénue Ellaline Terriss, her off-stage husband Seymour Hicks, and dancer Katie Seymour – disporting themselves in song and dance through a tale of mix-ups and misunderstandings in Paris and the circus. *The Circus Girl* proved a hit of *Shop Girl* dimensions, and Edwardes's new show went on to be produced by Augustin Daly at the famous Broadway theatre named after him, in Budapest, in Vienna, in Australia, in South Africa and everywhere else that British touring musical companies went. *The Circus Girl* confirmed, if it needed confirming, the rage for "musical comedy" of the Edwardes brand, a rage that would last for more than a decade.

As at the Savoy, the Gaiety musical comedies that followed the first great hits became built around a set of favourite players, and the stories, the scenes and the songs varied little from one show to the next. But no one wanted them to vary. *A Runaway Girl* had Ellaline Terriss running away from an unwanted marriage – pursued by the rest of the cast – through some picturesque European venues and introduced one of the most enduring of all Gaiety songs, Lionel Monckton's "Soldiers in the Park"; *The Messenger Boy* had Teddy Payne as the boy of the title rushing off with some vital papers to Egypt, pursued by those trying to stop him and those trying to stop them, and marked – Payne's top comic status obliging – the switch away from "girl" titles at the Gaiety; *The Toreador* plonked the Gaiety favourites down amongst the bombs and bulls of Carlist Spain; *The Orchid* had everyone chasing around trying to find the priceless flower of the title; and amongst them all they kept the Gaiety

Theatre – the old one and its successor – overflowing with success for seven full years, from 1898 to 1905, a triumph that equalled even that of the Savoy in its heyday.

During the years when the Gaiety reigned over the world of musical comedy, the rest of London's theatres and producers other than Edwardes also turned out some sizeable hits. A young army officer called Basil Hood put together some particularly impressive and well-written libretti, set with songs by composer Walter Slaughter, and the pair scored major successes with the saucy tale of the London cabby *Gentleman Joe*, who gets mistaken for a nobleman by a matchmaking society lady, and with the amorous South of France high-jinks surrounding *The French Maid*. *The Lady Slavey*'s author, George Dance, marked up another vast hit with the jolly tale of the blackmailing lassie who was *The Gay Parisienne*, before going on to supply variety comic Little Tich with a stage musical vehicle as *Lord Tom Noddy*, to detail to eager provincials the doings of *The Gay Grisette*, and then to provide the words to the music of the up-and-coming American-born musician Howard Talbot for the little tale of *A Chinese Honeymoon*.

A Chinese Honeymoon was written, as were many of Dance's shows, as a touring musical. It targeted the tastes and preferences of the less sophisticated British provincial audiences, and its ambitions were limited to the "country". When it was produced, in 1899, at Hanley in the British Potteries country, it was scheduled just for a short pre-Christmas tour. But fate and English audiences had other ideas. One tour led to another, then to the West End, and before it was finished *A Chinese Honeymoon* turned out to be the first musical ever –

Below: *A Runaway Girl*
"Oh, Listen to the Band..!"
Lionel Monckton's song marched across the world.

Opposite: *The Messenger Boy*
The camel didn't actually appear on the Gaiety stage, but Teddy Payne did. His star status meant that the Gaiety run of "Girl" shows gave way to one with a "Boy" in its title.

happen in China and they have to do with the local rules on kissing – rules such as: he who does it must wed she with whom he does it. Anyhow, Mr P. squabbles with his wifey, petulantly kisses a disguised local Princess in the street and – much to the despair of Tom who is in love with royal Soo Soo – is condemned to become her Chinese consort. Mrs Pineapple, in her turn, looks like falling into the clutches of ruling Papa. Things get so complex and so threatening that the British Navy has to be brought on to set all to rights.

The show's songs ranged from pretty ballads for Soo Soo and her Tom to comic songs for the Chinese Emperor and his Admiral and soubrette pieces for Mrs Pineapple ("The à la Girl") and her undetachable troupe of bridesmaids, but the musical highlights of the night were a bunch of cockney music-hall numbers served up by Fi Fi, an incidental and lovelorn (for Tom) Chinese waitress from Hoxton. When the plot wasn't on, Fi Fi delivered the story of "Sister Mary Jane's High Note", insisted "I Want to be a Lidy", described how her music-teacher taught her "The Twiddley Bits", and made herself the star turn of the evening.

Dance and Hood shared the very top branch of the music-comedy-writing tree through the turn-of-the-century years, but they shared it with one other man – the man who'd really given the whole genre its lift-off: the irrepressible Jimmy Davis, alias Owen Hall. Hall worked mostly for Edwardes, but in 1899 new-boy producer Tom B. Davis (no relation) hired him to manufacture the libretto for what was to be the first stage musical by top popular songwriter Leslie Stuart. Hall obliged by trotting out a South Seas story featuring a soprano leading lady done out of her rightful flower-plantation by a villainous perfume-maker, but eventually helped back to birthright and into marriage by his handsome baritonic Welsh overseer. The far-off Pacific setting and the bony Pacific plot didn't stop Hall from introducing into the proceedings plenty of society London folk with the slicing society London chatter he favoured as dialogue, and when his producer found that star soubrette Ada Reeve was willing to sign for the show, Hall unconcernedly popped in a suitably large and bon-motful character for her. Like Fi Fi in *A Chinese Honeymoon*, Lady Holyrood had only a little to do with the plot,

anywhere in the world – to run for over a thousand consecutive town performances. And that record-breaking London season was just a beginning. It proved a triumph for a new young American production outfit called the Shubert brothers, it broke records in Australia, it gallivanted through Central Europe in German and in Hungarian, and it spent years and years, after its London run, trouping the provinces of Britain.

Dance's tale was one that seemed to look back to the days of *Ba-ta-clan* and *Fleur de thé*, and it shared with both their cock-eyed oriental setting and their theme of Westerners caught out by funny foreign people with funny foreign customs in a funny foreign country. The Westerners here are Mr Pineapple and his new bride and the young naval officer Tom Hatherton, their funnies

but it was she, along with the evening's low comedian (playing the part of a peripatetic phrenologist), who were the stars of the show that was called, after the perfume in the story, *Florodora*.

Leslie Stuart's score for *Florodora* was a truly fine one. The soprano waltzed through "The Silver Star of Love", her baritone hymned "The Shade of the Palm", the number two gentleman proclaimed "I Want to be a Military Man", and his partner serenaded "The Fellow Who Might" in one of the era's sweetest melodies. As for the latecome Lady Holyrood, she got a couple of brisk point numbers ("Tact", "I've an Inkling") written by support songwriter Paul Rubens. However, even in a score as full of hits as these, there was one number that turned out bigger and better. And, unusually, it wasn't a solo or a duo, but an ensemble: six chorus boys and the six front-line girls parading up and down to an oddly long-lined melody called "Are There any More at Home Like You?". As it went on to international hitdom, it soon became better known by its first line: "Tell Me, Pretty Maiden".

Florodora was a huge hit in Britain, and it went promptly to all those corners of the earth – from Budapest to Sydney – where the good hits of the time went, but its biggest success of all came in America. The show ran for 549 consecutive nights on Broadway, the songs became American chart-toppers, the girls of the double sextet became showbusiness personalities, and *Florodora* itself evolved into a longtime tourer and even a revival prospect. The Shuberts mounted a major revival in New York in 1920.

Leslie Stuart went on to write several more successful musicals – and *The Silver Slipper* and *Havana* actually proved better liked in America than in their native Britain – but his first show remained his biggest winner, and he never succeeded in challenging the record of his nifty librettist.

For a man whose pen was fuelled by the need to keep the bookmakers and barkeepers of London in business, and who

George Dance showed he could challenge Gilbert when it came to writing libretti and George Edwardes when it came to producing, and both when it came to making money.

thus wrote not only for cash down and no royalties but to whatever order was required, Owen Hall had a remarkable record. In the 15 years between *A Gaiety Girl* and his early death he wrote 11 libretti, of which only one was a flop and eight were full-scale to world-circling hits.

The biggest of these hits was, in fact, the biggest international hit to come out of Britain in the nineteenth century – bigger than *Pinafore*, bigger than *The Mikado*, *Erminie*, *Florodora* or *A Chinese Honeymoon*. In real terms, in fact, probably the biggest international hit ever to come out of Britain until the late twentieth century and its series of multi-national mega-musicals. *The Geisha* was, unsurprisingly, a George Edwardes production, but it was not produced at either the Gaiety or the Prince of Wales, as the earlier hits had been, it was produced at Daly's Theatre in Leicester Square.

A Gaiety Girl played out the latter part of its career at Daly's, and when Edwardes – soon after the production of *The Shop Girl* – replaced it with a successor, it was a successor written by the same people – Hall, lyricist Harry Greenbank and composer Sidney Jones – who had done so well with the past piece. *A Naughty Girl* was, naturally, intended to be on the same lines as its predecessor. However, like *Florodora*, it underwent some expedient changes between page and stage. This time the artist who became suddenly available was star soprano Marie Tempest, so instead of the new show being built around American soubrette Marie Halton as a naughty schoolgirl in Paris, the plot was reshaped to become a double-headed one. The naughty schoolgirl (Miss Halton was re-routed to *The Shop Girl*, and the part was ultimately played by Letty Lind), her English family in Paris, her sparky schoolmistress and others sang and danced their way through a lively Gaiety-type imbroglio, whilst Miss Tempest with her superior soprano voice was cast as a former artist's model, now a wealthy and merry widow, who has returned to Paris and met up with the richly baritonic artist with whom she had whispered forevers in her young days. Like a later and better-known merry widow, she finds him proud and obdurate until a quarter to eleven.

An Artist's Model, as the show was finally called in homage to its soprano, turned out to be a major hit. Even bigger than *A Gaiety Girl*. But it was also, of course, given the prominent and wholly romantic "merry widow" plot that had been grafted onto the Gaiety-weight one, a show of a very different substance and flavour to Hall's earlier musical. It was like . . . well, what was it like? There hadn't been anything quite of the kind made in London since . . . since when?

In fact, the musical by accident, with its bipartite nature, was rather a novel one. And it was also one of which, given the success it had scored, Edwardes was not slow to order a repeat. Miss Tempest, Miss Lind and baritone Hayden Coffin who had played the poor but proud artist, were promptly put into Owen Hall's collimator to be turned into characters in a new Daly's Theatre musical. And that new Daly's Theatre musical, which came out in April of 1896, was *The Geisha*.

Above: **Florodora**
"Tell me, Pretty Maiden, are there any more at home like you?" The elegantly strolling boys and girls of Sidney Ellison's double sextet scored the biggest song-and-dance hit of the era with their routine.

Left: **An Artist's Model**
None of the Daly's stars got the feature spot on the frontispiece of their show's souvenir. That spot went to the deliciously stareable-at chorine Hetty Hamer, whose wordless appearance as a nearly-nude model was a much appreciated moment of the musical.

The Geisha

Owen Hall might not have known his horses very profitably, but he knew his actors. And his audiences. For the new show he cast Miss Tempest as a beautiful geisha girl, Coffin (who was now as big a star as she) was put into the spotless white and braided epaulettes of a British naval uniform, and Miss Lind (who'd suffered by comparison with neither of them in the public's favouritism) was written up as a little English lassie of a mischievous nature.

Background: O Mimosa Sans donned Japanese kimonos and wigs from St Petersburg to Hobart. This one got obi-ed up in Budapest.

Alongside those top-billed characters Hall placed one of the superior, charming ladies of a certain age with whom he'd succeeded so markedly in both earlier pieces, plus a couple of good male comedy parts: one little chap and one comic heavy. For these latter rôles Edwardes hired statuesque ex-Gaiety Girl Maud Hobson, the rising little comedian Huntley Wright (after this to join the three stars at the head of the Daly's team) and popular musical-comic Harry Monkhouse, and as a *bonne bouche* he added the little French ingénue Juliette Nesville, who had recently caused a *tempête* in her first London appearance.

The story that these folk were embroiled in was a fairly simple one, one on similar lines to that which *A Chinese Honeymoon* would follow a few years later, but told with a slightly more comic-operatic tone. Reggie Fairfax, RN (Coffin), is stationed out in the Orient. Far from his fiancée Molly (Miss Lind) and lonely for feminine company, he regularly spends his free time at the Tea House of Ten Thousand Joys, run by Chinaman Wun-Hi (Wright),

talking with the lovely geisha O Mimosa San (Miss Tempest). This proximity sends warning lights up in the mind of Lady Constance Wynne (Miss Hobson), who happens to be boating by, and she telegraphs pronto to Molly to get on the next P&O out. It also stirs up the local overlord Marquis Imari (Monkhouse), who fancies Mimosa for himself, and who orders the teahouse shut down and its girls sold off. The complications start on the day of the disposal sale. Molly has arrived and disguised herself as a geisha (since Reggie's tastes apparently run that way), and now she gets mixed up in the auction. Lady Constance stoutly outbids Imari for Mimosa's indentures, but then sees the Marquis instead help himself to the next lot – Molly! The British band set out to prevent Molly from being forcibly turned into a Japanese Marquise instead of Mrs Fairfax, and with Mimosa's help the ambitious little French interpreter Juliette (Mlle Nesville) ends up under the wedding canopy in Molly's place. The good old Royal Navy doesn't even have to intervene this time.

The Geisha saw young Sidney Jones, in his

third show, blossom as a theatre composer. Miss Tempest's rôle was just littered with lovely music: the little tongue-in-cheek tale of "The Amorous Goldfish", the waltzes in rueful description of "A Geisha's Life" and, with the star disguised as a fortune-teller, of "Love, Love", an additional piece by James Philp in which she described herself as "The Jewel of Asia", and a winning Kissing Duet with Reggie – he teaching her how. Coffin had a splendid baritone ballad, "Star of my Soul", as well as a jaunty "Jack's the Boy" provided by Lionel Monckton, and Miss Lind delivered a cute "Chon-Kina" in her Japanese disguise and scored a hit with the anthropomorphic tale of "The Interfering Parrot" and then another with Monckton's "The Toy Monkey". As for Wright, he drew what turned out to be the most popularly enduring piece of the score, a daft little ditty about the woes of a Chinaman in Japan called "Chin- Chin- Chinaman".

The Geisha ran for 760 performances at Daly's Theatre, but they were only the very small beginnings of an instant and long international career. Daly put the show into his highly respected repertoire on Broadway, and America, like all the other English-language centres, welcomed the show with a singular enthusiasm. It quickly established itself as one of the great hits of the English-language musical stage, and settled in for years and years of touring around the provinces and colonies. But Europe, which up to this time had given only *Der Mikado* amongst English shows a first-class reception, quite simply went mad for *Die Geisha, eine japanische Theehaus-geschichte*. The show caused a sensation when it was produced at Berlin's Lessing-Theater, and within months Budapest's Magyar Színház and Vienna's Carltheater had their versions on the boards to a similar reaction. France, Italy, Spain, Scandinavia, South America . . . productions sprouted everywhere, and in all sorts of languages, as *The Geisha* turned itself into the most famous example of a British musical ever known.

The Geisha was last seen on Broadway in 1931, and in the West End in 1934. But whereas British companies, in particular, have neglected the show in later years, preferring to play translated versions of foreign shows, Central Europe has stayed true to a piece which in the early 1920s was rated in all-time popularity inferior only to *Die Fledermaus, Die lustige Witwe* (*The Merry Widow*) and *Das Dreimäderlhaus* (*Blossom Time*). *Die Geisha* was played at the Vienna Raimundtheater as recently as 1973.

CREDITS

The Geisha

A Story of a Tea-House
  Japanese musical play in 2
  acts by Owen Hall

LYRICS

by Harry Greenbank

MUSIC

by Sidney Jones. Additional
  songs by Lionel Monckton
  and James Philp

Produced at Daly's Theatre,
  London, 25 April 1896
USA: Daly's Theater, New
  York, 9 September 1896
Germany: Lessing-Theater,
  Berlin, 1 May 1897
Austria: Carltheater, Vienna, 16
  November 1897
France: Théâtre de l'Athénée-
  Comique, Paris, 8 March
  1898

CAST

O Mimosa San Marie Tempest
Molly Seamore   Letty Lind
Reginald Fairfax, RN
                Hayden Coffin
Wun-Hi   Huntley Wright
Marquis Imari
              Harry Monkhouse
Lady Constance Wynne
                Maud Hobson
Juliette   Juliette Nesville

"Chin Chin Chinaman Chop Chop Chop."

"Chin, Chin, Chinaman" –
Huntley Wright details the
woes of his down-the-drain
career in business.

The Daly's musical continued on superbly after *The Geisha*. In the next show, Hall quit the Orient for ancient Rome, casting Miss Tempest as Maia, the soothsaying daughter of a hack magician (Wright) with a yen for a statuesque slave called Diomed (Coffin). Former Savoy star Rutland Barrington joined the company for *A Greek Slave* and played Marcus Pomponius, the rejected Prefect who gets Maia to help him in his revenge against his lofty Roman lady, a revenge in which Maia nearly loses her Diomed. Set with a score no less fine than that of *The Geisha*, *A Greek Slave* didn't score as highly as the earlier piece, and for his next show Edwardes went back to the Orient. He went, however, without Hall, as he needed to pander to a powerful journalist by using a libretto the man had submitted to him. But by the time *San Toy* got through rehearsals, the journalist's book had been all but rewritten by the actors and production team, and Jones's music, Greenbank's lyrics, and the Daly's stars did all the rest that was needed.

San Toy cast Miss Tempest as the umpteenth musical-theatre girl brought up as a boy ("The Petals of the Plum Tree"), Coffin played another fellow in uniform, a fellow who seems to have found out she's not a boy at all ("Love Has Come from Lotus Land"), whilst Wright was another funny Chinaman with another funny Chinaman song ("Chinee Soje-Man"), and Barrington was another Eastern potentate with a harem of little wives ("Six Little Wives", "I Mean to Introduce it into China"). Miss Lind had jumped ship – probably at the sight of the book of *San Toy*. Soon after the opening Miss Tempest followed suit, severing her connection not only with Edwardes but with the musical theatre, before going on to her famous second career as an actress.

Both ladies had misjudged the potential of *San Toy*. Although it was not in the class of its two predecessors, it obviously served, much better than *A Greek Slave* had done, the wants of those looking for a second *Geisha*. In the end it actually notched up an even longer run than its famous forebear at Daly's, had a long provincial afterlife and even followed *The Geisha* into Europe, where it joined that show and *Der Mikado* as the third successful – third oriental successful – English-language

musical of the nineteenth century.

San Toy was Sidney Jones's last musical to be produced by George Edwardes at Daly's. After five fine shows in a row, the last survivor of the great *Geisha* team moved on to other successes (*My Lady Molly*, *King of Cadonia*) and half-successes (*See See*, *The Girl from Utah*, *The Happy Day*), ultimately retiring when the kind of music he wrote went under in the dancing craze of wartime Britain. He was succeeded at Daly's by the man who had supplied him (and the Gaiety) for so many years with "additional songs", and amongst them a high ration of hits – Lionel Monckton. Monckton, aided by Adrian Ross and Jimmy Tanner of the Gaiety team, not to mention Coffin and Wright – the remnants of the Daly's star team – kept up the house average when they scored a fine success with the period English tale of *A Country Girl*, but thereafter the Daly's era that had been opened up by *A Gaiety Girl* and *An Artist's Model*, and which had peaked with *The Geisha*, puttered to a halt.

The West End, in the early days of the twentieth century, continued to supply the world with much of its musical theatre entertainment, and the gradual eclipse of Daly's Theatre by no means put an end to the flow of musical plays of all kinds rolling off the London stage and into packing cases labelled for abroad.

The writer whose name appeared most often through these years on winning playbills was Ivan Caryll, the same Ivan Caryll who had penned the songs for *Little Christopher Columbus* early in the 1890s. Since then, whilst acting as musical director at the Gaiety Theatre, he had been responsible for the bulk of the music to all of the Gaiety hits, and in the 1900s that series continued through such hits as *The Spring Chicken*, *The Girls of Gottenberg* and *Our Miss Gibbs*. At the same time, however, the copious Caryll was supplying further music for further shows, shows produced beyond the confines of his home theatre, and he scored hit after hit with such pieces as *The Girl from Kay's*, *The Earl and the Girl*, *The Cherry Girl* and the more than usually substantial *The Duchess of Dantzic*, at one stage going so far as to have five successful musicals running at the same time in the West End.

Background: ***A Greek Slave*** "I want to be popular" – Rutland Barrington as Marcus Pomponius, a Roman magistrate with a yen to be loved.

It was noticeable, in fact, that several of Caryll's pieces were "more than usually substantial", though not necessarily in their musical part. The composer, who shared what free time he had between homes in Britain and France, had kept close contact in the years since with the Parisian theatre where he had started his career, and several of his pieces had – unusually – used successful Parisian plays as the bases for their libretti. *The Duchess of Dantzic* was a musical version of Sardou's *Madame Sans-Gêne*, Owen Hall's book to *The Girl from Kay's* was taken from Léon Gandillot's *La Mariée recalcitrante*, and *The Spring Chicken* was a musical version of the French hit *Coquin de printemps*. Which meant that, even adapted as English musicals, they had much more consistent plotting and character, and much more dramatic shape than most turn-of-the-century musical comedies. And the man behind all this transplanting of French backbone into the British musical was the wheeler-dealing Caryll, with his solid background in French *opérette* and *vaudeville*.

The trend which Caryll helped take root soon influenced other writers, but it did not ever become a rule. There was still a place in the West End, and in theatres and countries beyond, for the flimsiest of musical comedy shows, and some of the very flimsiest came from the pen of Paul Rubens. Wealthy, well educated, and theatre-struck, Rubens wrote both the songs and the script for many of his musicals, beginning with two of the most blow-away light of the era, *Three Little Maids* and *Lady Madcap*. Both were successful, both were tuneful, and both were vaguely pitiful and/or distasteful in their emphasis on a sort of naughty-British-schoolboy humour. But Rubens eventually went on to prove that he had much better in him than this twee sort of material. First of all, he turned out a delicious little musical play called *Mr Popple of Ippleton*, and then he moved on to produce some of his happiest work in the merry "Dutch musical incident" called *Miss Hook of Holland*.

Miss Hook of Holland was a starring vehicle for George Huntley, the endearingly lubricated comedian who had made such a hit in the title-rôle of *Mr Popple*, and once again he played a charming, befuddled character with consummate skill. This time he was Mr Hook, the owner of a Dutch distillery that makes the famous liqueur Cream of the Sky. Unfortunately, one day Mr Hook takes his secret recipe out for a walk, and loses it, and the retrieval of the recipe becomes a point in the battle between a bandmaster and a military Captain for the hand of the titular Miss Hook. Rubens provided a pretty selection of what he false-naively called "jingles and tunes" of a Dutch-tinted variety to illustrate his story ("Little Miss Wooden Shoes", "Soldiers of the Netherlands", "The Flying Dutchman", "A Pretty Pink Petty from Peter", "Fly Away Kite", "The Sleepy Canal"), and the evening turned out to be both charming and probably the biggest hit of its already terminally ill writer's career. Rubens did less well following Holland with trips to the Côte d'Azur (*My Mimosa Maid*) and Scandinavia (*Dear Little Denmark*), but he scored further success with an unlikely attempt at a costume musical (*The Balkan Princess*) and in particular with the most vertebrate of all his shows, a musical version of the famous farce *Les dominos roses*, which was produced throughout the English theatre world as *Tonight's the Night*.

Basil Hood, who had written such fine musical comedies in the 1890s, was another who held his place on the theatrical front in the early part of the new century, but he found his prime success in these later years in an area far from the lusty *Gentleman Joe*s and *French Maid*s of his early years. Hood became the official "new W. S. Gilbert" (which can't have pleased the still living and trying-to-be-active Gilbert), pairing with Sullivan on the fine *The Rose of Persia* and *The*

The Spring Chicken
A poster-artist's picture-punful whimsy, instead of the usual colourful scene from the show.

Tom Jones

The first act finale. Tom (Hayden Coffin) has knocked down his beastly foster brother for the love of the fair Sophia (Ruth Vincent). It will be two acts of picaresque flight from Somerset to London for half the cast before the happy ending arrives.

Emerald Isle, and then with "the new Sullivan", Edward German, on perhaps the most enduring comic opera of the early twentieth century: *Merrie England*.

Merrie England told the three-cornered tale of Queen Elizabeth I who loves Sir Walter Raleigh who loves her lady-in-waiting, Bessie Throckmorton. Written in a whimsically theeing and thouing style, much more Savoy-Elizabethan than *The Yeomen of the Guard*, the show was illustrated by a fine, singable score that threw up several English concert classics: the baritone hymn to "The Yeomen of England", the tenor paean to "The English Rose", the Queen's contralto hymn "Peaceful England", and some brilliant soprano music for heroine Bessie ("Oh, Who Shall Say that Love is Cruel", "She Had a Letter from her Love"). The show had a disappointing career first time round, in the dying days of the Savoy régime, but it proved its durability, returning several times to London, decades later, and becoming a concert classic.

Sadly, Hood largely distanced himself from the lighter musical theatre after an uncomfortable encounter with the star system and modern producing methods. He was hired by American producer Charles Frohman as librettist/lyricist for a version of the Romeo and Juliet tale set in modern London – a kind of *West End Story*. But his carefully constructed book, with characters and scenes all neatly parallelling Shakespeare, got hacked up and around to suit Frohman's star-casting, and Hood withdrew his name from the bills. Public judgement, however, seemed to justify Frohman. *The Belle of Mayfair* turned out to be a big success, and the large bulk of the credit went to composer Leslie Stuart ("Come to St George's").

Stuart stayed around for some time. Apart from and as well as *The Belle of Mayfair*, he scored with the tale of *The School Girl* who winkled out a nasty secret from the stock exchange, with *Havana* at the Gaiety, and finally with *Peggy*, a London version of a fashionably French farce. But his career and his life both tailed away into gambling debt-ridden greyness, and in the end the composer of *Florodora* faded prematurely from the scene.

Frohman, too, was a presence in the West End around this time, often allied with George Edwardes, or with a man who, like himself, made no bones about the sort of integrity that mattered to Hood, but simply went for results. That man was Seymour Hicks, once the star juvenile of the Gaiety, and now with his wife, Ellaline Terriss, half of the West End's favourite musical comedy couple. The pair had their biggest success with an up-to-date London version of the Cinderella story called *The Catch of the Season*, and followed it up with *The Beauty of Bath* and *The Gay Gordons*, before their vein of favour also ran out. Even the most

successful Seymour Hicks pieces, however, were rarely noted for their scores: the most popular musical moments usually came – just as his *Shop Girl* hit had done – from songs simply plucked from the music-hall or minstrel world and stuck fairly incongruously into his shows. Miss Terriss's biggest hit was her rendition of the American song "The Honeysuckle and the Bee", glued into Walter Slaughter's score for the little Christmas show *Bluebell in Fairyland.* So, whilst writers like Caryll were taking the musical in one direction towards a more coherent comedy with musical numbers format, rather in the vein of a more sophisticated *vaudeville* or an upmarket *Posse mit Gesang,* Hicks and Frohman and others were pulling in the other direction – towards the old potpourri, pasticcio or variety musical with its slight story and movable musical parts. But there was no argument. Both kinds of show drew the town – though maybe a different part of the town – and both coexisted

quite happily in the West End and the musical theatre's other high and holy places.

Even though the English musical comedy was beginning to lose its hold on the world's stages as the first decade of the 1900s went by – no little thanks to the challenge presented by the new craze for everything that was Viennese – the decade before the war did, nevertheless, produce some of the finest musicals of the famous era of English musical comedy.

One of those pieces was *Tom Jones*. Following in behind shows based (more or less) on *Romeo and Juliet*, *Much Ado About Nothing* and *The Vicar of Wakefield*, it seemed like the vanguard of a musical theatre retaliation to the idea of Franco-English musical comedy, but what it turned out to be was another medium success, like *Merrie England*, that proved to have staying power. A neatly filleted version of Fielding's famous, and already thoroughly musicalized, story was attached to a splendidly suitable score by *Merrie England* composer Edward German that produced one of the most celebrate waltz-songs of the British stage ("For Tonight") and one of its prettiest soprano ballads ("Dream o' Day Jill"). *Tom Jones* never returned to the West End, as *Merrie England* did, but its songs are still sung to this day.

The other great hit of the Edwardian era was another piece mounted by *Tom Jones*

producer Robert Courtneidge. *The Arcadians* is probably the most complete of all the musical comedies of its age, and it is certainly the most complete of those that were composed to a wholly original libretto. That libretto, effectively written by the same Alexander Thompson who had produced *Tom Jones*, had something of the smartness of Owen Hall at his best as it followed the adventures of James Smith, the people's caterer, through what was little more than a trip to fairyland. Smith bails out of his deficient plane in the far-off realm of Arcadia, a place where all is perfect and an untruth unheard of. When the Arcadians hear about the horrors that exist in London town, they set proselytizingly forth, determined to bring truth and light to the beastly British. It takes two acts before – after all sorts of comic and romantic complications – they give up in their hopeless mission and go home.

The music to *The Arcadians* was the work of two proven men: Lionel Monckton, most recently triumphant in *The Country Girl* and as the sidekick to Caryll at the Gaiety, and Howard Talbot of *A Chinese Honeymoon* fame, who had delivered the songs for *The White Chrysanthemum*, *The Girl Behind the Counter* and *The Belle of Brittany* to the world's stages in the latest seasons. With *The Arcadians* the two men hit another and new peak. Their memorable score went from the

Left: *The Girl Behind The Counter*
Some of the original costume designs, by Karl, for the intimate musical comedy produced at Wyndham's Theatre in 1906.

lovely music of the first, Arcadian act ("The Pipes of Pan", "The Joy of Life") through the jollities of a race-course scene ("The Girl with the Brogue", "I've Got a Motter") and the hilarities of Smith's attempt to launch a fashionably Arcadian restaurant amid the tangle of romances and fibs ("Truth is so Beautiful", "Half Past Two", "All Down Piccadilly"), scoring hit after hit on the way. *The Arcadians* itself was also a hit, going on from its notable first London run to prove itself, in after years, as one of the most appreciable and appreciated pieces to have come from the prewar British stage.

Even after this, there were still hits to come from the British musical stage. Monckton – with the ever-faithful Tanner and Ross – turned out a winner in *The Quaker Girl*, and the early days of the war brought the French-based *Tonight's the Night*, followed by several others of its ilk, as well as Britain's favourite wartime entertainments *Chu Chin Chow, The Maid of the Mountains, The Boy* and *The Better 'Ole*, but these wartime shows belonged to another, a different era. The era of Gaiety George was done. Ivan Caryll had taken his ideas and expertise to America, and, as America sent back in return the new sounds that would shortly be the popular music of the postwar years, Monckton and Jones soon went head-shakingly into self-imposed silence. And

the great George himself? George Edwardes exited for ever in October of 1915, round about the same time that the kind of musical theatre he had fostered gave up its very last shreds of pretensions to leading the world.

It was time for something new. Not just the craze for Viennese musicals, that craze that Edwardes himself had been responsible for launching on the English-speaking world by his London production of *The Merry Widow*, but something even more foreign and different: musicals based on dance – on rhythms and beats that only a decade or two back had been unheard of in the theatres of Europe. The rhythms of American popular music.

Below: *The Arcadians*
The Deuce has carried the helpless Simplicitas to victory in the big race at Askwood, because the other horses decided it was his turn to win. And because a live horse on stage always makes a fine curtain picture.

Dance, little ladies . . .

A round dozen of delicious chorus
girls strut their stuff across the
pre-war stage of Broadway's New
Amsterdam Theater, in the wake
of their less leggy leading lady.

Broadway beginnings

Paris, Vienna, London. Turn by turn, they entertained and entranced the world with their different brands of happy and melodious musical stage shows in the last decades of the nineteenth and the earliest years of the twentieth century. But, during those years, what was happening on the musical stage beyond Europe and, most particularly, in America?

Oddly enough, America — which would later become, in its turn, the world leader in the production of new musical shows — was the slowest of all the important theatrical centres to develop a substantial and thriving tradition of home-grown musical theatre. Like other colonial countries, the United States of America for a long time imported the largest part of its best entertainments. But, unlike such colonies as Australia, which looked almost entirely to its "mother-country" and to the English-language stage for its plays, and which did little more than imitate those plays in such original work as it produced, America, with its more varied immigrant population, consumed, digested and reproduced its own versions of a much wider range of theatre, musical and non-musical, in its venturing days. German- and French-language theatres showing the original versions of the latest novelties from, and the classic repertoire of, the Vienna, Berlin and Paris stages flourished alongside the English-language shows in mid-nineteenth-century New York and a number of other American cities. The traditions that those theatres and the pieces they played represented would each go on to have its moment as midwife during the sometimes laborious birth of what was eventually to be called "the Broadway musical".

In the mid-nineteenth century, the preponderant, English-language part of America's musical theatre did indeed subsist largely on the same diet as that of England: a basic menu of romantic opera, marquis-and-milkmaid comic opera, and pasticcio burlesque. This was mostly imported and often adapted to what was considered local taste — and that usually meant a distinct lowering of the comedy and the addition of

75

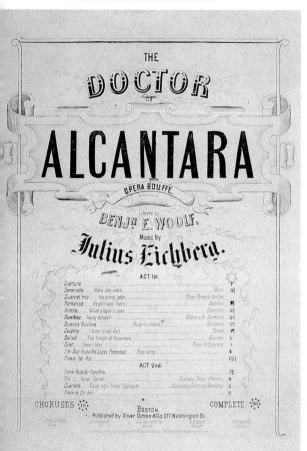

Above: **The Doctor of Alcantara**
Ben Woolf and Julius Eichberg's Boston show was the American theatre's first export-worthy musical.

currently popular songs – but just occasionally home-made. And just very occasionally worth more than an ephemeral showing.

Boston strikes first

The first genuine success on the American comic opera front was a piece called *The Doctor of Alcantara*. It was produced in Boston in 1862, and following its Boston showing it was not only played throughout America, but was even seen briefly in both Britain and Australia – which was altogether a novelty for an American musical in those days. *The Doctor of Alcantara* was, however, not very visibly American. It was written by Ben Woolf, an immigrant from London, composed by Julius Eichberg, who had come to Boston from Düsseldorf, and it was nothing more than a square-cornered comic opera that could have come out of any part of Europe at any time in the two previous centuries. Its story – centred on the efforts of the young Hispanic Carlos to woo his Isabella in spite of her parents' vigorous and sometimes comical efforts at opposition – was a virtual remake of the French play *La Guerre ouverte*, and its score was made up of wholly conventional, if often attractive, lyric and buffo items on the main, well-established comic opera models. But, derivative though it undoubtedly was, *The Doctor of Alcantara* was both soundly made and successful, and it undoubtedly deserves its place as the first real landmark in the American musical theatre.

Burlesque big and burlesque beauteous

The type of show that concentrated on lashings of scenery and gaggles of scantily clad ladies could be guaranteed – then as now, and in New York just like anywhere else – to do better at the box-office than classic comic opera, and some of the earliest American shows to book themselves long

stays on Broadway were built on these lines. Although it was neither the first, nor the first successful, such American piece to hit the stage, the one that's gone down in history – with a myth or two encrusted on it – is *The Black Crook*. This typical mixture of melodramatic fairytale, massed dancing, short skirts, low comedy and mostly second-hand tunes, constructed roughly along the lines of the French *grande opéra-bouffe féerie* or the German *grosse Spektakel-Feerie*, enumerated its customer-drawing attractions in its advertisements: "Tableaux, Costumes, Marches, Scenery", written very large, shared the top of the bill with the "Grand Parisienne Ballet Troupe" and the "Garde Imperiale" of those apparently bare-thighed girls in sheer-ish stockings known to the time as Amazons. The writers, and the actors and singers who performed the show's goodies versus baddies story, were ignored. But the story and its actors weren't what *The Black Crook*'s public came to see, and the show happily provided ever-changing, ah-inspiring entertainment to New York theatregoers for more than 15 months in 1867 and 1868 before going on to parade its charms to other parts of the continent.

Alongside these big, beautiful tableaux-and-thighs shows, the more conventionally sized pasticcio burlesque, with its high-spirited, jokey fun and jaunty songs and dances, also prospered. Many of the most popular such pieces were Americanized versions of the works of Britain's best burlesquers, but several local shows – amongst which the outstanding example proved John Brougham's 1855 perversion of the American tale of the Indian maid *Pocahontas* and the Englishman who told her his name was Smith – also made their mark. But in the latter part of the 1860s the American burlesque stage – indeed the American musical stage in general – was shaken to its foundations by the arrival of two visiting troupes from the other side of the Atlantic. The first was the 1867 French *opéra-bouffe* company headed by Lucille Tostée, bringing its production of Offenbach's brilliant burlesque *La Grande-Duchesse*; the second, the following year, was Samuel Colville and Alexander Henderson's English burlesque troupe, starring sexy Lydia Thompson and bursting its seams with what were advertised as her supporting company of "British blondes". Both these companies had enormous success, and both established a tremendous vogue throughout America for their own particular kind of burlesque entertainment, but it was the British kind of burlesque, with its often outrageous punning texts and lusciously leg-displaying starlets, rather than the more sophisticated French sort, that local writers went on to take as a model for their own efforts. In the wake of Lydia's visit, the emphasis in American burlesque shifted squarely from nimble pen to nubile legs, and it stayed there until the day when burlesque faded away into more modern entertainments.

The most successful local burlesque effort in the post-Lydia years did, however, take one very important cue from *La Grande-Duchesse*. For it sported not the scissors-and-paste score of the British burlesques that the "blondes" had played, but a set of songs that was specially written for the occasion. The 1874 *Evangeline, or the Belle of Acadia* came, as *The Doctor of Alcantara* had, from that cradle of the American musical theatre, Boston. It was written by the local actor-journalist J. Cheever Goodwin, and composed by the son-in-law of a Boston theatre owner, Edward E. Rice, and what did duty as its plot line parodied that of Longfellow's poem. Evicted heroine Evangeline and her sweetheart Gabriel (played Lydia-like by a buxom lady in tights) wandered the world, encountering all sorts of picturesque folk and creatures as they went. Their wanderings were accompanied and interrupted by a prolific mixture of sentimental and comical songs, and the whole made up into a kind of jolly variety show which pleased the American touring circuits for many years and left joyful memories of such highlights as its dancing heifer and its mute Lone Fisherman to a whole generation. Like *The Doctor of Alcantara*, *Evangeline* proved popular enough at home to win showings further afield in England and Australia, but the burlesque only did modestly abroad and did not manage, any more than the comic opera had, to score a first international hit for the American musical theatre.

French comic opera and British burlesque sowed their seeds on American ground, but perhaps even more influential than either was the product of the transplanted German stage, and most particularly its *Possen*. These were real musical comedies, in the true sense of the two words: comical, or sentimental-comical, plays with songs. The robust and powerful German-American theatre, which was responsible for introducing American musical-goers and producers to many an Austrian or German show which neither London nor Paris would ever witness, very quickly overflowed its first and foremost purpose as entertainment for new Americans from German-speaking countries, and both an Americanized version of the *Posse* kind of musical play and the character of the German-American himself became and for decades remained prominent on the American stage.

The most famous early example of this kind of entertainment was Charles Gayler's musical comedy drama *Fritz, Our Cousin German*. Its star, J. K. Emmet, made himself a career playing lovable Fritz, who set out to rescue his sweet Katrina from the clutches of an unbelievably melodramatic villain equipped with a heart of gold, a thick German accent (which was good for both laughs and heart-tweaks), a guitar, and a set of new, nearly new and self-made songs which included one of the earliest enduring hits of the American musical stage, "Fritz's Lullaby". Far from being just an incidental piece of music, the Lullaby actually had a place in the plot – it is the song by which Fritz and his long-lost sister finally recognize each other – but Emmet's renditions of "Sauer Kraut Receipt with Banjo" and "Kaiser, Don't You Want to Buy a Dog?", and his performance of five variations on "Home, Sweet Home" on "Dat Toy Harmonic", had less to do with the search in hand. But who cared? *Fritz* remained a firm

Above: *La Grande-Duchesse*
Mlle Tostée's impersonation of Meilhac and Halévy's mad-for-the-military little Duchess caused a sensation in America.

favourite on American stages for years and years, and when Emmet attempted other rôles public opinion quickly shoved him back into his adored persona and show.

In the decades that followed these first home-grown successes, the American musical theatre still dined very largely on the latest and best of overseas produce. The French and Austrian musical plays that were sweeping the rest of the world's stages swept those of the new world as well, and, following the stage-shaking triumph of *H. M. S. Pinafore*, a triumph that reached even the most unlikely corners of America, the all-conquering works of Gilbert and Sullivan and even some pieces by their less celebrated compatriots became country-wide favourites. But whilst these imported musicals held the vast part of the limelight, local writers were now, tardily, slowly but definitely, beginning to come to the fore, and in the 1880s and 1890s more successful home-made musicals on the lines of *The Doctor of Alcantara, Evangeline* and *Fritz, Our Cousin German* began to appear. And, as they appeared, they began, little by little, to develop. They grew gradually more "American" as the mostly new Americans who produced them grew more "American": less imitative, more individual.

The comic opera style of show, by its very nature, developed the least. In fact, it developed even less than it might have been expected to, for, when the first American comic opera hits arrived, they were not in any way modern or American in either their texts or their music. They were, as *The Doctor of Alcantara* had been, simply old-fashioned European-style musicals built on tried if now slightly tired light opera formats. To listen to them, you would have thought that the Tostée tour and *H. M. S. Pinafore* had never happened. But like the Boston show they were sound enough examples of their antique kind: sound enough to become decidedly successful.

American comic opera

Librettist Harry Bache Smith and composer Reginald De Koven struck American comic opera gold first, in 1891, and they did it with a piece that was sort of based on the old English tale of Robin Hood. *Robin Hood* was produced by the Boston Ideal Opera Company, a fine light-opera touring company that had started its life taking *H. M. S. Pinafore* around the country, but it bore little resemblance to Gilbert and Sullivan's famous work either in tone or in tale. It also had little in common with the history of Robin Hood as generally known, for Smith simply took the well-known names of the characters of the popular story and tacked them onto a plot line that had hardly anything to do with the Lincoln-green outlaw of Sherwood Forest. That story was nothing more than a slightly disguised patchwork of much the same elements that had long gone into making traditional comic operas of the *Doctor of Alcantara* type. The Sheriff of Nottingham is out to deprive Robin of both his lands and title, and the hand of the Sheriff's ward, Marian, that goes with them. An actful of pursuit – filled with the usual sort of amorous and comic complications – ends with Robin's betrayal and capture, and the final act, replete with even more than the regulation amount of disguises, even for a comic opera, culminates in his escape and an everyone-to-his-desserts finale. The plot did have a beginning and an end, but its middle was very largely given over to finding opportunities for the Sheriff – the chief comic player of the evening – to run the gamut of comic-opera comedy situations and the principal vocalists – and the vocalists of the Boston company were very fine – to sing a full book of light operatic music.

De Koven's music followed staunchly in the line of Eichberg's for the earlier show, but the score of *Robin Hood* was altogether more expansive than that for *The Doctor of Alcantara* had been. There was romantic music for Marian and for Robin, a set of comedy pieces for the Sheriff, and plenty of well-written concerted music as well, but the big song successes that emerged from *Robin Hood* were the solos allotted to three of the Merry Men: Little John's squarely baritonic counselling of "Brown October Ale" for what ails your heart, the disguised Will Scarlett's basso "Armourer's Song", and the Wedding Song, "O Promise Me" made famous by the Bostonians' contralto Jessie Bartlett Davis, who played a travesty Alan a Dale, and a wedding-day perennial in America for ever after.

De Koven wrote many more shows in the next thirty years but they rarely came anywhere near his first hit in popularity and longevity, and the comic opera initiative was taken up instead by a young Irishman from Stuttgart who had recently settled in America. In 1895 Victor Herbert teamed up with the same Harry Smith who had supplied De Koven not only with the book for *Robin Hood* but also with those for the best of his succeeding shows – *The Fencing Master*, *The Algerian* and *Rob Roy* – on a classy *opéra-bouffe* called *The Wizard of the Nile*. The result, if ultimately less enduring, was nevertheless rather more of a landmark than *Robin Hood*. For *The Wizard of the Nile* not only progressed to other English-language stages beyond the shores of America, it even took the American musical into Europe.

Smith's libretto was, once again, a combination of well- and even recently used plot elements. But its central comic rôle of the phoney rainmaker Kibosh allowed the star of the show plenty of opportunities for laughter-grabbing, and Herbert decorated both the comic and the romantic parts of the show with a kind of *opéra-bouffe* music that was altogether less straight-laced than De Koven's and altogether nearer in spirit to that of Offenbach or Sullivan. *The Wizard of the Nile*'s New York production topped the hundred-performance mark that was for so long the Plimsoll line of a Broadway hit, and the show then set out on its travels both round the country and overseas – to Vienna's Carltheater, to Budapest's Budai Színkör, to London's Shaftesbury Theatre and to Berlin's Metropol-theater. Its German adaptation even returned to base and was seen in New York's German-language theatre.

Smith and Herbert followed up this more than promising start with several other musicals on similar lines, but they found their biggest success with a pair of light operas that had very little to nothing at all of the *bouffe* about them. *The Serenade* and *The Fortune Teller* were standard romantic comic operas, set in the romantic neverlands of period Europe, and were little textually advanced from the nearly forty-year-old *Doctor of Alcantara*. But they were blessed with some lovely light operatic music, and music being the forte of both the Bostonians, who introduced *The Serenade*, and the breakaway Alice Nielsen company, which mounted *The Fortune Teller* both in America and Britain, songs such as the soprano "Romany Love" and the basso Gypsy Love Song "Go to Sleep, my

Little Gypsy Sweetheart" established themselves as classics of the American lyric stage. They also confirmed Herbert, at the turn of the century, as the foremost composer in the American comic opera field.

The Fortune Teller
Producer-singer Alice Nielsen double-starred herself as both leading ladies in her made-to-order musical.

Bye bye burlesque

The burlesque tradition, so long a feature of the musical stage all around the world, rather ran down in the last years of the nineteenth century, vacating the place it had occupied through the last half a century and more for newer fashions in musical theatre. In America, some elements of the old burlesque hived themselves upwards into what would become known as musical comedy, others went

downwards into girls-and-grinds "burleycue". But before this dissolution happened, the American burlesque stage produced its biggest success of all.

It was Edward Rice of *Evangeline* fame who was behind the production of *Adonis*, for which he was listed variously as co-librettist and composer. The text for the show was, however, the work of the Australian theatrical jobber-of-all-work Willie Gill, who pasted together the series of scenes and set-pieces which, in good old *schöne Galathee* style, followed a statue (male this time) come to life through a series of amorous adventures and disguises and, of course, of songs and dances in the popular vein. Those songs and dances were mostly scissors-and-paste stuff, with Mozart and Offenbach standing crotchet to crotchet with such local musicians as Dave Braham, but Rice contributed some of his own melodies too, and it was his topical song "It's English, You Know" which turned out one of the hits of the evening. The other hit was the show's star, the handsome young Henry E. Dixey, who – displaying as much of his physique as a *Black Crook* Amazon, as well as a much greater talent for comedy and a number – played a very large part in helping *Adonis* to a notable record. It became the first musical to notch up 500 consecutive nights on Broadway on its way to a second record – a total of 603 first-run performances.

Rice took both *Adonis* and his later burlesque success, a new parody version of Byron's *The Corsair*, abroad, but – like *Evangeline* – they were dismissed over the oceans as glorified variety shows, and at the end of the day the elderly *Pocahontas* was left as the sole example of the American burlesque to have found favour beyond its native shores.

America's American musicals

By far the most interesting part of the American musical theatre in the last quarter of the nineteenth century was neither its comic opera nor its burlesque. It was that part which Americans – new and not so new – succeeded best in making their own: the *Posse* area, the musical comedies, plays with songs – call them what you will. Often, as they frequently were in Europe, these shows were star vehicles, pieces constructed largely to allow an actor or an actress to show off all the things he or she did best. On other occasions they were loose-limbed farcical plays built to allow the maximum of high-jinks and illustrated with whatever musical numbers the performers fancied. The musical part of these shows could be decidedly chequered: old or remade popular songs shared the scene with special material, made-to-measure numbers and even chunks of pasticcio. But often, too, they were just regular musical comedies, lively plays full of recognizable, if exaggerated, character types and characteristic songs – American character types and American songs. But whatever they were, however "low-brow" they were, the best of these shows were a vigorous and unpretentious evening's entertainment, and many a hit show and even a hit song emerged from amongst them.

The two most famous, and certainly the two best, writers of this kind of musical were Ned Harrigan and Charles Hoyt. Ned Harrigan began his career playing in that most singularly American kind of entertainment, the minstrel show, and in variety as part of a comic double act. But the humorous and musical sketches that he wrote for himself and his partner Tony Hart to perform, as a featured part of their variety programmes, proved so popular that he eventually expanded them into full-scale musical comedies, and through the 1870s and the 1880s Harrigan and Hart (and then Harrigan without Hart) purveyed their own very special brand of musical from their base at their very own Broadway theatre to their own special audience with memorable success.

Harrigan's shows were broadly comic tales of Irish New Yorkers, German New Yorkers, black New Yorkers and other kinds of new or nearly new Americans, told in a joyously un-hung-up, self-knowing, rumbustious style that would give galloping nightmares to today's watchpuppies of the "politically correct", but which, in an era when folk hadn't lost the health-giving gift of laughing at themselves, made for the very best kind of comedy – the self-reflecting kind. His comical plots were usually based on the ridiculous and extravagantly serious rivalries that set one over-exclusive group of these immigrant New Yorkers – the Irish Mulligans, the German Lochmullers, the black Skidmore Guards – against another in their efforts for social or cock-of-the-street supremacy, and he took a happy pleasure in his plays in puncturing all that was pretentious, whether it was a spot of social climbing or the posturings of the pseudo-military parade groups.

Harrigan took his favourite characters through from one show to another, as if they were part of a nineteenth-century stage soap opera, and he scored his own most particular performing success as the incorrigible Irish New Yorker Dan Mulligan. He played Dan, with Annie Yeamans as his frustrated, upwardly immobile wife, Cordelia, through a whole series of Mulligan shows, in which Hart appeared both as their son, Tommy, and – with huge success – as the Harrigan household's loud-mouthed negro maid, Rebecca Allup, and their characters became as well known and as well loved as those of any modern-day television series.

The "musical" part of Harrigan's musical comedies was no less successful than the "comedy" part. The lyrics which Harrigan provided as part of his plays were set to music by the theatre's musical director Dave Braham (who was also Harrigan's father-in-law) and the result was a whole canon of popularly flavoured songs, including several that stayed on people's lips for decades: "Maggie Murphy's Home", "The Babies on our Block", "McNally's Row of Flats", "The Mulligan Guards". Some even made their way beyond America for, although the very nature of Harrigan's plays ensured that they would not have meant much to non-American audiences, his songs travelled well, and a version of his "Hush, the Bogie" became a hit at the London Gaiety itself.

A decade on from their first essay with the short *The Mulligan Guards*, the Harrigan and Hart series peaked with the comical tale of the deflating of *Cordelia's Aspirations*. The partners then split, but Harrigan continued

Opposite: *Adonis*
Henry Dixey did for those who appreciated male thighs what the *Evangeline* girls did for the other half, and got chased around the stage a record number of times as a result.

Below: **Ned Harrigan**
In the days when being different was fun, Harrigan made fun of being different and created some the best musical-stage Americans of his century.

to turn out popular hits in the style he had made his own for another five years before his fashion started to fade, and when he laid down his pen in 1896 he left behind him a body of truly "popular" musical theatre that was quite unique.

If Harrigan stayed longer in the limelight, thanks to his multi-highlighted career as playwright, producer and performer, it was nevertheless the Boston-based Charles Hoyt who, just a few years on from Harrigan and Hart's heyday, scored the biggest single hit on the nineteenth-century American musical comedy stage. The show that gave him that hit was called *A Trip to Chinatown* and, like the nine earlier shows that he had launched around the touring circuits of America in the 1880s, it was a rag-bag of musical comedy, a loosely constructed framework of plot and action filled up with lively, actable characters and a catching mixture of used, slightly used and occasionally freshly brewed songs and dances. In some ways, a Hoyt show had more in common with *Adonis* and its ilk than it did with the Harrigan musicals, for it was built on the same format as the burlesques had been, simply replacing the fanciful far-off tale they used with a piece of comical action set in the here and now. But the point that Hoyt's "farce-comedies" did have in common with Harrigan's shows was that very here-and-nowness that made them such thoroughly American musical comedies.

The notion that was the starting-off point for *A Trip to Chinatown* was a familiar one, one that had done the rounds of the French and German stages, in particular, many years earlier, but one that was no less effective for its purpose for all that. Two young San Franciscans are planning a night out dancing and dining with their girlfriends. They are good young San Franciscans, and they've arranged a chaperone, but they don't want strict papa along, so they pretend that they are going on an educational visit to the city's Chinatown. Unfortunately the confirming letter from the pretty young widow who is to be their chaperone is mistakenly delivered to papa, and he thinks he's on to a good thing. Off he sets, out into the wicked world of San Francisco eateries and niteries, and the comedy starts to build up to its most extravagant heights.

Much of that comedy came, just as in

Evangeline days, from the incidental folk who peopled the plot-folks' night out – the imaginary invalid Welland Strong, the hard-done-by Slavin Payne, the serving girl Flirt, the precocious lad Willie Grow – for, as in the burlesques, it was the content of *A Trip to Chinatown* rather than its outline that was the attraction.

An important part of that content was, of course, the songs and the dances. The company's musical director, Percy Gaunt, was responsible for this part of the show, and he produced a score that proved – for all that it was a hotch-potch – to be remarkably solid. Over the many, many years that *A Trip to Chinatown* survived on the stage, its musical backbone actually stayed intact. One important vertebra in that backbone was a number actually written by Hoyt and Gaunt themselves and detailing, with topical gusto, the ghastly things that go on "On the Bowery"; another, equally topical, and with its lyrics duly updated to take in the latest talk of the town, was a piece made up by Gaunt on the bones of an old negro tune and called "Reuben and Cynthia". However, the biggest and most lasting *Chinatown* hit of all was neither a new song nor a remade song, but a song that was simply picked up and stuck in. But there is no doubt that it was its inclusion in *A Trip to Chinatown* that made Charles K. Harris's "After the Ball" such a hit that, nearly forty years later, Jerome Kern chose to reuse it in his score to *Show Boat* as an example of a period song.

A Trip to Chinatown played for a whole year on the touring circuits for which it had been built before it ventured onto Broadway. But when it got there, it stayed, and by the time it left, 657 performances later, it had outlasted all the opposition, becoming the longest-running home-made musical New York had seen up to that time. Then *A Trip to Chinatown* went further, for not only did it cover the theatres of America year after year well into the new century, it also laid siege to the provinces of England where, alongside other examples of American fare such as *My Sweetheart* and *Hans the Boatman*, it found enthusiastic audiences for many years. Even the West End gave it stage room for a good 125 nights.

The end of the nineteenth century was approaching, and, although it was now trotting

Minnie Palmer
She played a teenager till her 'teens were a distant memory, but even at (an unadmitted) 40, she was still *My Sweetheart* to her adoring audiences.

Opposite: ***A Trip to Chinatown***
John Tresahar goes extravagantly oriental in the British production of Charlie Hoyt's endlessly touring idyll of San Francisco.

along happily, the American musical stage had yet to spawn a real international hit. *A Trip to Chinatown* had certainly done well in Britain and, like the ingenuous, *Fritz*-ish musical melodrama *My Sweetheart*, whose babyish star, Minnie Palmer, had won it a surprising 167 London nights in 1884, it had held its own in the West End. Again like *My Sweetheart*, however, its real popularity had come in the less than sophisticated country theatres. *Robin Hood* and *The Wizard of the Nile* had won themselves London productions and American companies had presented *The Fortune Teller, Adonis* and John Philip Sousa's *El Capitan* and *The Charlatan* in the West End, but none of these had been a real hit. Only *The Wizard of the Nile* had so far tempted producers on the right-hand side of the English Channel. But, just a few years before the century finally ticked over, Broadway at last turned out the show that would launch America as a presence on the international musical stage. It was called *The Belle of New York.*

The Belle of New York

The Belle of New York *was a "musical comedy", and, although it certainly had something of the Hoyt brand of musical comedy in its make-up, it owed more to the English tradition of musical comedy that had blossomed under George Edwardes in 1890s Britain – more particularly to the "variety musical" typified by such British musicals as* Morocco Bound *and the endlessly touring* The Lady Slavey.

Background: **'She is the Belle of New York ...'**
Pretty, cottonwool-voiced Edna May entranced London in the title-rôle of the Casino Theater's musical.

Opposite: Kerker churned out years of music that came and quickly went, but his *Belle of New York* numbers endured through endless rearrangements on the strength of the success of the show.

The show was the work of New York journalist Charles Morton Stewart McLellan, on this occasion temporarily calling himself "Hugh Morton", who had recently been employed writing and adapting revue and musical comedy for the Casino Theater. One of his jobs there had been to take a hand in the rather brutal reorganization of *The Lady Slavey* for Broadway consumption. The musical part of the show was in the hands of the theatre's musical director and prolific journeyman composer, Gustave Kerker.

The Belle of New York was organized on classic "variety musical" lines. A story was let loose in the first act, and looked like working itself out through the length of the evening. But then, in the second act, that story was for some reason (or sometimes none at all) put on hold whilst the members of the company got to do their "turn", and it reappeared only in time for what was often a very perfunctory wind up just before the final curtain. McLellan's story centred on high-living Harry Bronson, a jolly lad who is going merrily through provincial papa's money whilst courting a whole selection of lovable ladies down in naughty New York. When Ichabod Bronson turns up and catches him at it, Bronson junior finds himself disinherited, and he has to give up his fancy ways and his fancy girls and go to work as a soda jerk. All Ichabod's money is instead settled on his old partner's daughter, the Salvation Army lassie Violet Gray. The whole cast then gets whisked off to Narragansett for the "entertainment" part of the show, after which Harry and Violet are united – just as papa had plotted all along.

Harry and Violet and the conniving, not-so-strict Ichabod stayed firmly at the centre of things throughout the evening, but there were plenty of colourful subsidiary characters to supply the comical and musical extras of the show – the gold-digging comic opera star Cora Angélique, whom Harry has promised to marry and Karl Pumpernik, the polite madman who adores her and stalks both Mr Bronsons with revengeful but well-mannered murder in mind, the music-hall floosie, Kissie Fitzgarter, and Fifi the French chef's daughter both of whom have also been intermittently on Harry's marriage list, the whistling boxer

Blinky Bill, and his downtown girlfriend, Mamie Clancy, and even a pair of Portuguese twin aristocrats. Each of these merry folk had his or her moment, and most of them also had a number to perform.

Kerker's score was a collection of bright, if not particularly distinguished numbers in the Gaiety-variety mode, but the vogue which the show ultimately won helped several of its numbers to a good life beyond the production – the waltzing title-song, Violet's "They All Follow Me", and Harry and Fifi's little duet "Teach Me How to Kiss".

The vogue for *The Belle of New York* didn't start in New York. The show ran at the Casino for only 56 nights. But, after it had put up rather a better showing in Boston, Australian producer George Musgrove, who had been caught with his stalls empty, decided to take what looked like a pretty long-odds risk and whisked the whole Casino company and their

show across to London to fill what might otherwise have been an expensive gap at his Shaftesbury Theatre. And in London *The Belle of New York* caused a sensation. Londoners hadn't ever seen a show quite like this and performers quite like these before and they were taken by storm. They loved all the boisterous high spirits of the piece, they loved the lusty chorines and their energetic dancing, they loved the unfamiliar American character types portrayed by the show's comedians. What was old hat on Broadway was a breath of fresh air on Shaftesbury Avenue, and *The Belle of New York* quickly became the West End's novelty hit of the year – and much of the next one. For the musical that had been played just 56 times on Broadway pulled in audiences for a Gaiety-sized run of 697 nights on the London stage, and established itself as a major favourite through years of touring round the British Isles and several return visits to London.

The recent success of some of the Gaiety Theatre shows and other British musicals on the Continent encouraged European managers to look at and to reach out for this latest hit on the London stage, and as a result *The Belle of New York* ended up going where almost no American musical had gone before – and none under such favourable circumstances. It made its way triumphantly across the Channel to conquer all the main European theatre capitals. The deed was done. For all that there were undoubtedly better musicals back home in America, it was *The Belle of New York* that well and truly brought the Broadway musical onto the world's stages.

CREDITS

The Belle of New York

Musical comedy in 2 acts by Hugh Morton

MUSIC
by Gustave Kerker

Produced at the Casino Theater, New York, 28 September 1897
UK: Shaftesbury Theatre, London, 12 April 1898
Hungary: Magyar Színház, Budapest, 30 January 1900
Austria: Venedig in Wien, Vienna, 18 July 1900
Germany: Centraltheater, Berlin, 22 December 1900
France: Moulin Rouge, Paris, 29 May 1903

CAST

Harry Bronson	
	Harry Davenport
Ichabod Bronson	Dan Daly
Violet Gray	Edna May
Cora Angélique	Helen Dupont
Kissy Fitzgarter	Mabel Howe
Karl von Pumpernick	
	John E Sullivan
Fifi	Phyllis Rankin
Mamie Clancy	Paula Edwards
Blinky Bill	Frank Lawton

The international success of *The Belle of New York* didn't actually have a comprehensive follow-up. It was a novelty hit, and the novelty didn't work in the same way twice. Although one or two other American "musical comedies" – notably the Casino Theater's attempt at a clone with *The Casino Girl* – did well enough both at home and abroad in the first years of the twentieth century, it was still to be nearly two more decades before the American musical would again raise its head to such far-flung effect on the world's stages. But during those decades American writers and composers turned out plenty of shows that kept the patrons of the English-language theatre very happily entertained. And some of those shows would be the most interesting and the most finely made that the American stage had yet produced.

Victor Herbert was amongst those writers whose works failed almost completely to travel beyond America. For some reason he never managed to score a hit outside his adopted homeland, and the away-from-home record chalked up by his early *The Wizard of the Nile* remained his best international reference. At home, however, things were entirely different. Herbert, skating with delicious versatility from comic or romantic opera to bare-boned farcical comedy, from spectacular or kiddie show to streamlined musical play, was the most visible and the most appreciated composer working on Broadway in the prewar years of the new century. Between 1900 and 1915 he supplied the score for 23 full-sized musicals. They were a mixed bag, but they included a good number of well-liked shows of all styles and sizes.

The one that is remembered most widely today, largely thanks to an MGM reincarnation on the singing screen a quarter of a century after its original production, is *Naughty Marietta*. *Naughty Marietta* was a romantic period piece – though one with altogether more spirit than pieces such as *The Fortune Teller* – put together to order as a vehicle for the out-of-work members of a flopped opera company. This meant that Herbert was able to let himself go thoroughly with the vocal lines of his star music, and the result was not only some splendid solo songs – the contralto "'Neath a Southern Moon", the baritone's marching song "Tramp, Tramp, Tramp" and

Victor Herbert

He started out as the fellow with the 'cello, but went on to become Broadway's favourite musical-theatre composer.

tender, waltzing "I'm Falling in Love with Someone", the showy soprano Italian Street Song and the plot-worthy "Ah! Sweet Mystery of Life" – but some exciting, almost operatic ensemble music, topped by the dramatic "Live for Today". The screen Marietta, Jeanette MacDonald, and her partner Nelson Eddy didn't get round to "Live for Today" so, whilst the rest of the best of the *Marietta* score survives as classic Broadway show music, it very rarely gets an outing today.

Rida Johnson Young's libretto for *Naughty Marietta* told the story of a French countess who hitches a boat-ride to the American colonies to escape an unwanted marriage. But the boat she hitches is a bride-ship, and Marietta has to run away all over again when she hits New Orleans, because she has this *idée fixe* that she'll only marry the man who can put the ending on a song that's running about in her brain. Fortunately for her, with the final curtain in sight, it's the handsome baritonic ranger, Captain Dick, who, in double-quick time, cleans out the corrupt local administration, bests his beastly rival-in-love-and-in-war, and comes up with the missing cadences.

There was more than a flash of Ruritania and old-style comic opera libretto in this text, but Mrs Young's work (for all that the piece was written for an Italian soprano, Emma Trentini, and a French contralto, Marie Duchêne) was noteworthy in that it was actually set – as Harrigan and Hoyt musical comedy had so long now been – in an at least partly recognizable America. This wasn't altogether new – shows such as Sydney Rosenfeld's Louisianan *The Mocking Bird* and Stan Stange's Civil Wartime *When Johnny Comes Marching Home* had gone the same way several years previously – but *Naughty Marietta* was a more notable piece than either of those works, and the choice of its setting showed that American writers were, even with such small steps, gradually freeing themselves of a copycatlike allegiance to European writing.

Herbert's other early-century hits had, indeed, included pieces which were firmly fixed in the European or pseudo-European settings that had so long been standard in this type of show: the pretty *Mlle Modiste*, in which another ex-opera singer, Fritzi Scheff, introduced his "A Kiss in the Dark", was a tale of a French aristocrat and his little French milliner (who, like all comic opera milliners, ends up a prima donna), whilst the more comically orientated *It Happened in Nordland*, which had an American lady impersonating the Queen of that Ruritanian land, happened indeed right there. Even the composer's most swingeingly low-comic musical was set in foreign parts, for American librettists of these years, just like their foreign fellows from the days of *Ba-ta-clan* to those of *A Chinese Honeymoon*, often drew their fun from plonking their own nationals down amongst funny foreign folk.

In Herbert's *The Red Mill*, it wasn't the foreign folk who were funny – it was the Yankees. The favourite comedy team of Dave Montgomery and Fred Stone appeared, in Henry Blossom's libretto, as a pair of crazy Americans let loose in a Dutch setting. The stars spent part of the evening burlesquing Sherlock Holmes, part getting tangled up in the juveniles' romance and (physically) in the allegedly haunted red mill of the title, and part giving out some comic song and dance that was leagues in style from the music of Herbert's *Naughty Marietta* or *Mlle Modiste* ("The Streets of New York", "Go While the Goin' is Good"). The composer did, however, score his biggest musical successes in *The Red Mill* with numbers in a more lyrical vein – the sweet soprano "Moonbeams" and the bouncy baritonic "Every Day is Ladies' Day with Me".

The Red Mill was a fine Broadway hit, and Herbert went on to supply the comedy team with the songs for another first-rate success in the Cinderella musical *The Lady of the Slipper*, but he also spread himself into other areas with equal success. The for-children-of-all-ages musical *Babes in Toyland* was staged by the men who had made a stack the previous season with a spectacularly mounted version of *The Wizard of Oz*. Like that piece, the new one relied largely on its visuals for its success, but this year the producers went upmarket and, instead of hiring the hack musicians who had put the songs to the earlier show, they hired Herbert. So *Babes in Toyland*, as well as having its scene changes and its huge cast to decorate its little story of the adventures of a couple of children amongst the characters of nursery rhyme, had a score of music ("March

Above: ***The Red Mill***
Amy Augarde insists that "A Woman Has Ways" in London's première of Henry Blossom and Victor Herbert's comical musical.

of the Toys", "Toyland", "I Can't Do That Sum", "Go to Sleep, Slumber Deep") of a quality not usually found in such spectaculars. It was undoubtedly that score that helped the show to survive into repeated revivals, whilst *The Wizard of Oz* – in their version, at least – went the way of most scenery shows.

Herbert wrote the music for another spectacular children's show, based on the cartoon character *Little Nemo*, he went more Ruritanian than was possible in the preposterous but tuneful *Sweethearts*, he dipped into fantasy, into burlesque and, repeatedly, into lyrical musicals with a Continental flavour, but the show that gave him his longest Broadway run in the later part of his career fell into none of those categories. It was a modern musical play of the year 1914 – a musical play of the new kind that had been becoming more and more prominent on Broadway in those years since the turn of the century. *The Only Girl* was an up-to-date piece of small-house, small-cast musical comedy based on an established and successful play, Ludwig Fulda's German comedy *Jugendfreude*, and it was produced by ex-comedian Joe Weber, who had had a fine success a few years previously with another small-house, small-cast, German-extracted musical called *Alma, Where Do You Live?* Herbert, who had been such an important part of the American musical of the past decades, was right there as the new-style American musical play began to get up steam.

Background: **George M. Cohan**
The author-star pictured with his father, Jerry Cohan, in one of his earliest musicals, *Running for Office* (1903).

Right: ***The Prince of Pilsen***
The pretty widow (Trixie Friganza) provides only a tiny bit of the action at Nice's International Hotel in the summer of '02.

He illustrated his up-to-date musical with up-to-date music – including a ragtime number – and, even though the musical's best-liked song was the straight soprano "When You're Away", the results were fine. *The Only Girl* notched up 240 nights on Broadway, and was even seen – as few of his shows were – in Britain.

Herbert, of course, did not have Broadway all to himself. He even had some very worthwhile rivals in the field of the romantic and lyrical musical where he had always shone the brightest. And one of those rivals went so far as to chalk up the international success that Herbert failed to win.

Gustave Luders was another new American, a native of Bremen who had come to America in his early twenties and whose first musicals were produced in Chicago. *The Burgomaster* and *King Dodo* did grand business on the American tour circuits, but it was Luders's 1902 Boston show *The Prince of Pilsen* (which was brought to New York the following year) that proved his biggest hit. A jolly piece of Americans-in-far-off-places comedy, it centred on a low-comical German-American brewer who goes on holiday to the South of France and (thanks to the similarity of

"Pilsen" and "Pilsener") gets mistaken for a Central European prince. Frank Pixley's libretto mixed good-humoured comedy with plenty of funny situations and a touch of juvenile romance, and Luders supplied a winning, well-written musical score – ranging from the lusty Germanic "Stein Song" to the romantic "The Tale of a Sea-Shell", "The Message of the Violet" and the topical "The American Girl" – that combined with Pixley's work to make up arguably the most satisfying Broadway musical of its era. Overseas certainly thought so. In spite of the fact that *The Belle of New York* had taken the shine off the American musical as a novelty, London gave the show 160 nights before it was exported to the Paris Olympia, and ultimately to Australia, whilst all the while continuing its long life round the American circuits.

Luders struck again in 1904 when he set George Ade's *The Sho-Gun*, a Chicago piece that followed very closely in the mode of *A Chinese Honeymoon*, and saw it produced as far afield as Budapest, but he proved to have less staying-power than Herbert, and his later shows failed.

Luders had not long faded from contention when a new rival to Herbert came on the scene. Rudolf Friml was from Prague, and he came by his first chance at a Broadway score courtesy of Herbert himself. Herbert refused to write a new show for his *Naughty Marietta* star, Trentini, whose unprofessional behaviour ultimately made her unemployable, so the little-known Friml was given the job. His score to Otto Harbach's text for *The Firefly* ("Giannina mia", "When a Maid Comes Knocking at your Heart", "Sympathy", "Love is Like a Firefly") established him instantly at the top of the profession in which, a little later, he would become a worldwide name.

Whilst Herbert, Luders, Friml and their colleagues kept the lyric musical boiling, the Harrigan and Hoyt style of show also prospered. And it prospered largely through the talents of one man – George M. Cohan. Star, author, composer and often producer as well, Cohan was responsible for a twenty-year series of vigorous, true red-white-and-blue musical comedies that not only made him a theatrical institution, but also left a legacy of popular songs that outshone even the Harrigan list to the Broadway songbook –

from "Give my Regards to Broadway" and "The Yankee Doodle Boy" to "Nellie Kelly, I Love You" and "Mary, it's a Grand Old Name".

Like Harrigan, Cohan came to the musical from the world of variety, and like Harrigan he had written his earliest stage pieces as sketches for himself, and the members of his family who made up their act, to perform. Those sketches lengthened into shows, and in 1904 *Little Johnny Jones* – with Cohan as the little American jockey of the title, who gets accused of throwing the British Derby – set the series rolling. In between his activities as a performer and a highly successful producer, Cohan turned out 15 more musicals which, if they didn't always suit Broadway, found many, many fans in other centres.

Another piece that didn't suit Broadway, but found favour elsewhere, was the musical *In Dahomey*. *In Dahomey* was unusual in that it was a musical written largely by black writers and songwriters for black actors and singers. Musicals of this kind had been around for a number of years, but they were mostly played in the fringe houses which supplied entertainment for black audiences. Suddenly it had seemed that there might be commercial possibilities in showing such a piece in a regular Broadway house, and this one was switched to play at the New York Theater.

Its book, by actor Jesse Shipp, was written round the popular vaudeville team of Williams and Walker and was full of fun. Walker played a slickster, and Williams his pal and patsy from whom he woos cash for a venture to export all the down-and-out blacks of America back to a promised land in Africa. The story, which whizzed from America to Africa and back, was accompanied by a set of songs from various hands, black and white, and if some – particularly those from top-billed composer Will Marion Cook – showed evidence of rather too much exposure to the Victorian parlour ballad and other elderly European forms, others just swung with danceable vivacity.

The gamble didn't come off – Broadway of 1903 couldn't muster more than 53 nights' worth of enthusiasm for its first full-scale black musical. But a second gamble elsewhere did. The whole cast and production of *In Dahomey* was shipped to London's West End, and London – which had never seen anything blacker than a Christy Minstrel show – was

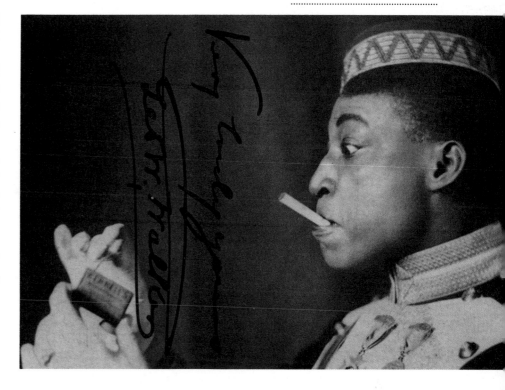

In Dahomey
Broadway gave short shrift to George Walker (above) and his partner Bert Williams in Jesse Shipp's show, but they cakewalked to success as a lively curiosity on the London stage.

knocked sideways by its vivacity and energy, its cakewalk dancers and its sheer novelty. The novelty held good for 251 performances, and a command performance at Buckingham Palace for the little prince's birthday, before the adventure ended and the players went back home.

EDWARD MARRIS' Company.

Take one French play...

The Girl from Kay's
This musicalized English version
of a cross-Channel comedy
signalled the coming of a new
stiffening of play-worthy plot to
the musical comedy.

Lend Me a Libretto

The early years of the new century on the London musical stage had been marked by the coming of a new kind of libretto — the "more than usually substantial" libretto, a text with a thoroughly well-made comic or romantic-comic plot that would have done just as well for a straight play without songs as for a libretto — and in most of these early cases, already had. A number of these shows received Broadway showings after their London seasons were done, and pieces such as The Girl from Kay's, The Duchess of Dantzic *and* The Spring Chicken *proved just as popular to the west of the Atlantic as they had in the West End. Plot, construction, and a more coherent and self-contained kind of libretto were on their way.*

Soon American writers started to look in the same direction that Britain's Ivan Caryll and his collaborators had done – and, at least to start with, that mostly meant towards France, where the best-built comedies susceptible to musicalization were currently being produced. Actor-manager-writer Richard Carle, who had profitably Americanized the Gaiety Theatre's *The Spring Chicken* to his own starry measure, manufactured a "French" musical out of a version of the comedy *Madame Mongodin* (aka *Mrs Ponderbury's Past*) and toured it successfully as *Mary's Lamb*, while Otto Harbach remade Maurice Ordonneau's French-born libretto for the German musical *Madame Sherry*, and, reset with fresh songs by Karl Hoschna, it turned into a sizeable Broadway hit.

Musical comedy, which had so long relied on libretti that would have had trouble crawling had they not been decorated with song and dance, was starting to get books that resembled, more and more, an evening in the comedy theatre.

Les Fêtards

Opérette in 3 acts by Antony Mars and Maurice Hennequin. Music by Victor Roger. Produced at the Théâtre du Palais-Royal, Paris, 28 October 1897.

The French theatre, with its bristling tradition of *vaudeville* or *vaudeville-opérette*, had been there for years, and some of its product – from *Niniche* to *Josephine Sold by her Sisters* – had, over those years, been exported to English-language stages. One of the finest examples of this type of show was *Les Fêtards*, a musical which was made over and remade over as it toured the world, everywhere with success.

American Quaker heiress Edith has married a French marquis but, to her dismay, he doesn't stay at home. As soon as he gets the opportunity, he leaves his pretty but prudish wife and heads for the fleshpots of Paris. Fearing a fate worse than widowhood, Edith follows him, all the way to the dressing room of the famous dancer, Théa. The kindly dancer advises the pious marquise that, if she wants to keep her husband to herself, she'll have to loosen up a bit. Then the libidinous King of Illyria arrives to lay court to Théa, and mistakes Edith for the dancer. The women don't disillusion him and the farcical action of the piece gets under way. It ends with the chastened marquis taking home a rather more with-it wife.

Alongside the principals of the story – but with important parts to play in it – there were show-stopping rôles for a silly-ass Frenchman and for the buxom, ageing theatre wardrobe mistress who, in her time, had been the plaything of a Prince.

Victor Roger's score included some fine plotful pieces for the marquise, as she took her lesson from the dancer ("C'est par le coquetterie") or tranformed herself into "Théa" ("Si le révérend me voyait"), and for her husband, lusting over "La p'tit' Théa", but the comedy highlights of the night fell to the expansive Madame Maréchale, instructing the theatre chorines to get into "du bon trois pour cent" or sending apologies heavenwards, to her deceased husband, for her over-generous sex life ("Grégoire, Grégoire").

Les Fêtards did well in Paris, but that was just the beginning of its career. It was a mega-hit in Austria and Germany under the more pungent title of *Wie man Männer fesselt* (How to tie up men) and in Hungary as *A bibliás asszony* (The bible girl), and George Edwardes took it to London as a straight play before realizing that a musical could have a proper plot and refashioning it with Lionel Monckton and Howard Talbot tunes as the hit musical *Kitty Grey*. On 1899 Broadway, *Les Fêtards* became *The Rounders*, and although the piece was remade to feature a more conventional kind of comedy – the King became an Irish-Turkish pasha, the silly-ass Frenchman a broadly comic Duke de Paty du Clam – and a rather ordinary score (music: Ludwig Englander), the combination of vigorous, comedy-filled plot and scenes and jolly numbers won it yet another success. And Broadway then went on to host both the German and English versions of the show!

The Girl from Kay's

Musical in 2 acts by Owen Hall, based on *La Mariée recalcitrante* by Léon Gandillot. Lyrics by Adrian Ross and Claude Aveling. Music by Ivan Caryll, Cecil Cook et al. Produced at the Apollo Theatre, London, 15 November 1902.

London wasn't used to seeing musicals based on established plays. Operas, yes, but musicals? In between the songs and the dances and the almost stand-up comic scenes, there simply wasn't room (or the wish?) for lashings of plot. The normal amount of "play" in a Gaiety Theatre show wouldn't have filled a champagne glass. So *The Girl from Kay's* was a bit different. Only a bit, though, because whizz librettist Owen Hall didn't actually admit that he was pilfering his libretto from the French. Perhaps he thought no one would notice, for he remade the original thoroughly, in his very special English style. Unfortunately for him – and for producer Edwardes – Gandillot found out, sued, and won himself a royalty.

The Girl from Kay's
Willie Edouin created one of the great musical-comedy characters of the era as the lovable "Piggy" Hoggenheimer.

His story was one familiar on the French stage. A young man who has just been tidily married now has to say goodbye to the mistress of his pre-wifed days. But whilst he is saying goodbye, he gets caught. And the little wife who has just said "I will" now decides that she's going to say "I won't". She keeps on saying "I won't" until the final curtain is in sight. Of course, in the English version the mistress was a friendly shop-girl (from Kay's emporium) and the goodbye was nothing more than a peck on the cheek, but the principle was the same.

The story was, like that of *Les Fêtards*, enlivened by some subsidiary characters with more or less to do with the plot and some comedy and/or a song to provide. *The Girl from Kay's* had the now customary goofy Englishman or dude, several spare shop-girl friends of the girl from Kay's, and a comical Yankee. That comical Yankee, Mr "Piggy" Hoggenheimer of Park Lane, with his pretentions to a place in London society and his catchphrase "I'm not rude, I'm rich", became the most popular feature of the show.

The songs were a delightful bunch. The little bride sniffled on her father's shoulder over her husband's lightning infidelity in the waltzing "Papa" and declared in duo with the unfortunate spouse that they would henceforth live "Semi-Detached", whilst he tried to pretend musically "I Don't Care". Other numbers were less plot- and character-ful – one shop-girl sang jauntily about "Smiling Sambo', for coon songs were the fashion of the day – in a score that mixed the relevant and the decorative in equal parts.

The Girl from Kay's ran for over a year in London before it was picked up for Broadway and scored all over again. In fact, such a success did comedian Sam Bernard have in the star comic rôle created by Willie Edouin that he returned to the part repeatedly in remakes and musequels (*The Rich Mr Hoggenheimer*, *The Belle of Bond Street*, *Piggy*) for a quarter of a century.

Alma, Where Do You Live?

Vaudeville in 3 acts by Adolf Philipp. Produced at the Wintergarten "Zum schwarzen Adler", New York, 25 October 1909.

Although the French comic tradition was the most pluckable for musical comedy plays and plots of the new, strong-backed kind, the

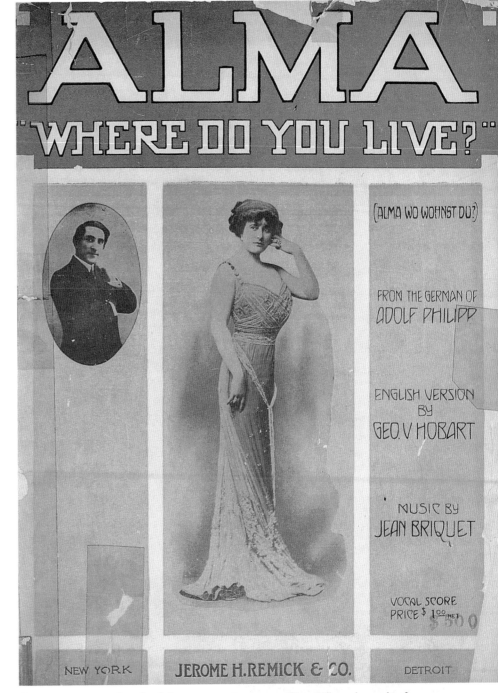

German stage also had its moments as a fruitful source. Not only the German stage, but the American-German stage. And, at this moment in time, that American-German stage was largely under the sway of one rather amazing man: actor-singer-author-composer-producer Adolf Philipp, who had made himself huge writing and starring in such German-Yiddish-American musical plays as *Der Corner Grocer aus der Avenue A* and *Der Pawnbroker von der East Side*. The first of those two pieces had even been translated to the regular Broadway stage – as early as 1894

Alma, Where do you Live?
Her publicist insisted that Kitty Gordon, who played Alma, was "famous for her back". But her front didn't serve her badly either.

– souped up unrecognizably as a revusical musical.

In 1909 Philipp wrote and composed – under a group of fashionably French pseudonyms – what he advisedly called a *vaudeville* in the French style for his little German-language theatre. *Alma, wo wohnst du?* was, indeed, a play with songs and dances – a *Posse mit Gesang und Tanz*. Not, perhaps, as coherently constructed as a piece like *Les Fêtards*, but striving in that direction.

The Alma of the title was a little French lassie of considerable physical charms, and it is those charms that she is called on to employ to entrap the unsuspecting Pierre Le Peach. For Pierre has been left a lot of money in a will, under certain conditions, and those folk who stand to inherit should he fail to keep those conditions are out to make him stumble. Alma is the stumbling block. The action was perforated by a series of not terribly to-the-point numbers, but Philipp was more concerned with imitating most of the most fashionable types of song of the day. His score included pieces called "Childhood Days", "The Land of the Beautiful Dream", a waltzing instruction to "Kiss Me, my Love" and a comic dance piece about "The Boogie Boo".

The small-stage, small-cast *Alma* proved so popular in her little German theatre that producer Joe Weber decided to transfer her to Broadway. And there she triumphed. This undersized (by normal standards) show – in no way hindered by a well-publicized complaint to the mayor of New York over its "indecency" – turned out one of the biggest hits of the vintage 1910–11 season, outrunning *Naughty Marietta*, equalling *Madame Sherry* and giving best only to the most successful of all the new style of musicals, *The Pink Lady*, before going on to be seen in both Germany and Austria. There, with "The Boogie Boo" and its fellows replaced by local music, Philipp's *vaudeville* gave at least part of the new sort of American musical comedy its first Continental showing.

The Pink Lady

Musical comedy in 3 acts by C. M. S. McLellan, based on *Le Satyre* by Georges Berr and Marcel Guillemaud. Music by Ivan Caryll. Produced at the Globe Theater, New York, 13 March 1911.

Composer and theatrical wheeler-dealer Ivan Caryll had been responsible for some of the first and best London attempts at the new kind of book-strong musical play, and when he emigrated to America in 1910 he carried on as he had done on the other side of the seas. He teamed up with *Belle of New York* librettist C.M.S. McLellan, and between 1910 and 1913 the two of them turned out four "French" musicals, pieces of musical theatre of a kind and a substance to rival the real French vaudevilles, but wholly "(re)-made in America". The second of the four shows, and the one which both made the greatest hit and – as much as any one show can – might be said to have established the strong-backed musical play on the American and English-language stage, was *The Pink Lady*.

The story of the piece was – in part – not dissimilar to that of *The Girl from Kay's*. The lady of the title is the demi-mondaine Claudine, and she is out having a last fling with her lover Lucien before he retires to marriage when his wife-to-be turns up at the same restaurant. Pretences swirl, complicated by the fact that "the satyr", a mysterious chap who's been snatching unawares kisses from local ladies, suddenly strikes again. The culprit turns out to be a mild little antiquarian whom the caught-out Claudine had hurriedly pretended was her husband, and who is delighted to find that his "weakness" has made him a celebrity with the ladies.

McLellan's sprightly adaptation of the French play was accompanied by a hit-filled Ivan Caryll score, topped by a gloriously gliding waltz tune, "Beautiful Lady", with which Hazel Dawn in the rôle of Claudine almost out-widowed *The Merry Widow* waltz, and by a jaunty, dancing piece – which sounded 100 per cent American and not a whit Belgian – about what goes on "By the Banks of the Saskatchewan". And, with a hand wholly different to the one he had wielded at the Gaiety Theatre, Caryll also introduced some fine ensemble music.

The Pink Lady was a first-class hit through 316 Broadway nights before the production transferred bodily – as *The Belle of New York* had done – to London. In fact, in the end, it did better on the international circuits than any American musical since McLellan's earlier hit, as it went on to be seen in Australia, at the Paris Théâtre des Bouffes-Parisiens and even in Budapest.

Mr Popple (of Ippleton)

Comedy with music in 3 acts by Paul Rubens. Produced at the Apollo Theatre, London, 14 November 1905.

Paul Rubens wasn't generally known for fine, characterful modern farce writing, so his *Mr Popple* was both atypical and a pleasant surprise. It was difficult to believe that the writer hadn't "borrowed" his story from across the English Channel, so much did the show's libretto rustle with the well-made fun of the *vaudeville*.

Mr Freddie Popple, from very little Ippleton, makes an unaccustomed visit to the big city and can't find an hotel room. So he accepts the loan of a flat from an actress, La Boléro. The flat is actually being paid for by not one but two gentlemen who are "interested in" the actress, so events get pretty hectic when both gentlemen turn up, followed by their wives. Freddie is jolly glad when he can stop being a pretend "husband" and get off back to sleepy Ippleton.

The show's songs fitted their characters delightfully. The "country mouse" Freddie – a memorable creation by G. P. Huntley – sang about how he was much more at ease with "Rabbits" than women, La Boléro serenaded him with a fond, friendly "You're Such a Dear, Sweet, Clumsy Old Thing", and the only concession to traditional "musical comedy" was the introduction of six chorines and a picturesque final scene at the Bexhill Kursaal. The little, aptly described comedy with music played 173 times in London in a run curtailed by a sagging theatre roof, toured the country and colonies, and then, in 1915, turned up in New York in the hands of producer F. Ray Comstock. In the usual New York way, Comstock had it doctored up to local tastes and infiltrated by local songs, but on this occasion to such an extent that, by the time the show got on, all Rubens's gentle, shaded songs were gone, to be replaced by a full set of new ones by Jerome Kern. The title had

Left: **Ray Comstock**
The producer bares his knees on Palm Beach. His pal is Mammy-singer Al Jolson, out without his blackface.

Below: *Mr Popple*
G. P. Huntley as the "country mouse" Freddie Popple gets his tie straightened by the friendly La Boléro (Ethel Irving).

gone too. Now the piece was called *Nobody Home*, and simply credited to Kern and to Guy Bolton. *Nobody Home* was produced at the Princess Theater, a struggling little house that had been unable to find a hit, or sometimes a tenant, during its handful of years of existence. But Comstock's publicists cleverly spread about the idea of the very smallness of their house, and of their musical, as being something novel and special, the public and the papers took them at their word, and the Americanized version of *Mr Popple* won itself a fair run (135 performances). It was sufficient to encourage Comstock to try more of the same, and the more of the same did even better.

This multi-coloured group of strongly built and often play-based musical comedies quickly encouraged others. Following *The Pink Lady* Caryll scored further "French" hits with the delicious, wife-swapping *Oh! Oh! Delphine* and *The Girl Behind the Gun*, both of which struck gold on English-language stages all round the world, Rudolf Friml and Otto Harbach produced one of the biggest musical comedy hits of the era with a version of *Les Dragées d'Hercule* called *High Jinks*,

and many another show with Gallic ancestry passed happily across the Broadway stage. However, it was obvious that it was perfectly possible to base a strong-booked musical on a goodish play that wasn't French or otherwise foreign, and also that it was possible to write a libretto that might have been a play first but hadn't bothered.

American material had, in fact, served as musical-comedy fodder quite early on. Mrs Pacheco's *Incog* had been successfully transmuted into *Three Twins* as early as 1908, Colonel Savage's hit novel *His Official Wife* had served as source for the internationally played *The Red Widow* in 1911, and, down at the Princess Theater, Ray Comstock followed up *Nobody Home* with a musical version of an American play called *Over Night*. The small and perfectly formed *Very Good Eddie* upheld the house's "bigger isn't better" policy splendidly, and its adapter, Bolton, then went on to turn out a long list of libretti – some French-based, some American-based, and some simply un-based – scoring a wide selection of successes as the Broadway musical play danced merrily towards its most satisfying and successful years to date.

'Dein ist mein Herz . . .'

Das Dreimäderlhaus
This fanciful version of the love-
life of Schubert, with a shaken-
not-stirred selection of his music,
turned out to be the most widely
successful musical of its era.

They All Waltzed

In these years when the musical comedy of Britain and of Broadway was busy getting itself a backbone, turning itself from a Gaiety-weight entertainment into a more solid piece of theatre, it didn't by any means have the front of the stage all to itself. In fact, it had only a smallish share of it. For there were other things going on in the musical theatre. More specifically, there was one very all-pervasive something else going on in the musical theatre.

Inset: Oscar Straus, Franz Lehár and Leo Fall

Three of the greatest musicians of the Central European theatre.

It came to be known as Viennese operetta. And, in the half-dozen or so years leading up to the war, it was *the* big thing on the singing, dancing stages of the world. As big as *opéra-bouffe* had been, as big as Gilbert and Sullivan but much more international than they had ever been, and as big as or bigger than the Victorian and Edwardian musical comedy that was then coming into its lattermost days.

Hit after funny, romantic, tuneful hit tumbled out of Central Europe onto the stages of the world in the 1900s and the 1910s, and such was the rest of the world's appetite for more and more of this glittering, joyous type of musical play that eventually Austrian, Hungarian and German authors and composers began to write their shows not with their own home-town audiences in mind, but quite simply as musical meat for the greedy and lucrative export market – and, most particularly, the English-language stages of the British Empire and of America.

The best and/or most popular of the shows that came out in the first thirty or so years of the new century have combined with a tiny handful of nineteenth-century ones to make up the backbone of the standard repertoire that is still played today on German-language stages. But, for some strange reason, only one

Das süsse Mädel

Heinrich Reinhardt's jaunty tunes sent some musically pretentious noses skywards, but both his show and his songs were a distinct popular success.

Kálmán all had the kind of hits at home and abroad that challenged not only the very best of Lehár, but anything else the musical-theatre world was turning out.

The "golden age" of Suppé, Strauss, Millöcker and Co. had come to an end virtually in unison with the nineteenth century, and it seemed, momentarily, that the Viennese musical theatre was going to go into a decline. Where, now, would local theatre managers go for the scores to their musicals? It didn't take them long to find out. Within just a handful of seasons, Vienna was simply rustling with melodious new shows, and the names that were attached to their music were nearly all new names.

The open-air Venedig in Wien summer theatre mounted a lively musical comedy called *Die Landstreicher* (1899) with music by the only really established musician to stay prominent through this "change-over period", the popular conductor and composer Carl Michael Ziehrer. But although there was no question about the attractiveness of Ziehrer's pretty and thoroughly Viennesy light music, the best of the more than dozen shows he would turn out in later years (*Ein tolles Mädel, Liebeswalzer*) were really only second-rung successes.

The bigger houses went very largely for the new men. The Theater an der Wien had a sizeable hit with the merry masked-ball musical *Der Opernball* (1898), an adaptation of the famous French farce *Les Dominos roses* with a pretty score ("Geh'n wir in's chambre séparée") by first-timer Richard Heuberger, but Heuberger never managed to pull it off again. Then the rival Carltheater found a winner with *Das süsse Mädel* (1901) a jolly little tale of a wealthy uncle, a naughty nephew, a missing heir and the not entirely 'sweet girl' of the title, with music by another new boy, Heinrich Reinhardt. Reinhardt was definitely no Suppé or Millöcker. His music was of the simplest, most obviously tuneful kind, full of catchy, dancing rhythms – frothy, folksy, looser and more lightly orchestrated. And very popular: *Das süsse Mädel*'s title-song ("So g'waschen wie a Damerl") became a round-the-town hit.

The same theatre followed up Reinhardt's hit with another winner, *Der Rastelbinder*, an endearing piece with a comic-sentimental tale

pre-war Viennese musical is a regular in today's English-language theatres: Franz Lehár's *Die lustige Witwe*, better known to us as *The Merry Widow*. And the name of Lehár has become as much a synonym for the slickly christened "silver age" of European musical theatre as has that of Johann Strauss for the "golden age". The other great shows of this period, and their composers, are all but forgotten outside Central Europe. And yet, in their day, Edmund Eysler, Oscar Straus (one "s" and no relation to those with two), Leo Fall, Victor Jacobi, Georg Jarno and Emmerich

about a couple of young tinker folk who end up – after a few ins and outs – gratefully not fulfilling their childhood betrothal. The show featured a star-making central character rôle – a Jewish onion-seller – which undoubtedly helped to ensure the show's popularity, but it also boasted a decidedly attractive score by a young Hungarian composer whose first work for the Vienna stage had been heard only weeks earlier – Franz Lehár. *Der Rastelbinder* and its comical peddler remained favourites in Central Europe for several decades. So, of course, did Lehár.

Theater an der Wien supremo Wilhelm Karczag, the so-so playwright-turned-inspired manager who had given his fellow Hungarian, Lehár, his first Viennese chance, had done only respectably with the young composer's maiden musical *Wiener Frauen*, but he had a full-scale hit when he mounted another new *Operette* with a score by another untried composer, Edmund Eysler. Like *Der Rastelbinder, Bruder Straubinger* had at its centre a virtuoso star rôle, and that rôle – an in-problems young man who is forced, for much of the evening, to masquerade as a very old one – was played by Viennese mega-star Alexander Girardi. But it wasn't just the splendid rôle or even the skill and pull of Girardi that made the piece a hit. The music more than did its part too, and the star of the show scored the biggest show-song success in years in Eysler's loping waltz number with its claim that "kissing's no sin" ("Küssen ist keine Sünd").

By the time the first few years of the decade had gone, it was clear that the Viennese musical theatre was in fine condition. New musical talents seemed to be surfacing annually – Hugo Felix, Pepi Hellmesberger, Oscar Straus, Leo Fall, Leo Ascher. But, although all was healthy on the banks of the Danube, these splendid Central European shows that were rolling out at such a rate were, for the moment, being seen and appreciated only in Central Europe. Further afield, hardly anyone was taking any notice. It needed that one international mega-hit – an *H. M. S. Pinafore* or a *La Grande-Duchesse* – to provoke a wider audience interest in the new kind of German-language *Operette*. That mega-hit wasn't too long in coming, and it was, of course, *Die lustige Witwe – The Merry Widow*.

Karl Streitman and Mizzi Günther (left) introduced the top song of Lehar's first hit show, *Der Rastelbinder*, but even their sprightly duetting couldn't compete with Alexander Girardi's big number from Edmund Eysler's *Bruder Straubinger*, "Küssen ist keine Sünd" (below).

Die lustige Witwe

French plays had been traditional source material for Viennese musicals since the days when Genée and Zell merrily plundered Paris for texts to remake as Operetten, *and playwright Victor Léon had been a particular adept of the practice during the last decade.* Der Opernball *had been one of his. So when he refashioned Henri Meilhac's old play* L'Attaché d'ambassade *as a libretto for the Theater an der Wien, it was Richard Heuberger who was scheduled to write the music.*

pparently he did produce a score, but manager Karczag didn't like it, and in the end – against the wishes of the librettist, so it is said – it was Léon's *Rastelbinder* partner, Lehár, who got the job of illustrating his piece (the writer would admit on the playbill only that it was "partly based on a foreign idea") with music.

Pontevedrian Hanna Glawari is a widow, and she is also deeply, seriously rich. She is so rich, that the idea of her marrying a foreigner and taking all that lovely money out of financially shaky Pontevedro gives the government the blue horrors. So Baron Zeta, the Pontevedrian ambassador in Paris – where the widow is off enjoying herself amongst a swarm of suitors – is deputed swiftly to find her a healthily home-made husband. He picks for this delicate, patriotic mission the boozy, womanizing, but indubitably charming Count Danilowitsch. It's a tricky choice, because Danilo missed out on Hanna first time round, and has a pretty poor opinion of her for preferring Mr Glawari to his enamoured self. And now he has to woo her all over again! For the sake of the fatherland he swallows his pride, but he almost brings it right up again when Hanna is caught in a compromising position with a sexy young Parisian who sings high notes. However, Hanna has only been covering up for the embarrassed Baroness Zeta, and by the end of the evening pride and the Glawari millions have both been saved.

Lehár's score caught the light-hearted Balkan-Parisian romanticism of the story and its characters marvellously, as it ranged from

Background: **Louis Treumann and Mizzi Günther,** the original stars of what would become the most famous European musical of its century.

Left: An artist's impression of George Edwardes' London production of *The Merry Widow*.

CREDITS

Die lustige Witwe

Operette in 3 acts by Victor Léon and Leo Stein, based on *L'Attaché d' ambassade* by Henri Meilhac

MUSIC

by Franz Lehár

Produced at the Theater an der Wien, Vienna, 30 December 1905

Germany: Neues Theater, Hamburg, 3 March 1906

Hungary: Magyar Színház, Budapest, 27 November 1906

UK: Daly's Theatre, London, 8 June 1907

USA: New Amsterdam Theater, New York, 21 October 1907

France: Théâtre Apollo, Paris, 28 April 1909

CAST

Baron Mirko Zeta Siegmund Natzler

Valencienne Annie Wünsch

Hanna Glawari Mizzi Günther

Count Danilo Danilowitsch Louis Treumann

Camille de Rosillon Karl Meister

Cascada Carlo Böhm

Saint-Brioche Leo von Keller

light comedy ("Dummer Reitersmann", "Da geh' ich zu Maxim"), romance ("Lippen schweigen") and even a showpiece ("Vilia") for Hanna and/or Danilo – both of whom were played by comically talented "actors-who-sing" – to more earnestly sung romance in a series of duos for the vocalists cast as the Parisian and the Baroness Valencienne ("Wie eine Rosenknospe", "Ich bin eine anständige Frau"). There was also full-blooded comedy for the buffo Baron and his friends, comedy that was topped by a swinging march octet about "women" ("Ja, das Studium der Weiber ist schwer"). Even the girlie element was not neglected, as Valencienne led the grisettes of Maxim's in a vigorous song-and-dance routine to the strains of "Ja, wir sind es die Grisetten".

Die lustige Witwe was an immediate hit, and a hit of proportions never before seen on the Viennese stage. It was played 400 times in its first 16 months in the repertoire, and it soon went forth to conquer the rest of the world in the same way it had taken the Austrian capital. Hamburg got its production, with Marie Ottmann and Gustave Matzner in the central rôles, little more than two months after the Vienna opening, and within two further months that production had headed Berlinwards. In not much more than a year and a half, it too had passed its 400th night. Before then, Croatian, Czech, Hungarian, Italian, Norwegian, Russian and Swedish widows had all made it to the stage, and in 1907 the first English adaptation appeared, produced under the management of George Edwardes himself, at Daly's Theatre in London. *The Merry Widow* was not entirely a straight English rewrite of *Die lustige Witwe*. Edwardes ordered a few "typically English" alterations, to make his first attempt at giving his public a Viennese musical less of a shock. Lehár provided two new numbers, two others were reorganized and reallotted, and the girls and the comedy were given a bit more exposure than before. In a cast that didn't exactly ripple with top star names, comedian George Graves, cast as Zeta, was given his head and promptly inserted all sorts of irrelevant chatter, including a music-hally monologue about a hen called Hetty who laid misshapen eggs. But lovely young Lily Elsie, in the rôle of Sonia (as the widow had been rechristened), and American light comedy actor Joe Coyne, previously seen mostly in dude parts, kept the limelight firmly on the central story as the show gambolled on for 778 nights in London.

American impresario Henry Savage soon picked up Edwardes's slightly remade hit, and Ethel Jackson and Donald Brian headed a Broadway production of *The Merry Widow* through 419 performances, as the show and, in its wake, the Viennese musical in general established themselves as firmly on both sides of the English-speaking Atlantic as they had all round Europe.

As *Die lustige Witwe* went triumphantly round the world, the flag-bearer of what would quickly become the latest fashion in musical theatre, other Viennese shows and other Viennese (or, at least, Vienna-based) writers and composers quickly found their works being snatched up – sometimes more than a touch indiscriminately – to follow, and to feed the new demand for more *Merry Widows*. In the eternally inexplicable way of the theatre, it wasn't always the biggest home-town hits that proved the overseas favourites, but the next two decades and a bit produced a rich and varied set of musicals, from a whole variety of authors and musicians, which scored memorable successes both in Europe and/or further afield.

Operette for all

A couple of the most attractive *Operetten* that came out in and of Vienna in the years between *Die lustige Witwe* and the war were again the work of Lehár. Although his up-to-date musical comedy about a trigamist travelling salesman, *Der Mann mit den drei Frauen*, didn't take off, and the Greek bandits musical (with a tactfully American sailor hero) *Das Fürstenkind* didn't live up to its home reputation abroad, he scored consecutive and noteworthy hits with another tale of aristocratic romancing in Paris, *Der Graf von Luxemburg*, and an altogether more tempestuous and gypsyish piece, evocatively titled *Zigeunerliebe*. If the first of these – which duly followed *Die lustige Witwe* to all the main centres of the world – reproduced the bubbling musical tones of Lehár's most famous work as an accompaniment to its sparkling story of a marriage of convenience that turns serious, the latter went for some altogether more dramatic effects in its music, effects that foreshadowed Lehár's later abandonment of musical comedy for the lusher and more lugubrious pastures of the romantic musical. But *Zigeunerliebe,* a passionate piece rather than a conventionally romantic one, found the composer writing with all the flair and flavour of his native land, and this tale of an Hungarian girl torn between wild romanticism and a life of comfortable love remains a case alone amongst Lehár's successful shows.

The first major hit to follow *Die lustige Witwe* out of Vienna was a piece which insisted that its libretto wasn't taken from the French, or even "partly based on a foreign idea". It almost certainly was but, be that as it may, it was as colourful a tale of high society love and marriage as *Die lustige Witwe*, and its score of Oscar Straus music was in the same delicious and "Viennese" mode. It was a mode highlighted by the show's title: *Ein Walzertraum* – a waltz dream.

The hero of the piece has married a Princess – at the beginning of the operetta, please note, and not at the end. But he's Viennese, she has courtly duties to perform, and he soon gets bored and homesick. He finds consolation with a little lady who runs a touring Viennese café orchestra, but when she finds out who he is she renounces her love and instead teaches the distressed royal wife how to make her husband feel at home. The show's musical highlight was the two-tenor duo for the Consort and his pal ("Leise, ganz leise"), on their first hearing the music of the Viennese band floating through the palace gates.

Somewhat curiously, *Ein Walzertraum* didn't prove a big hit in the English language, but it was a huge success at home, and went on to become one of the top favourites amongst Viennese shows in France, where it is still played today, nearly a century on.

If Straus's biggest home-town winner didn't travel as well as it might have, he more than made up for it with another show which did only fairly first up but became an enormous success in its English edition. *Der tapfere Soldat* (The brave soldier) ran for only sixty performances in Vienna, but Stan Stange's English version, more winsomely retitled *The Chocolate Soldier*, became one of the biggest ex-Viennese hits of all in both America and England. *Der tapfere Soldat* was a musicalized version of G. B. Shaw's *Arms and the Man*, from which some of the subsidiary action (and the musical-comedy maid) had been excised. Those excised bits were replaced by a score of charming music which included both the heroine's "Komm' komm'! Held meiner Träume" (to become

Below: ***Der Graf von Luxemburg***

Lehár made a hit out of the same Parisian story of a temporary marriage which had earlier been a flop when set by Strauss.

famous as "My Hero" in Stange's version) and some splendid ensemble work.

Although he composed some forty further musicals, a number of which ran up fine records in Europe, *The Chocolate Soldier* remains Straus's one real reference on the English-language stage.

The frivolous, Frenchified style of musical show was well and truly *à la mode* in the years following *Die lustige Witwe*'s arrival on the scene, but European high or highish society was in no way obligatory as the setting for a hit. One of the earliest post-*Witwe* hits, indeed, chose to plonk its action down in a much more romantic bit of Ruritanian countryside – the United States of America. The heroine of *Die Dollarprinzessin* was a rich (Operettic Americans were always rich – it was their theatrical *raison d'être*) mining heiress, the hero a poor but proud émigré Continental nobleman who can't face marrying her until he's got as much cash as she has. The show opened with a ditsy chorus of young lady typewriters, and went on to some of the fleetest-footed music yet to have come out of Vienna, ranging from a title quartet in waltz time to an of-the-moment song-and-dance routine that was the hit of the night ("Wir tanzen Ringelreih'n").

That music was the work of Leo Fall, another young composer to have recently been given a chance by producer Karczag. Fall's début show at the Theater an der Wien had actually been a flop, but his very next, the sweetly rural *Der fidele Bauer*, had been a huge triumph throughout Germany, and Karczag's production of *Die Dollarprinzessin* more than made up for the earlier flop.

Die Dollarprinzessin proved a splendid successor to *The Merry Widow* in Britain and in America, but the show that really made Fall into a household name in Britain was his next, the saucy courtroom tale of *Die geschiedene Frau*. Victor Léon's "divorced woman" gets divorced because she thinks her husband has been up to no good with a free-loving actress in a railway carriage. Of course it's all a mistake, and in the end the actress gets paired off, *Trial by Jury*-fashion, with the divorce-court judge, whilst the two principals get relievedly back together again. It was the soubrette – as actress Gonda van der Loo – who had the evening's juiciest and dancingest

moments, swooping into a description of the pleasures of horizontal railway travel in "O Schlafcoupé, O Schlafcoupé" or demonstrating a new dance to the march rhythms of "Ich und du, Müllers Kuh", but Fall supplied a multicoloured score – from waltzes to a burlesque funeral march – which helped *The Girl on the Train* to a major West End success, *La Divorcée* to a fine Parisian run, and *Elvált asszony* to a long life in Hungary.

Fall varied his subjects and styles thoroughly in the regular flow of musicals he produced up to the war years – real French comedy with a musical version of *Miquette et sa mère* done as *Das Puppenmädel*, a glamorous French spy story in *Die Sirene*, an olde Austrian fable in *Die schöne Risette* and a delicious remake of his first flop show (with a royal baby-mixup, no less!) as the tale of the princess and her piano-teacher who was called *Der liebe Augustin* – but he didn't yet, in these years, top those big, early hits that had made his fame.

Die geschiedene Frau
Anny Dirkens, as good-time Gonda, introduced Victor Léon and Leo Fall's song in praise of the possibilities of a railway sleeping car.

Like Lehár, Georg Jarno was Hungarian by birth, and like Lehár he did his first theatre composing trying to write opera. Again like Lehár, he got his big chance in Vienna thanks to a fellow-Hungarian in high places. Only, in Jarno's case, that fellow-Hungarian was his brother. Josef Jarno ran the Theater in der Josefstadt, where the star attraction was his wife, Hansi Niese, the most popular soubrette on the Vienna stage. But Hansi wasn't just a cute actress, she was also a fine singer, and many of her made-to-measure shows had songs in them. In 1907 she starred in *Die Förster-Christl*, the story of little country Christl who goes up to town to see the Kaiser and beg from him a pardon for her deserter lover. She discovers that the Kaiser is a man who, like any other, can fall in love. And does. But the ill-matched pair are strong enough to resist the impossible temptation.

Right: **Edmund Eysler**
He wrote as much gloriously Viennese music as the most famous of his contemporaries, but none of his hometown hits carried his name to fame overseas.

Below: *Ein Herbstmanöver*
Soubrette Luise Kartousch and leading lady Grete Holm in the Vienna version of Kálmán's Hungarian hit *Tatárjárás*.

Brother Georg was hired to do the Hungarian-flavoured music for what turned out to be his and Hansi's biggest hit, and *Die Förster-Christl* went on to a long, long life in Central Europe and a Broadway showing as *The Girl and the Kaiser.*

Lehár and Jarno had already given Hungary a strong representation on the Viennese stage, but soon after their first big hits they found reinforcement from home in no uncertain way. In 1909, Karczag imported a hit musical from Budapest's Vigszinház. It was a piece about romance and fun on army manoeuvres, and its score was by one Imre Kálmán. The rechristened *Ein Herbstmanöver* turned out to be a major Viennese hit, and soon Kálmán had moved to Vienna, was calling himself Emmerich instead of Imre, and had had his first Vienna-built musical produced at the Johann Strauss-Theater with none other than the great Girardi starring. Girardi was getting on a touch by now, and *Der Zigeunerprimás* (1912) cast him as a famous old gypsy violinist who ultimately loses both the girl and his fame to his own son. He didn't lose the evening's biggest number, though, and Vienna's favourite musical star scored his umpteenth great show-song hit with the gypsy's description of what his violin means to him ("Mein alter Stradivari"). The career of *Der Zigeunerprimás* outside Central Europe was undoubtedly cut short by wartime considerations and the virtually effective banning of "German" musicals in Britain and France, but America – where such considerations weren't considered – took the show in, and under the title of *Sari* it turned out to be one of the most successful of all Broadway-Viennese shows.

Some of Girardi's best rôles – and best songs – in these years came in shows composed by the most tunefully Viennesey of all Viennese composers, Edmund Eysler. Eysler never scored the one big overseas hit that Lehár, Fall and Kálmán all managed, and his fame has suffered accordingly, but at home he turned out a remarkable run of melodious and long-running musical plays – *Pufferl* (1905), *Die Schützenliesel* (1905), *Künstlerblut* (1906), *Vera Violetta* (1907), *Der unsterbliche Lump* (1910), *Der Frauenfresser* (1911), *Der lachende Ehemann* (1913) and *Ein Tag im Paradies* (1913). Germany and

Hungary welcomed Eysler's works liberally in the aftermath of their often long Vienna runs, but, although several made their way to English stages, the nearest the unlucky Eysler got to a success beyond Europe was a heavily botched version of *Ein Tag im Paradies* produced on Broadway as *The Blue Paradise*.

Downriver and upriver

What's become popularly known as "Viennese operetta" wasn't – as we've seen – entirely Viennese, even though many of the shows that we've passed by were first produced in the Austrian capital. The surrounding countries – some of them, of course, parts of the then Austro-Hungarian Empire – contributed their bit as well, and none contributed more and more memorably than Hungary. Even though Budapest had – then as now – a thriving and exciting theatre world of its own, many Hungarians left their home for the more obvious and substantial rewards on offer in Vienna. But if Lehár, Jarno, Kálmán, Karczag and a very appreciable list of others made most of their career in Austria, other fine musicians, writers and producers stayed at home, and at home they produced a wide range of remarkable musical theatre.

One of the most remarkable amongst all the pieces which appeared in Hungary at this time – and one which, in spite of being regarded to this day virtually as Hungary's "national musical", has rarely been seen elsewhere – is *János vitéz* (1904). "Brave John" is a shepherd boy who is chased from his home and job by the wicked stepmother of his beloved Iluska. He joins the army, rises to command and helps the King of France defeat the Turks, but, rejecting the King's offer of his daughter's hand and half his kingdom, he then goes in search of Iluska. She is dead, murdered by the witch, her stepmother, but János braves the afterworld, defeats the witch, and brings Iluska back from the depths of the Lake of Life to be his wife. The text for this *daljáték* or song-play, based on Sándor Petöfi's dramatic poem, was illustrated by a score of embracing folkish simplicity, warm and plaintive in turn and ravishingly beautiful at times, composed by Pongrác Kacsoh.

The very special success of *János vitéz* naturally prompted other Hungarian writers and composers to attempt shows in the same

style, and one who succeeded as well as any was the young Victor Jacobi. But Jacobi's greatest moments in the musical theatre did not come until he forsook the realm of fairytale and fabular musicals and switched to the more widely appreciated romantic *Operette* mode. He found his first international success when George Edwardes chose his 1911 show *Leányvásár* (*The Marriage Market*), a piece set in America and mixing a *Martha*-like story of mistaken marriages with a good deal of the kind of lowish comedy popular with UK and US audiences, for Daly's Theatre. But his greatest international success came with his next show, *Szibill*, the tale of an in-the-process-of-breaking-the-law opera-singer who gets mistaken for a Grand Duchess. The Grand Duke wickedly sang romantic music ("Illúzió, a szerelem") with his temporary Duchess whilst she was hiding her deserter lover in her hotel room, and at the same time the comedy characters of the piece – Sybil's impresario and his wife – performed the jaunty, light-comic but heavily rhythmed dance numbers ("Gombhaz, sej, hogyha leszakad", "Van valami") which Jacobi composed so infectiously. *Szibill* went round the world, and some of the top singing ladies of the era (Julia Sanderson, José Collins, Gladys Moncrieff, Fritzi Massary) took on the rôle created by Sári Fedák, as the show established itself as the most widely successful Hungarian musical of its time.

If the 1914 *Szibill* gave Hungary – with a decent delay caused by the war – possibly her finest hour on the international musical stage, there is no doubt that the same period also saw Germany making her most impressive mark abroad. For, before and during the war years, Berlin saw the production of a whole run of home-made musical comedies, many more of which might have gone, from there, round and

Below: *János vitéz*
A fairytale musical of unbounded charm, this unusual and beautiful show has a very special – and wholly deserved – place in the Hungarian theatre.

round the world, had times been different.

From 1909, and the production of his merry, farcical *Polnische Wirtschaft* at Cottbus, composer Jean Gilbert (whose real name was Max Winterfeld) wrote a whole series of comical, tuneful hit shows for the Central European stage, shows that sent forth a whole series of songs which would become the whistleable tunes of their day ("Puppchen, du bist mein Augenstern", "Ja, das haben die Mädel so gern", "In der Nacht"). Gilbert's *The Girl in the Taxi* and *The Cinema Star* – otherwise *Die keusche Susanne* and *Die Kino-Königin* – progressed from Germany to great success in Britain, and George Edwardes had two further Gilbert shows slated and the composer lined up to write an original score for him when the war broke out. All such German-tinted projects were cancelled forthwith, and Gilbert's main outlet and his opportunity for wider fame were summarily sealed off.

Much the same fate befell another busy Berlin composer, Walter Kollo, who in 1914 had been just a couple of years in the limelight and who had just had his first real overseas exposure with the production of his *Filmzauber* (*The Girl on the Film*) in Britain and on Broadway. Whatever wider prospects Kollo might have had never matured, but if he had nothing like the success that Gilbert won abroad, he nevertheless kept up a steady supply of long-running musical comedies to the German stage for many years, including several – especially the pre-war *Wie einst im Mai* (1913) – that would have a recurring life.

Musicals to make war by

There was no doubt that the memorable shows and show music of the Great War came almost entirely from the losing side. Not from Germany, where Gilbert and Kollo's one-after-another shows monopolized the main Berlin houses, but from Austria. During the war years, such stars of the pre-war Vienna stage as Kálmán, Eysler and Fall all turned out marvellous scores as illustration for the kind of happily escapist, "good-old-days" texts that always flourish so thoroughly in wartime.

Kálmán actually had an unusual worldwide run of productions with one of his shows, a musical play about a soldier which had started life in Budapest in 1910 as *Az obsitos*, and was seen, during the war, in various patriotic versions not only in Vienna and Berlin (*Gold gab' ich für Eisen*) but also both on Broadway and in Britain (*Her Soldier Boy*). But his big success during those years was a new show, mounted at Vienna's Johann Strauss-Theater in 1915, and called *Die Csárdásfürstin*. *Die Csárdásfürstin* had a conventional enough plot – the aristocrat and the cabaret singer – but that plot was adjoined to a really delightful score of romantic melodies ("Tausend kleine Engel singen"), light-footed dance pieces (Schwalbenduett), singer's showpieces ("Heia, heia, in den Bergen ist mein Heimatland") and light comic numbers ("Die Mädis vom Chantant"), all rolled together in what was to prove to be this very successful composer's most wholly and widely successful score. *Die Csárdásfürstin* ran for 533 performances first up in Vienna, became a fixture in the Central European repertoire, and even if the English version, curiously retitled *The Gipsy Princess* (she isn't), didn't do quite as well, the French version, *Princesse Czardas*, is firmly established as one of the handful of Viennese shows still seen on the French stage.

The Theater an der Wien had its biggest hit since *Die lustige Witwe* with its wartime production of Leo Fall's 1916 musical *Die Rose von Stambul*. The romantic part of the story – a Turkish woman's attempt to escape an arranged marriage and wed a poet who's into women's lib – produced some of the greatest lyric tenor music of the musical theatre ("O Rose von Stambul", "Ihr stillen, süssen Frauen", "Heut' wär ich"), and the parallel comic part, with the lead comedian dragged up in a knee-length gown and picture hat in his efforts to liberate his girl from the local harem, brought forth both some memorable high-jinks (especially for him) and a set of lilting, dancing soubret duos. *Die Rose von Stambul* ran for a straight 15 months on the stage of its famous house, before going on to other countries and other productions, and the show, with its two rare star rôles, still gets revived in Austria. The failure of a really rotten Broadway production in 1922, however, effectively finished its prospects outside Central Europe. More's the pity.

Edmund Eysler's biggest successes in these years were produced at the Apollotheater, a venue that had moved on from playing variety programmes with a bit of *Operette* in them to mounting full-length shows. It still sported a slightly night-clubby atmosphere, but that didn't stop it getting big stars (and star composers) to work there. Two of the biggest, soubrette Mizzi Zwerenz and leading man Fritz Werner, were around when Eysler scored hits with his *Hanni geht's tanzen* and *Graf Toni*.

The biggest Vienna hit, the biggest anywhere and everywhere hit of all the war years, was, however, none of these top-notch musicals. It was a show that was quite simply as good-old-days as it was possible to be. It was called *Das Dreimäderlhaus* (The house of the three little girls), although eventually the rest of the world would come to know it as *Lilac Time, Blossom Time*, or – a more apt title – *Chanson d'amour*. The piece even had a good-old-days score. For, since its libretto was a women's-mag version of the life and love story of composer Franz Schubert, its music was quite simply a cocktail of emulsified Schubert – a cocktail that was remixed for each country the show visited, getting stickier and sugarier and more sentimental the further it went – but one that was clearly addictive. The show topped 650 nights in wartime Vienna, ran for more than a thousand performances in wartime Berlin, and when it was staged, in the early 1920s, in France, Britain and America it became – in all three places – a huge favourite, and a touring and revivable prospect for decades thereafter.

There was just a touch more than a decade between the production of *Die lustige Witwe* and *Das Dreimäderlhaus,* but in that decade the theatres of Central Europe started a veritable flood of fine musical plays on their way around the world. And there were plenty more of them to come in the years that were to follow, in those wonderfully rich years of the 1920s, the one and only time in history when all the main centres of musical theatre were producing fine new musical plays at one and the same time.

Below: *Die Rose von Stambul*
The lady made it to the sheet-music cover, but it was the tenor who got the solid gold solos in Leo Fall's soaring score.

Opposite: **Sári Fedák**
The great star of the Hungarian musical theatre of her time poses as the "queen of the movies" in Budapest's production of *Die Kino-Königin*.

Days of dance and laughter . . .

Darling, I Love You
Ella Logan and the Gaiety company pose for a picture on the stage of the no-longer-quite so-famous theatre.

Mad, Glad Musical World

Les années folles, *the French called them. The English expressions ranged from the "era of wonderful nonsense" to "the jazz age" and the rather less atmospheric "the roaring twenties". But I like "les années folles" best. It somehow catches the all-but-uncatchable spirit of the madcap years that followed the most horrible war in history.*

Those post-war years were remarkable ones, bringing important changes in the very fabric and functioning of society from one side of the world to the other. And they were remarkable years, too, in the merry, decorative, little world of entertainment, particularly in the musical theatre. For the 1920s turned out to be arguably the most memorable and the most widely productive years that the musical theatre had ever seen, or would ever see.

In America, in that time, the native-born musical stage burst fully and finally into blossom, as a double strand of light-hearted, light-footed, songwriters' shows and richly romantic musical plays went exploding out from Broadway to establish American musicals and music firmly on the stages of the world in general; in Central Europe the prosperous *Operette* tradition drew itself up to its highest peak of pleasurability in what would be the last grand decade before its decline; in France the almost wholly run-down *opérette* genre moved over and out, making space for some of the most sophisticated and dazzling musical comedies the world would ever see; whilst in Britain the musical stage – with a little help from its overseas friends – simply danced and laughed with a real, madcap vengeance that fitted in thoroughly with the mood of the times. Never before had the international musical stage flourished like this. Never would it again. But right then, who cared about tomorrow?

Yes, yes, the Yankees!

The American musical – the really American musical, the one that would go out and take the world by dancing up a storm – almost happened all of a sudden. And it didn't happen just through that growing up of its libretti that had taken place in *The Pink Lady* days. It happened, rather, thanks to the coupling of those better-than-before libretti with a kind of music that was recognizably not European, not British, not anything else, but to all intents and purposes home-grown.

The words "ragtime" and, later and more frequently, "jazz" were tossed pretty liberally around as a description of this fresh and merrily rhythmic kind of music, but more often than not they were tossed wrongly. Neither real ragtime, which had been heard here and there on the musical stage since the 1890s (when one show was actually described as a "ragtime opera"), nor genuine jazz, with its inherently improvisational nature, was or would have been suitable as the score for a whole tradition of theatre shows. The music in question was, quite simply, up-to-the-minute American popular music: music that came from the same melting-pot of cultures – the Jewish, the negro, the Continental, the Anglo-Saxon – that had produced that grand new multicultural thing that was up-to-the-minute America itself.

In these early years of the twentieth century, however, the American music that grabbed the attention of the world at large was American dance music. In the 1910s and the 1920s, the world went mad for dancing, and the music it liked best to dance to – or watch others dance to – was the jaunty, rhythmic

and/or syncopated strains that were coming out of America: the fox-trot, the shimmy, the Boston and the two-step, the tango, the one-step or any other of the foot-stirring, hip-swivelling, two-at-a-time dances of the day. Britons and Germans and Hungarians might try to ape the American writers and their styles in an attempt to hitchike a ride on this marvellous musical bandwagon, but almost always the best and most high-heeled of this seemingly patented kind of music was the music that came from beyond the Atlantic. And during the 1910s and the 1920s those tunes, those dances, those dance-musicked songs were even delivered attached to equally jaunty, fun-and-dance-filled musical plays. How could the world resist?

The answer was, of course, that it didn't. The world quite frankly took the dances and songs and tales and shows that were tumbling out from the theatres of the now not-so-new world firmly to its light heart. But, just as had been the case with the other, earlier international waves in the musical theatre, it took the regulation amount of time before the "big" show of the era, the one that would go down in history as the flag-bearer for its genre, put in its appearance. The year was 1923, the place was Chicago, and the show was *No, No, Nanette*.

Right: **Miss Amerika**
American dance-music was still all the rage in Europe in 1929. Eisemann's Hungarian musical left no doubt as to the source of its inspiration.

Opposite: **"Tutenkhamen Shimmy"**
The dance rhythms of America didn't quite go back to the Egypt of the pharaohs, but they certainly invaded 1910s Germany. Beda, the lyricist of this jolly knees-about, went on to write some forty *Operetten* and composer Beneš also scored both musicals and films.

No, No, Nanette

In 1919, producer Harry Frazee had had a profitable share in a play called My Lady Friends. *By now, it had become regular practice to use local, rather than imported, plays – sometimes when the original had barely moved off the stage – as the bases for new musicals, and so in 1923 Frazee, with a second pocket-filling bite at this particular apple in view, duly had* My Lady Friends *remade with music.*

Background: **France's Isola brothers kept the familiar title for their record-breaking production, even though Loulou Hegoburu sang "Non, non, Nanette!"**

Opposite: **Louise Groody was Chicago's Nanette and New York's Nanette, but she only got the part after a tanked-up Frazee sacked his original ingénue.**

Otto Harbach, who had so successfully recreated the German *Madame Sherry* for him, joined original playwright Frank Mandel on the libretto, and Frazee let himself be convinced by a sizeable investment from the mother of the songwriter Vincent Youmans, recently credited with his first Broadway half-score, that her not-so-experienced son should supply the music.

Publisher Jimmy Smith has made a lot of money, but he can't get his careful wife, Sue, to spend any of it. So, rather than have it go mouldy in the bank, he gives himself pleasure by opening charge accounts at some nice stores for a trio of pretty girlies with no qualms at all about spending someone else's cash. But the girlies eventually become a bit of a liability, and Jimmy's lawyer pal, Billy Early, is called on tidily to terminate all his friend's "arrangements". He chooses far-off

Atlantic City as the venue for this little feminine showdown, but it turns out not to be far off enough. Jimmy, his ward Nanette, his wife, Billy's wife Lucille, and the three suspiciously choice-looking girlies all get mixed up in an actful of Atlantic City understandings and misunderstandings before Jimmy's affairs are put happily in order.

The songs for the show were a charming lot, with Lucille Early pulling most of the best – the lively "Too Many Rings Around Rosie", the truly blue "Where Has my Hubby Gone?" Blues and the confident wifely "You Can Dance with Any Girl at All" – until some rewrites following the show's Detroit tryout introduced two new numbers. One was Jimmy's generously loping explanation "I Want to Be Happy", the other was a bouncing duo for ingénue Nanette and her ingénu Tom about taking "Tea for Two".

was already on her way round the world. And wherever she went the reaction was most definitely "yes, yes".

The production team which had helped to make the London *Nanette* such a success crossed to Paris to stage an ever more dance-filled French version of the show, and, while "Thé pour deux" and "Heureux tous les deux" made themselves hits all over again, it racked up a superb run, establishing itself as a frantic favourite in such a way that it has stayed in the French repertoire through many, many a revival ever since. The London version was also taken up for Berlin with equally happy results, and that production then toured to Vienna and Budapest. By this time the dancers of the very prominent chorus had second billing only to star Irene Palasty, for the further that it went into Europe the further the show went in for spectacle and massed dance effects. *Nanette*, as seen in central Europe, had grown into an altogether more sizeable show than it had been in Detroit and Chicago.

No, No Nanette has remained the quintessential American 1920s musical on the world's stages, its popularity given a fresh boost by a 1971 Broadway revival of a version that – with its heavy accent on dance content and period glamour – resembled the show as played on the Continent more than the original "musical comedy". But in whatever version, *No, No, Nanette* lives on, secure in its niche alongside such pieces as *H. M. S. Pinafore* and *Die lustige Witwe* as one of the landmarks in the happy history of the musical theatre.

No, No, Nanette – which had originally been scheduled as Broadway bound – proved so successful in Chicago that it simply didn't move on, but instead – whilst its hit tunes danced their way infectiously round the country – stayed and played there for a whole year. This meant that the show was seen in London before New York, and the two novice producers who had picked up the British rights to the piece early on in what was supposed to be just its out-of-town tryout were rewarded for their pluck when their version of *Nanette* scored every bit as big a hit in the West End as the original had in Chicago. Companies began to tour the show all around America, and it had been seen as far south as Australia before Frazee finally brought his Chicago production to Broadway. New York sulked a touch at having had to wait so long for the hit half America had already seen, and gave it a shorter stay than Chicago and London had done, but *Nanette*

CREDITS

No, No, Nanette

Musical comedy in 3 acts by Frank Mandel, Otto Harbach and Irving Caesar, based on the play *My Lady Friends* by Mandel and Emil Nyitray

MUSIC

by Vincent Youmans

Produced at the Harris Theater, Chicago, 7 May 1923

UK: Palace Theatre, London, 11 March 1925

USA: Globe Theater, New York, 16 September 1925

France: Théâtre Mogador, Paris, 29 April 1926

Germany: Metropoltheater, Berlin, 7 November 1926

Austria: Wiener Bürgertheater, Vienna, 23 December 1927

Hungary: Király Színház, Budapest, 17 March 1928

CAST

Jimmy Smith	Charles Winninger
Sue Smith	Juliette Day
Billy Early	Bernard Granville
Lucille Early	Blanche Ring
Nanette	Louise Groody
Pauline	Georgia O'Ramey
Tom	Jack Barker

Inset: *Mercenary Mary*
Peggy O'Neil was the Mary of the title when Broadway's successor to *No, No, Nanette* reached London. Here, she and Sonnie Hale (as Jerry) plot the marital pretence that's at the heart of the show's plot.

Background: *Oh, Kay!*
The show's star rôle – the title's titled English lady – was written for British actress Gertrude Lawrence. The authors originally went so far as to call their ex-French farce *Cheerio!* for her benefit, but thought better of it before Broadway.

So this was the new recipe. A light-hearted and fairly simple tale of romance and fun, illustrated by a great deal of energetic dancing and by the kind of songs that would undoubtedly have been the hit-parade material of their time, had hit parades then existed. Many of those songs were written by writers such as Jerome Kern or Louis Hirsch, who had already been prominent before and during the war, but they were joined now by a whole host of newer composers as providers of show music to this bright and blooming era. Some of those writers' names are still familiar to us today, either for good and obvious reasons or through diligent plugging – Kern himself, the Rodgers and Hart team, George Gershwin and his brother Ira, and so forth – whilst others, who wrote both hit songs and shows in their time, amongst them Harry Archer, Con Conrad, Youmans himself and Harry Tierney, are pretty well forgotten.

Harry Tierney was the tunesmith responsible for one of the biggest American hits of the immediate post-war years. It was called *Irene*, and its little heroine rose winsomely from American-Irish poverty, via adventures both romantic and comic, to wealth and social position as the wife of an American equivalent of a fairy prince, and she did it to the accompaniment of a pretty 1919 score from which its heroine's remembrance of her "Alice Blue Gown" has proved the lasting item. The sort of story used in *Irene* was, for a while, all the rage, but an ingénue in what actually became known as "the Cinderella era" in the Broadway musical didn't always get just a handsome home-grown aristocrat as a last-act prize. Often she ended up becoming a Broadway star as well.

The title-lassie of another major hit of the period, *Sally*, was one such. With a helping hand from the standard low, accented comedian, this little blonde dishwasher danced her way to both wealthy wedded bliss and a Broadway star's dressing-room. And on the way she got to share with her prince one of Jerome Kern's most durable songs, "Look for the Silver Lining".

Irene and *Sally* both proved grand hits all around the English-speaking world, but other made-in-America shows from the turn of the decade proved even better liked than they did. One of these was *Going Up*. A fine piece of altogether more real comedy than the Cinderella shows, it was a musicalized version of the successful play *The Aviator*, and its central character was a fellow who writes a fictional book about flying and then finds himself challenged to a race by an air ace, with the girl they love as the prize. Louis Hirsch supplied the numbers, topped by the dizzy dance routine known as the "Tickle-Toe", to this fun-filled text, and *Going Up* proved a major hit wherever English was sung, from Sydney to London.

Hirsch would go on to write such successful shows as *The Rainbow Girl* ("The Rainbow Girl", "I'll Think of You"), *Mary* ("The Love Nest") and *The O'Brien Girl*, shows that included some of the happiest melodies of his era. But, like Tierney, he never became a fashionable "name", and his position in the history of the musical theatre is more secure in London – where he was largely responsible for helping to popularize the new kind of American music – than on his native Broadway.

Probably the biggest American-bred musical comedy success to play the international circuits in the wake of *No, No, Nanette* was *Mercenary Mary*. *Mercenary Mary* is now thoroughly forgotten, just as her composer Con Conrad, for all that he wrote the very first Oscar-winning song, "The Continental", is forgotten. This merry musical comedy was, in fact, a 1925 remake of a 1923 play, full of mixups and marriages and money and set with a jazzy, dancey score. It did only fairly on Broadway, but in London it turned out second only to *Nanette* in popularity amongst American musical comedies of the era, and it went on to be seen in Australia, in France and, in its most remarkable stand of all, in Budapest. There, *Mersz-e, Mary?* quite simply topped the poll, *Nanette* and all, and became the archetypical American jazz-age musical.

Back home, however, shows that travelled less well, and composers other than Youmans, Conrad and Hirsch, won more lasting favour. Jerome Kern, who had topped a run of happy and often successful shows with *Sally* in 1920, had his best musical comedy runs of the decade with *Good Morning, Dearie* (1921) and *Sunny* (1925); the

young songwriting team of Richard Rodgers and Lorenz Hart took their careers flying towards the heights with pieces such as *The Girl Friend* (1926) and *A Connecticut Yankee* (1927); and George Gershwin turned out some delightful dancing melodies as the musical part of such star-vehicle shows as *Lady, Be Good!* (1924), *Tip-Toes* (1925), *Oh, Kay!* (1926) and *Funny Face* (1927).

Three of these four pieces were – like so many musicals of the time – written for the benefit of dancing stars, and thus they featured many moments and numbers built around the fanciest and finest of up-to-date footwork, but the fourth, *Oh, Kay!*, was constructed for comedienne Gertrude Lawrence and, in consequence, was a more than usually solidly built comical musical. The reason for the solidity wasn't far to find. Like *Going Up, Oh, Kay!* was built on the bones of a hit play, in this case the famous French farce *La Présidente*. Its smartly farcical plot of impersonations and improbabilities had its star (with the evening's chief comedian in tow) getting herself mixed up in a little bootlegging at the American seaside, and its score introduced such favourites as "Someone to Watch Over Me", "Do, Do, Do" and the exhortation (apropos of very little) to "Clap Yo' Hands". The combination of nifty text and attractive numbers ensured the show, if not vast original runs, a regularly revivable life.

The flow of fine musicals from the

Above Left: *Sunny*
Jerome Kern's musical comedies were ignored by a Europe that was producing brilliant ones of its own, but his show songs exported happily.

Above: **Lorenz Hart** (left), **Richard Rodgers** (seated) and a piano. An aerial view.

Left: *Lady, Be Good!*
Fred and Adele Astaire stepped out to George Gershwin's rhythms through fine seasons on Broadway and in Britain.

Above: **Irving Berlin**

He wrote just one Broadway musical in the 1920s – for the barely musical Marx brothers.

Opposite: **Hit the Deck!**

The French retitled it *Hallelujah!*, after its most rousing song, but Paris didn't respond.

Below: **The Cocoanuts**

The Marx brothers – with a flock of southern belles – in the second of their three Broadway musicals.

Broadway stage in the 1920s wasn't just limited to these few titles. The list of hits, and of exportable hits, was long, and so was the list of contributors. Youmans scored a second time with *Hit the Deck!* (1927), George M. Cohan shifted into the modern mode with *Little Nellie Kelly* (1922), forgotten Conrad hit the mark again with *Kitty's Kisses* (1926), and Harry Archer and Harlan Thompson impressed with a series of the small-scale musicals like those Ray Comstock had mounted in the 1910s. The happiest of the group did better than any of Comstock's, though, for *Little Jessie James* – a splendid bit of bed-cum-drawingroom-farcical nonsense illustrated with dancing songs which included a genuine world-travelling hit in "I Love You" – went right through Europe when Broadway had done with her.

Harry Ruby and Bert Kalmar went comedywards with *The Ramblers* (1926), Cinderella-ry with *The Five o'Clock Girl* (1927) and loony with the Marx brothers vehicle *Animal Crackers* (1928), whilst Irving Berlin provided the same brothers with the songs that decorated their zany *The Cocoanuts* (1925). Walter Donaldson wrote the songs for the comical *Whoopee!* (1928), songwriting team DeSylva, Brown and Henderson hit the theatre world between the eyes with their first musical, the collegiate *Good News* (1927), and followed it up with *Manhattan Mary* (1927), *Hold Everything!* (1928) and *Follow Thru'* (1929), and even much less considered songmakers won hits with shows such as *Tangerine* and *Queen High*.

It was a delightfully happy list, but, as if all this bright, danceworthy musical theatre wasn't enough in the way of entertainment to a nation, there was a whole second – and equally successful – side to the musical theatre of 1920s Broadway: the romantic musicals. Not musicals that were necessarily "romantic" in the boy-meets-girl way that the Cinderella shows were, but romantic in their use of colourful times and places as their setting, of dashing and even dramatic tales as their subjects, and, of course, of a much wider – if less thoroughly "American" – musical palette than the songwriters allowed themselves in their shows.

The two most successful composers for this series of musicals were both newish Americans. Rudolf Friml had come from Prague in 1906 and Sigmund Romberg from Nagykanizsa in Hungary three years later. But both men had been working in the American theatre since before the war and both had established a career and a name on Broadway before their careers peaked, almost simultaneously, in the 1920s.

In 1924, Friml's *Rose Marie* and Romberg's *The Student Prince* came out just three months apart, and over the next four years Friml turned out the music for *The Vagabond King* and *The Three Musketeers*, and Romberg for *The Desert Song* and *The New Moon*. A very large part of the heart of the American classic romantic musical repertoire had appeared in double-quick time. Time and the musical-theatre world – with varying amounts of influence from movieland and the record industry – have treated this list of works variously, but in their own first-time-round time there was no doubt as to which was the big, international favourite amongst them. It was *Rose Marie*.

Rose Marie

The romantic musical had been rather abandoned by American writers since the heyday of Victor Herbert, but following the huge success of the American version of Das Dreimäderlhaus – the lushly sentimental Blossom Time *with its final-curtain death-of-a-broken heart – producers started once more to give a fair share of their attention to this side of the musical theatre.*

Background: **Mira Nirska**, as the murderous Wanda, leads a vast squadron of Drury Lane dancers in the show's most breath-catchingly spectacular moment: the "Totem Tom-Tom" routine.

Opposite: "Door of my Dreams" – **Cloë Vidiane** as the ready-to-wed heroine in the show's hit French production.

The Canadian-set "romantic" musical that producer Arthur Hammerstein conceived and ordered took no half measures. No musical comedy, this. It began with a murder (even if it was the principal danseuse who did it) and, in a tale very reminiscent of the 1917 Broadway drama *Tiger Rose*, went on to follow the flight of the falsely accused miner, Kenyon, and the trials and tribulations of the pretty trapper's sister, Rose Marie, who loves him. Needless to say, she manages to avoid being married off to the city man her brother favours long enough for the danseuse to come clean and for Kenyon to be cleared. The drama and the romance of the piece were lightened with a traditional comical subplot and characters, another romantic triangle featuring soubrette, straight man and the comical and risibly named Hard-Boiled Herman.

There were comical moments in the score, too, but – give or take a ton of scenery and costumes – it was its romantic music that was perhaps the single most important element in the success of *Rose Marie*. Hero and heroine serenaded each other in the plotful "Indian Love Call", a piece whose "yoo-oo-oo" refrain

would later be mocked by "sophisticates" as an example of old-fashioned musical theatre. In 1924 it wasn't thought of as any more ridiculous than any other operatic or verse-and-chorus song convention, and it was a very big hit. The baritone hymn to "Rose Marie", the heroine's dainty "Pretty Things", the waltzing "Door of my Dreams" and the driving strains of the "Totem Tom-Tom", danced by a colourful squadron of painted Indians headed by the evening's villainess, were others amongst the musical items that went towards making *Rose Marie* a remarkable success.

Rose Marie – romantic, dramatic, musical, spectacular in its staging and classy in its casting – was a grand hit through 557 performances on Broadway before it began its remarkable afterlife. At London's Theatre Royal, Drury Lane, it ran for two years and resulted in the famous theatre being firmly turned over to large, romantic musicals in the decades that followed, in Australia it triumphed once again, and only Germany rejected it, puzzled apparently by the incoherencies of the libretto and its dancing murderess. But *Rose Marie's* greatest hit of all

NUMÉRO 1   LES PREMIÈRES ILLUSTRÉES   PRIX 10 FRS.

Rose-Marie

THÉÂTRE
MOGADOR
PARIS

Cloé Vidiane
dans le rôle de
Rose-Marie

ÉDITIONS ARTISTIQUES DE PARIS – 32, RUE LOUIS-LE-GRAND – PARIS

CREDITS

Rose Marie

Musical play in 2 acts by Otto Harbach and Oscar Hammerstein II

MUSIC

by Rudolf Friml and Herbert Stothart

Produced at the Imperial Theater, New York, 2 September 1924

UK: Theatre Royal, Drury Lane, London, 20 March 1925

France: Théâtre Mogador, Paris, 9 April 1927

Germany: Admiralspalast, Berlin, 30 March 1928

Hungary: Király Színház, Budapest, 31 March 1928

CAST

Rose Marie La Flamme
Mary Ellis

Jim Kenyon   Dennis King

Hard-Boiled Herman
William Kent

Lady Jane   Dorothy Mackaye

Captain Malone
Arthur Deagon

Wanda   Pearl Regay

came in, of all places, the traditionally xenophobic France. The Isola Brothers' huge production of *Rose Marie* followed *No, No, Nanette* into the Théâtre Mogador, and promptly wiped out the earlier piece's record for an anglophone musical on the Paris stage. It ran for 1,250 nights, created a new fashion for *opérette à grand spectacle* in France, and set itself up for half a century of revivals in its French version.

Rose Marie went through many a revival in its original language as well, but at the end of the twentieth century we seem to have caught up with the Germans. The dancing murderess libretto does seem rather gauche. And the knockers of the "Indian Love Call" have had their effect, too. But *Rose Marie* has entertained, and thoroughly entertained, more than half a century of theatre and filmgoers, and, whilst it was big, it was just about the biggest there was.

The same Harbach and Hammerstein who created *Rose Marie* also turned out (with Frank Mandel) a much more durable book for what was probably, all things considered, the best of this group of shows. The reason for the durability is that, intentionally or not, there is more than a glint of humour, of the tongue-in-cheek, in the libretto to the "Elinor Glyn meets Rudolf Valentino" musical called *The Desert Song*. The heroine who dreams of wild romance finds herself rushed off into the desert by a masked hero . . . who turns out two and a bit hours later to be a chap she had always thought a halfwit. The show sported another dancing villainess (even played by the same actress as in *Rose Marie*) but this one limited her villainies to telling tales that helped the plot to its final climax. Romberg's score complemented the libretto superbly, rising to *Sheik*-like heights in its waltzing title-song and the heroine's heavily decorated longings for "Romance", and yet finding serious sentiment in an "Eastern and Western Love" segment which contrasted the extravagant romantic feelings of the leading pair with some more pragmatic expressions of love from the show's Arab characters ("Let Love Go"/"One Flower Grows Alone in your Garden"/"One Alone").

The Desert Song was every bit as big and enduring a hit as *Rose Marie* on English-language stages, not to mention on film, and it survives today in a notably more revivable condition, but in spite of a fair Paris run as *Le Chant du Désert*, it didn't ever manage to win the vast first-up favour that the earlier show did on a wider, thoroughly international basis.

Romberg's earlier *The Student Prince* also had a huge career on stage and on film in America, but curiously enough this musical version of the old German royal love versus royal duty play *Alt Heidelberg* made its impression in other countries more through the most popular of its songs – the rousing student's drinking song ("Drink, Drink, Drink"), the celebrated Serenade ("Overhead the Moon is Beaming"), the rich hymn to youth's "Golden Days" and the evening's big love duet, "Deep in my Heart, Dear" all disseminated to the world's cinema audiences by the voice of Mario Lanza – rather than as a stage show. Even a tally of songs as impressive as this, however, could not top the record put up by the composer's later *The New Moon*. The score of *The New Moon* probably boasts more popularly known and loved numbers than any other romantic musical in the Broadway canon – and yet almost every one of them was a replacement. When the original show, with its tale of a wanted French gentleman pursued to New Orleans by the lawkeepers of his country, was tried out at Philadelphia the producers cancelled its Broadway trip and Romberg was ordered to re-compose. He saved one piece called "Shoulder to Shoulder", but rechristened it "Stout-Hearted Men", and to it he added "Softly, as in a Morning Sunrise", "Lover, Come Back to Me", "Wanting You" and "One Kiss" – each and every one destined to become a standard, as the show, again with the help of the cinema, established itself as a romantic musical classic.

Not all the best music for the great romantic shows of the American 1920s was the work of musicians born and trained in Hungary or Czechoslovakia. Home-town had its word to say too, and said it most effectively in the musical that has been quoted in recent years as the single most outstanding product of pre-war Broadway. That show is *Show Boat*, and its score was the work of New York-born Jerome Kern, previously known almost entirely as one of the most effective, and most prolific contributors to the songwriters' musical comedies of two decades.

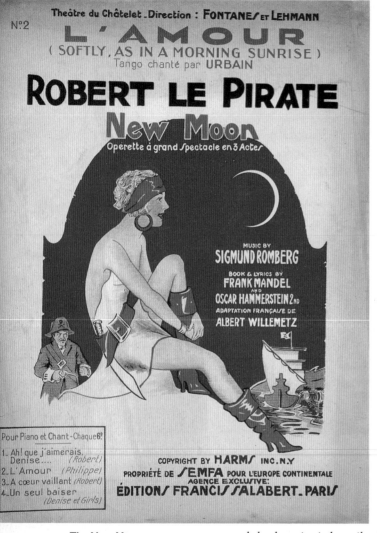

The New Moon

The show's title-song was cut in tryout, leaving the title a pretty meaningless one. The French changed it to the more apt *Robert, le Pirate*.

Show Boat

In his remaking of the Mississippi novel Show Boat *as a libretto, Oscar Hammerstein had no latitude for the* Rose Marie *"dancing murderess" kind of book, nor for the more sweepingly romantic tongue-in-sheikeries of* The Desert Song. *Unlike the two earlier hits,* Show Boat *was a straightforward American period piece, with "real" American period characters, and – even though he tactfully lightened one or two of the novelist's more sombre colourings – the librettist kept both the straightforwardness and the "reality" in his adaptation.*

Inset: Helen Morgan's sweet soprano voice had a strange tear-tugging power.

When Julie La Verne and her husband have hurriedly to quit their job on a Mississippi show-boat, the young daughter of the boat's owners deputizes as leading lady alongside a hastily recruited, but sexy, riverboat gambler. The two fall in love, marry, and leave the river, but Ravenal's betting leads them into money troubles. He leaves Magnolia and their child to fend for themselves. Thanks to an unseen, selfless gesture by a sadly fallen Julie, the desperate Magnolia gets a start as a club singer, and she ultimately rises to fame on Broadway. Thirty years on, with daughter Kim now a star in her turn, Magnolia is at last reunited with Ravenal on the banks of the Mississippi.

If the plot line, with its heroine's *Sally*-like rise to Broadway stage-stardom, seemed sometimes conventional, the scenes in which the story was told were not. There were many splendid moments. Touching ones such as Cap'n Andy's off-the-leash discovery of his daughter making her nervous début in a city dive, where with loving encouragement he turns what might have been disaster into the successful beginning of Magnolia's new career. Comic ones, such as Andy's re-enactment of half the plot of a play to his showboat audience after the actors have fled from the stage under the bullets of an over-involved hillbilly. And many musical ones.

Background: **Ziegfeld Theater** The Broadway house, modestly named for himself, where *Show Boat*'s producer launched his musical.

CREDITS

Show Boat

Musical play in 2 acts by Oscar
Hammerstein II, based on
the novel by Edna Ferber

MUSIC

by Jerome Kern

Produced at the Ziegfeld
Theater, New York, 27
December 1927
UK: Theatre Royal, Drury Lane,
London, 3 May 1928
France: Théâtre du Châtelet,
Paris, 15 March 1929
Germany: Städtische Bühne,
Freiburg, 31 October 1970

CAST

Cap'n Andy Hawkes
Charles Winninger

Parthy Ann Hawkes
Edna May Oliver

Magnolia Hawkes
Norma Terris

Gaylord Ravenal
Howard Marsh

Julie La Verne Helen Morgan

Ellie May Chipley Eva Puck

Frank Schultz Sammy White

Joe Jules Bledsoe

Above right: **London's Frank
(Leslie Sarony) and Ellie
(Dorothy Lena) give a quayside
sampler of what the show boat
has to offer.**

Right: **The French re-titled it
Mississipi but by far preferred
Rose Marie.**

Show Boat's score mixed such traditional romantic pieces as the lovers' soaring "Make Believe" and "You Are Love" with some dashingly carefree numbers for the hero, some song-and-dances for the soubrets of the showboat troupe ("Life on the Wicked Stage", "I Might Fall Back on You"), a helping of stand-up performance material (Julie's club-song "Bill") and a group of highly effective negro-flavoured numbers: a lazy baritone hymn to "Ol' Man River", a ripsnorting ballyhoo ("C'mon Folks!"), and a beautiful ensemble, "Can't Help Lovin' That Man". And Kern even introduced a small handful of genuine period pieces from the turn of the century (Charles Harris's "After the Ball", Joe Howard's "Goodbye, my Lady Love") for the sake of verisimilitude.

Show Boat ran for a fine 575 nights in New York before going on to be seen abroad. If it did not manage anywhere to challenge the success of *Rose Marie* or *The Desert Song*, it nevertheless did well enough in London, totting up a run of 350 nights at Drury Lane, but it disappointed sadly in a Paris eager for more *Rose Marie* when *Mississippi* could only hold up for 115 performances. The rest of Europe passed.

Show Boat was filmed several times over the decades that followed, and it was revived, without notable success, in both New York and London. At this stage it was generally regarded as "just another operetta" (the word operetta said in a knowingly pejorative tone) of the *Rose Marie* or *Blossom Time* variety. But the show was to win a remarkable rehabilitation which began nearly a half-century after its first run. A 1971 revival in London gave the piece its longest metropolitan run to date, a whole book was devoted to detailing its history, opera companies and other countries started looking at it, and little by little *Show Boat*'s reputation started to climb.

Now, in the 1990s, at a time when a reshaped version of the show has returned to Broadway in a lavishly mounted and praised new production, Hammerstein and Kern's musical play is hailed as the great American musical – of its period, that is. And it may very well be just that.

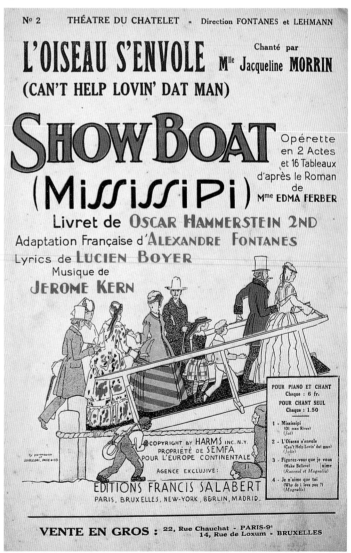

The romantic musical stages of Broadway had for many years been fed largely by imports from the Continent, and, although America itself put out fine shows in the romantic mode throughout the 1920s, this didn't mean that the flow of imports from Europe in any way slowed. Vienna, Berlin and Budapest still had plenty of exciting musical theatre to give to the world, and in the 1920s they gave a very large part of what they had left. And they gave it lavishly.

After the war was over

The years after the war were what might be called the mature period of the musical theatre in Central Europe. In the 1920s, fine new musicals practically elbowed each other onto and off the main stages of Vienna, Berlin and Budapest in the first showings of what was often a trip around the world. It was only in the early 1930s that the maturity gave place to over-ripeness, and – with a helping hand from Hitler – the mid-European musical theatre went into a decline from which it has never yet recovered.

Many of the writers responsible for the great shows of the 1920s were the same ones who had so happily sustained Europe at the top of the international musical heap in the previous twenty years or so. But several of them had switched their allegiances, and they were now supplying shows to the richer and more competitive Berlin theatre rather than to Vienna. One such was Oscar Straus, and he turned out one of the first outstanding musicals of the post-war era for the Berliner Theater and its prima donna, Fritzi Massary. In *Der letzte Walzer* the star played a sort of operetta Tosca, a woman trying to save the man she loves from being put to death by a vindictive prince whose advances she's refused. Straus went on to write several more shows for the queen of the Berlin stage, but Massary found perhaps her finest vehicle in a piece composed by Leo Fall and produced at the Berliner in 1922. *Madame Pompadour* allowed her a much more comical rôle than had the predominantly romantic *Der letzte Walzer*, casting its star as a distinctly over-sexed Marquise in a bedroom-farcical story full of misunderstandings and deceptions. It scored a full-blooded triumph, and when Massary had finished with her show it too went round the world.

Fritzi Massary
Berlin's favourite prima donna shares the Theater am Nollendorfplatz stage with Elise Hess and Susanne Bachrich in Leo Fall's 1913 musical *Die Studentengräfin*.

Germany received a fine addition to its rather short list of top-flight musical theatre composers with the arrival on the scene of Eduard Künneke. Künneke had his first show produced in 1919, and within months he was installed as composer-in-chief to producer Hermann Haller at Berlin's Theater am Nollendorfplatz. The best of the shows that he wrote for that house over the next few years, and the one that has survived into revivals up to today, was *Der Vetter aus Dingsda* (The cousin from thingummyjig). This piece had a different flavour to both the Berliner shows, for it was just a tiny Dutch tale about a girl who carries a candle for a cousin she hasn't seen since childhood. She won't marry the man she should, she simply sits and dreams of Cousin Roderich in far-off Batavia. But she comes to her senses before it's too late. Künneke's pretty and rather intimate score illustrated the intimate little piece with great charm, and *The Cousin from Nowhere* went on to be seen half a world away from Berlin.

Although much was going on in Berlin in the early 1920s, Vienna was by no means insignificant: pieces by such composers as Kálmán, Lehár, Gilbert and Robert Stolz all began international careers there between 1920 and 1925. The most successful of these was Kálmán's *Gräfin Mariza* (1924), a piece set in the composer's native Hungary and allowing him to indulge freely in those

GRÄFIN MARIZA

Operette in 3 Akten

Musik von
EMMERICH KÁLMÁN

Text von
Julius Brammer & Alfred Grünwald

Sämtliche Verlags-, Übersetzungs-, Arrangements- und Aufführungsrechte vorbehalten — Eigentum des
Verlegers für alle Länder — Eingetragen in das Vereinsarchiv

W. KARCZAG
MUSIKVERLAG, BÜHNENVERLAG UND VERTRIEB
INHABER: HUBERT MARISCHKA-KARCZAG
LEIPZIG, NÜRNBERGERSTRASSE 36/38   WIEN, VI., LINKE WIENZEILE 6
Copyright 1924 by W. Karczag, Leipzig, Wien, for Great Britain and United States of America
by Emmerich Kálmán, Julius Brammer and Alfred Grünwald

Für Gesang und Klavier:
Nr. 1. Grüß' mir mein Wien. Lied
    2. Komm mit nach Varasdin! Shimmy
    3. Komm Zigány! Lied
    4. Einmal möcht' ich wieder tanzen.
       Walzerlied
    5. Ich möchte träumen. Lied-Foxtrot
    6. Sag' ja, mein Lieb', sag' ja! Walzer-
       lied
    7. Behüt' dich Gott, komm gut nach
       Haus. Lied-Foxtrot
    8. Braunes Mädel von der Puszta.
       Shimmy-Fox

Für Klavier zu 2 Händen:
Mariza-Walzer
Großes Potpourri

Gräfin Mariza

A return to a piece set in his native Hungary allowed composer Kálmán to pour out some of his most colourful music.

reminiscences of the good life in "Grüss mir die süssen, die reizende Frauen" and the soprano's stylish csárdás "Hör' ich Zigeunergeigen" shared Kálmán's score with such sprightly soubret numbers as the unexpected bridegroom's offer – first to Mariza, later to his soubrette – to "Komm' mit nach Varasdin". Like *Die Csárdásfürstin*, *Gräfin Mariza* was a great hit in middle Europe, but not always as well liked further afield. In America, however, it proved Kálmán's single most popular work.

Although musical shows in the now established "Vienna" style continued to come out of Berlin, Vienna and Budapest in the early part of the 1920s, none of these venues was impermeable to what was going on around the world – a world where songwriters' musical comedies largely topped the popularity polls and where popular dance music and what was then and there called "jazz" were regular musical theatre fodder. Before long, mid-European composers started introducing the rhythms of the shimmy, the Boston, the tango or the fox-trot into their scores alongside the more normal waltzes and marches. One of the cleverest exponents of this kind of music and musical was a former singer-songwriter called Bruno Granichstädten. Granichstädten actually made his name with his very first stage musical, in 1908, and he was well into his forties when he scored his biggest hit.

Der Orlow was a musical about a fabulous diamond, a ballerina, and the battle between an American motor magnate and his employee (an ex-Russian Grand Duke) for both lady and jewel. Guess who won. One of its musical highlights was the song in which the carworker Duke, cigarette in hand, hymned the properties of nicotine – according to him, it cured love-sickness. *Der Orlow* and its composer are forgotten today, but the show, which played for more than 650 nights between 1925 and 1927, was quite simply the longest-running Viennese hit of its time.

The introduction of musicals like *Der Orlow* didn't by any means put an end to traditional Vienna music and musicals, and men such as Edmund Eysler were still there to keep the flag of tradition flying. Two years after its triumph with Granichstädten's work the Theater an der Wien had another fine hit with his *Die gold'ne Meisterin* (1927) – a piece

Hungarian musical colourings that are a feature of most of his finest work. The very rich and excessively unmarried Countess Mariza escapes the bachelors of Vienna by announcing her engagement to a fictitious Baron and sweeping off to her estates in Hungary. But then someone who answers to the phoney name she has chosen turns up with marriage in mind! By the end of the evening she has found true love with her noble steward, and the claimant has been happily joined with the hero's sister. Musical numbers such as the vibrant tenor "Komm' Zigán'", the strapped-for-cash hero's waltzing more old Vienna than ever, and glittering with soprano music that a prima donna would do almost anything to get her hands on. But, curiously, no prima donna outside Europe was tempted by the rôle of the lady goldsmith who mistakes her own workman for a nobleman.

It wasn't the sopranos that got the plum rôles in the most important *Operetten* composed in the post-war years by Franz Lehár. It was the tenors. And that bit of male orientation was quite simply due to the composer's friendship and admiration for popular tenor Richard Tauber.

Lehár was, in the 1910s and early 1920s, rather at a loss for a real, world-sized hit. The likeable, light romantic musical-up-a-mountain *Endlich allein* (1914) did well enough, and a rustic-flavoured 1918 Budapest piece, *A Pacsirta* (*Wo die Lerche singt*), ran well at home, but neither ever looked like turning into a hit on a grander scale any more than the musical comedies *Die blaue Mazur* (1920) and *Cloclo* (1924) did. And that even though the first-named – a bit of froth about a sulky bride and the bunch of old bachelors she runs away to on her wedding night – had a splendid first Viennese run. An attempt at something more exotic with the Spanish-tasting *Frasquita* (1922) and the oriental *Die gelbe Jacke* (1923) were, again, received well rather than enthusiastically or internationally. They were not *Die lustige Witwe*, *Der Graf von Luxemburg* or *Zigeunerliebe*.

It was, in one way, an unsolicited libretto that set Lehár off on his new path. Author and musician Paul Knepler sent the composer the script of his biomusical *Paganini*, and the result was a collaboration and one of Lehár's lushest musical scores to date. Actor-turned-Heldentenor Carl Clewing created the part of the lusty violinist (and the famous song "Gern hab' ich die Frau'n geküsst") in Vienna in 1925, but in the Berlin production it was Tauber who was Paganini, and the association of star and composer had begun.

Lehár wrote four new or nearly-new musicals between 1926 and 1930, and each was built around a ringing "Tauber-*Rolle*". The 1927 *Der Zarewitsch*, a musical based on a Polish play which had got as far as Broadway, was the story of an apparently homosexual Russian prince on whom his elders force the company of a dancing girl in an attempt to

Left: ***Der Orlow***
The dancer, the diamond and the saxophones in the orchestra all went towards making Bruno Granichstädten's musical the biggest Viennese hit of the 1920s.

Below: ***Cloclo***
Luise Kartousch introduced Bela Jenbach and Franz Lehár's little French heroine to Vienna, but success was in a sulk with the composer of *Die lustige Witwe* and the show had only a fair run.

CHAPTER 8

Gitta Alpár, Franz Lehár and Richard Tauber

The soprano, the composer and the tenor: three of the brightest stars of the European musical theatre of the 1930s.

"wake him up". He has actually fallen in love with her by the time his state marriage is arranged and, like *The Student Prince*, he has to give up love for duty. *Der Zarewitsch* was, in spite of some tacked in soubret comedy, a pretty unrelievedly glum piece, and although the tenor had most of the music, the soprano actually got the night's gem ("Einer wird kommen") in Lehár's thoroughly romantic score. The unhappy ending idea, which he had started to enjoy in *Paganini*, was to become a feature of latter-day Lehár shows, but it was a feature that finally became as much of a cliché as the old happy endings. Still, the composer's later shows generally had more happy moments in them than *Der Zarewitsch* did.

Next up, Tauber was cast as a singing Goethe in a fictional tale of the poet's youthful amours with the pretty country *Friederike*, who gives him up rather than harm his career prospects. This time the tenor did have the bon-bon, and Tauber serenaded "O Mädchen, mein Mädchen" to grand effect.

It was, however, the third of the post-*Paganini* musicals which turned out to be the biggest and the best. Lehár had never been chary of making over his old works, even works which had been not unsuccessful, and even more than once. So in 1929 he had a new version (unhappy ending obligatory) of the 1923 *Die gelbe Jacke* written, with the star rôle of the Chinese prince, originally created by Hubert Marischka, whooped up into a Tauber-*Rolle*. The new show was called *Das Land des Lächelns* (The land of smiles).

Tauber was the inscrutable Prince Sou Chong of China who gently woos and weds a Viennese lady and, having wed her, takes her home. Western Lisa has some difficulty adapting to the ways of the East, and the last straw comes when she finds that her husband will be traditionally taking other, Chinese wives. Although she still loves him, she flees and he, though his heart is breaking, does not try to stop her. Tauber was magnificently musically served, with a blockbuster hit in the rapturous "Dein ist mein ganzes Herz"

contrasting with a delicate "Von Apfelblüten einen Kranz" and the philosophical "Immer nur lächeln" alongside some full-blooded romantic duets. But he was not alone. His prima donna had a fine varied rôle, too, one which rose to super-operettic heights in one of the most thrilling moments in all Viennese musical theatre as she longed desperately for her home in the West – "Ich möcht wieder einmal die Heimat seh'n" – how I long to see my homeland again. And the soubrette, too, cast as the little Chinese Princess, Mi, longing in her turn for some of the freedom a Western woman has, had several delightful musical moments in solo ("Im Salon zur blau'n Pagoda") and duet.

The great success of *Das Land des Lächelns* was followed by another remake – the Tauberizing of *Endlich allein*. Without rewriting the whole story and changing the colour of the whole show, it was really impossible to put an unhappy ending on this one, so for once the tenor actually got the girl. Since he had spent the whole of the second act up a mountain in a snowstorm with her, it was just as well. He also got some splendid tenor music, but there was no big bon-bon in *Schön ist die Welt* such as those with which he'd been served in the two previous shows.

All four Tauber shows did well, indeed very well, throughout Central Europe, but, even though the star himself tried to take *The Land of Smiles* to English-speaking audiences, not one of the four succeeded in establishing itself in theatres beyond Continental Europe. The songs travelled beautifully, but the shows somehow would not. Lehár's on-stage fame beyond the English Channel would remain based on his three great pre-war hits, and very largely on *The Merry Widow*.

Musical theatre in Vienna and Berlin wasn't, of course, all romantic *Operette* of the Lehár-Tauber kind, nor comic *Operette*, nor even modern musical comedy with a transatlantic tinge. There were all shades and sizes of shows going on, and some of them were quite unlikely. One of these turned up in Berlin in 1928.

In 1920 the Lyric Theatre, Hammersmith, in London, produced a version of the eighteenth-century hit *The Beggar's Opera* with its music arranged afresh by Frederic Austin. It proved a great success, and other venues soon copycatted the Lyric's lucky choice. One of those venues was the Vienna Carltheater. In 1924 it staged a German remake of Gay's show called *Der Liebling von London* (The darling of London) adapted by Felix Dörmann, the author of *Ein Walzertraum*, and with the music re-re-arranged by Hans Ewald Heller. *Der Liebling von London* ran only for a month, but it prompted yet another version. This one was adapted by Elisabeth Hauptmann, done over by Bertolt Brecht, and had, not a re-re-re-adapted score, but original music by Kurt Weill.

Die Dreigroschenoper was a *Beggar's Opera* with jackboots on. Whereas the squirmingly satirical original had taken a rapier to its subject, this one used a meataxe. But that didn't worry 1920s Berlin. By and large, 1920s Berlin liked it. After the show became a success, the rampantly political Brecht tarted it up with dollops of dogma and, even though it flopped its way round the world first time, changes in political and theatrical fashions saw it catch on further afield in the 1950s. Thereafter – particularly in smaller and subsidized theatres – *Die Dreigroschenoper* has thrived and thrived. Nowadays, it is probably the most frequently produced of all German musicals.

Too hot to handle

The passion for laughing, dancing musical comedy that engulfed the world's stages in the post-war years saw writers and composers everywhere swirl into action. And nowhere did they swirl with more style, with more élan, with more dazzling wit and thrilling tunefulness than in newly liberated Paris.

The musical comedies of the French *années folles* were truly *folle, folle, folle*. Their texts simply bristled with sophisticated, sexy fun set in – or, more correctly, leaping out from – original and well-constructed farcical stories full of adorably comical characters. And their music? Why, it was simply a combination of the best of the two worlds of musical comedy music. On the one hand there were the most superb songwriters' songs – dance numbers, love songs, comedy point numbers – all equipped with the cleverest, the most witty, and often the most unforcedly risqué of lyrics. And, on the other, there were the composers' numbers: ravishingly written duos, trios and ensembles

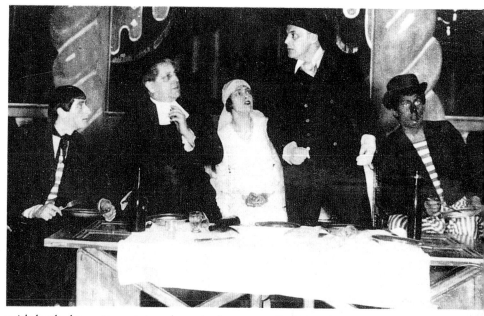

with both dramatic point and music that was no less attractive for being "well written".

Nowhere else in the world, and at no other time, did these same musical elements come together both with each other and with libretto writing of such quality. The best musical comedies of the *années folles* have a very special place in the history of the musical theatre.

So, why then haven't we in countries other than France heard more of them? Why don't we still hear these marvellous songs, and see these hilarious musical plays? The answer comes in one word. Three letters: S.E.X. Well, it has four letters in French, and anyway they would call it "amour". Every single French jazz-age libretto is based on it, half the shows' song lyrics are permeated by it, and even the music seems to swell with it. But the uncomplicated attitude that the post-war French had to their own and other people's sex-lives wasn't shared by the more uptight folk of other nations, and so, when these shows were sent abroad, they were almost everywhere expurgated. Emasculated. Their stories were changed, lyrics or entire songs were replaced, the music was dosed in musical bromide. Not surprisingly they failed. And, having failed, they were never seen again. Of the main centres, only Budapest proved up to regularly sharing the unfig-leaved fun of the Paris stage, and so France and Hungary virtually kept to themselves the caviare of what the world's musical comedy stages of the 1920s had to offer.

Die Dreigroschenoper
Harald Paulsen, Berlin's original Mackie Messer, in Vienna's production of Hauptmann and Brecht's remake of *The Beggar's Opera*.

Phi-Phi

It's very often the first big hit of a tradition that becomes its most famous representative, and such was the case with années folles *musical comedy. There had been small-scale musical comedies played in Paris back before the war, but it wasn't till 1918 that* Phi-Phi *came along and set the new kind of show in orbit.*

Phi-Phi wasn't a little French *poule*. To start with, she was a he. It's the nickname used by his little models for the famous Ancient Greek sculptor Phidias. For, yes, just as with *Orphée aux enfers, Die schöne Galathee* or *Thespis,* once again the eternal classical burlesque turned up in a landmark spot in theatre history. Though the classical folk of *Phi-Phi* are very Parisian under the Greek garments that they seem determined to take off as often as possible.

Phidias is looking for a suitably virginal model for his new statue of "Virtue", so when he spots this innocent little creature called Aspasie wandering up the Ancient Greek street (she's so innocent, bless her, she calls it "doing the beat"), he brings her right on home. Madame Phi-Phi is usually pretty watchful about this sort of thing, but right now she's rather distracted. She's been out shopping, and this young man has followed her home. And now he's trying – in delicious 3/4 – to get her to drop her chlamys. Mme Phi-Phi isn't like that – she's a respectable married woman. But the young man gets to stay, for – after a quick strip-off audition – he's booked to be "Love" in the new statue.

The farce winds up to all sorts of comical (and semi- to un-clad) heights, but, of course, the ending has to tally with Ancient History. So Aspasie gets sculpted and so forth, but then – as per the history books – she encounters wealthy and powerful Périclès. And we all know what happened then. So the comedy ends with a good old French-farcical

ménage à cinq along the footlights: the middle-aged husband, his mistress and her wealthy (he buys the statue) protector, the wife and her young lover. What could be more happily-ever-after?

This demi-Greek story was illustrated with a wholly French score – one that rippled with a light-hearted kind of melody and a gaiety such as had rarely been heard on the stage since the heyday of Offenbach. Aspasie twinkled out a lightsome set of soprano songs – songs both winsome and topical (including one about a woman's necessity for a good wardrobe, and another where Mabel Normand and Douglas Fairbanks made it into the lyrics), Madame Phidias attempted to keep her clothes on to the accompaniment of a swoopingly waltzing duo with her Ardimédon ("Ah! Tais-toi") and delivered a nude, mock-operatic prayer for help to Vénus, whilst the comedy star of the piece gurgled his way through a paean to the glory of the mammary gland (Chanson des petits païens) and another to the charms of Aspasie in general ("Une gamine charmante"). And never for a moment did the music stop sparkling and dancing.

Phi-Phi was initially scheduled for a tiny, underground wartime theatre, and was constructed accordingly for six actors, eight chorines, two dancers and a small orchestra. But a theatrical vagary saw it switched instead to no less a venue than the Bouffes-Parisiens. The show's play-like compactness and its lack of traditional musical-theatre accoutrements proved no bar to success. *Phi-Phi*, with its focus

CREDITS

Phi-Phi

Opérette legère in 3 acts by
   Albert Willemetz and
   Fabien Sollar

MUSIC

by Henri Christiné

Produced at the Théâtre des
   Bouffes-Parisiens, Paris,
   12 November 1918
Hungary: Lujza Blaha Színház,
   Budapest, 16 August 1921.
   Revised editions:
UK: London Pavilion, 16 August
   1922
USA: Atlantic City, NJ, 1922

CAST

Phi-Phi	Urban
Aspasie	Alice Cocéa
Mme Phidias	Pierrette Madd
Ardimédon	Ferréal
Le Pirée	Dréan

One step too many. Anglo-Saxon
attitudes required the de-sexing
of French musicals in the 1920s.

on witty, sexy fun and merry, leg-swinging music, thoroughly caught the mood of the moment, becoming Paris's victory musical, the show with which the city celebrated freedom, as it continued to a total of over a thousand first-run nights in the French capital. There would be plenty of other runs later.

The show went round France and across to Hungary, but then the contents of the champagne bottle got switched. What was mounted under the title *Phi-Phi* by C. B. Cochran in Britain and the Shuberts in America was *vin ordinaire*. Both mangled musicals were swiftly gone, the Shubert version even being aborted pre-Broadway. *Phi-Phi* is still played in what remains of the musical theatre in modern France, and it holds its place there as the most memorable of the shows that set the French stage of three-quarters of a century ago off on one of its greatest periods of success.

Needless to say, others quickly followed where *Phi-Phi* and its creators – co-librettist Willemetz, composer Christiné (a man with many a popular song to his credit, but little previous stage success) and producer Gustave Quinson – had so successfully pointed out the path. And no one followed them more successfully than themselves.

The team's 1921 follow-up to the surface-Greek *Phi-Phi* was an undisguisedly Parisian piece, and to capitalize on the earlier hit they called it *Dédé*. Dédé (short for André) is a young Frenchman with a violent passion for a married lady whom he's met at a tango tea. In order to have a place where they can meet for a bit of teatime hanky-panky without attracting attention, he buys a shoe shop, and thence he attempts to inveigle her. A lot of other people – from shopworkers' union men to a lovesick lawyer – turn up (none to buy shoes) before the lady does, but nearly all of them fit neatly in to the satisfied (or about to be) situation that reigns at the final curtain.

The star of *Dédé* wasn't Dédé (played by *Phi-Phi* star Urban) and it wasn't his lady. It was one of those maddeningly smart-ass hero's-best-friend characters. For the rôle of Robert Dauvergne was written to be the musical-comedy début of the music-hall's Maurice Chevalier. Christiné supplied him with a set of numbers to die for: leering forth his sexual availability in "Je m'donne", shrugging off the responsibilities of life in "Dans la vie faut pas s'en faire", or pairing with *Phi-Phi*'s Mlle Cocéa (as the shoe-shop bossess) in the delightful "Si j'avais su".

Dédé proved a second major hit – and a durable one, for the show has had a major revival in the 1990s – and both Christiné (*Madame*, *P.L.M.*, *J'aime*, *Arthur*, *Encore cinquante centimes*, etc) and Willemetz carried on as they had begun, turning out hit

Dédé

No, it's not foot-fetishism. It is merely our hero starting at the bottom before wooing his way upwards – to music, of course.

after hit, together and separately, for the rest of the decade.

Chevalier, however, didn't last. After the hit of *Dédé,* Quinson hurried the man who looked like being Paris's new comedy musical star into a new show, written by a couple of new writers. Well, not that new – for playwright Yves Mirande and composer Maurice Yvain, whose fame outside France rests just on his song "My Man", already had a big, big musical comedy hit behind them.

The wheeler-dealing Quinson had paired these two musical-comedy novices (with Willemetz for lyrics) on a 1922 musical called *Ta bouche*, and *Ta bouche* turned out to be one of the very funniest and most melodious of all French musicals – and a huge success. The libretto – built on the modern scale with nine principals and no chorus – told the story of two young folk who spend three whole acts rehearsing (off-stage) for their wedding night. The only thing is, simply everything – from greedy parents to marriages to other people – keeps pre-empting that wedding night. Years go by, the comic situations (and the musical numbers) succeed one to another, but at the final curtain an older, and hopefully not over-rehearsed Bastien and Eva actually do make it to marriage.

Yvain's score for *Ta bouche* immediately established him alongside Christiné in the musical-comedy songwriting top spot, for so popular were the numbers of the show – the all-pervading title-song, Bastien and Eva's discovery that "La seconde étreinte" is even better than the first, his lilting "Ça, c'est une chose", her heartfull wish for "Un petit amant" for every girl in the world, and even the more characterful songs that fell to the parents, their servants and the trio of gossipy girls who completed the cast – that a songsheet was let down to allow theatre audiences to join the artists in their singing!

The show that Mirande, Willemetz and Yvain supplied for Chevalier was less intricately plotted than the superb *Ta bouche*, but it needfully gave as many, if not more, opportunities for louchely libertinical lines and croonable melodies. The star was cast as a car-crash victim who is allowed to go back from heaven to earth for one last "goodbye" to his wife. The fact that he makes the trip under supervision doesn't seem to hamper his idea of how a man says "goodbye". Chevalier's blushing guardian angel was played by another music-hall star, Dranem, and unfortunately for the pecking order it was Dranem who turned out to be the real star of the show. So Chevalier walked out, leaving Dranem to become one of France's top musical comedy favourites, whilst he turned himself into the Plastic Hollywood Frenchman. As for *Là-haut*, it and its made-for-Maurice songs – the sexy "Si vous n'aimez pas ça", the "Ç'est Paris" fox-trot – went on to a long, long life.

Yvain scored many, many other hits in the decade to come (*Gosse de riche, Un bon garçon, Yes, Encore cinquante centimes, Oh! Papa*, etc), but by far the most enduring of them was another "bouche" musical, *Pas sur la bouche* (1925). This show had a text by the third top librettist of the age, André Barde, who had been turning out fine, funny musicals and revues for mostly smaller houses for nearly twenty years, and its plot turned around a businessman who is supremely and scientifically confident in his wife's fidelity. He trusts implicity in the metallurgical principle of he-who-puts-the-first-mark. So what does she do when her unconfessed former spouse turns up, anxious to renew "acquaintance" under her new husband's very nose? The show's songs included a jaunty title number, pieces waltzing and fox-trotting, topical, comical, wryly philosopical, novel (a hiccoughing song), and even a pair sporting the newly fashionable South American flavour. The mixture proved as potent as before, and *Pas sur la bouche* survives as one of the most popular still-played items of the 1920s French repertoire.

Many other writers and song- and dance-writers contributed to the *années folles* musical theatre, and a number of them scored at-the-time hits which have lasted a mite less well than this handful of particularly popular and played pieces. There was Raoul Moretti – less skilled than a Christiné or an Yvain, but eminently danceworthy – who musicked a quartet of winners with the Dranem-vehicle *Troublez-moi!* (1924), the horrifying 1925 tale of *Trois jeune filles . . . nues!* (they weren't, but they went on the stage, which was almost like being), the comical story of the lift-boy who inherits a fortune and goes into society as *Comte Obligado* (1927), and the light-hearted

tale of what went on *Un soir de reveillon* (1932). There was singer-songwriter-leading man Gaston Gabaroche, who topped his output with the jolly 1929 invitation to *Enlevez-moi!* (whisk me away), the pairing of Georges van Parys and Philippe Parès, whose *Lulu* introduced them to Paris in 1927, and most notably of all there was the great survivor of the preceeding era, André Messager. For Messager, years on from *Les P'tites Michu* and *Véronique*, was still there, and perfectly willing to switch from *gentille opérette* to up-to-date tastes and tunes. To prove that willingness, he turned out the scores for a little group of modern musicals which have survived to this day on the list of revivables: the advisedly titled *Passionnément* (1926), a tale of musical bunks afloat on the *Coups de roulis* (1928), and most particularly the exquisite Sacha Guitry musical play *L'amour masqué* (1923), in which – in his seventieth year – the composer turned out one of his most popular songs ever, "J'ai deux amants".

Eventually, in the early 1930s, both the vein of comedy and the fashion in dance-music that fuelled this famous run of musicals almost simultaneously ran out. The musical theatre in France turned its attention from the small-scale, must-be-listened-to kind of show to the large-scale, heavily decorated and romantically inclined must-be-looked-at kind of show. Yvain, Christiné and, especially, Willemetz went with the trend and proved themselves all over again as workable men of the musical theatre, but their new musicals, and those of the men who – more than they – developed and fed the next era of shows on the French stage were not in the same class as what had come out of the 1920s. All good things have to end sometime.

Transatlantic tidal wave

In the decade or so after the war, America, Austria and France all produced shows that were both of-the-moment hits and also durable and revivable pieces of musical theatre, but

Comte Obligado
André Barde's comical tale of the got-rich-quick liftboy Count featured *Phi-Phi* star Urban in a dandy tango called "Mio padre".

Britain – although it kept its musical stages merrily dancing and laughing through those years – didn't turn out a body of work with quite the same staying power. The home-made musicals that were played alongside the avalanche of imported shows, and the new kind of virtual variety shows that were called "revues", on the London stage were light, bright and mostly ephemeral, and the songs that decorated them, squarely in the time signatures and dotted rhythms of the American music that had swept British stages since just before the war, mostly didn't survive their shows by very long.

Chu Chin Chow

Lily Brayton as the dramatic barely singing slavegirl spy tacked into the traditional Ali Baba story for her by her author-producer-director-star husband, Oscar Asche.

The war years had actually seen a whole series of successful and long-running new musicals appear on the London stage, and the two longest-running of them all were pieces thoroughly in that escapist mode that has been the making of so many successful wartime shows over the years. *Chu Chin Chow* – which set up a West End long-run record that would last many years – was a spectacular remake of the Ali Baba tale, and *The Maid of the Mountains* was a straightforward romance-with-bandits show. Both musicals left behind standard songs ("The Cobbler's Song" and "Anytime's Kissing Time" for the first, "A Bachelor Gay" and "Love Will Find a Way" for the second) and both established themselves for many years of reprises, but it is doubtful whether they would have known quite such success, first time round, in less turbulent times.

The other triumphs of Britain's wartime years included some meatier stuff in a swatch of musicalized comedies of the *Pink Lady* genre (*Theodore & Co*, *Yes, Uncle !*, *The Boy*, *Tonight's the Night* et al), a revusical piece celebrating the common Briton at war (*The Better 'Ole*), and even – surprisingly – one

German musical. Perhaps, because it was composed by a Frenchman and came via America in the hands of a South African producer, no one noticed. But *The Lilac Domino* – almost alone of its kind in a West End starved of anything that might resemble "enemy" music – was a first-class success.

The Continental musical soon worked its way back onto the London stages once peace had redescended, and shows such as *Madame Pompadour*, *Katja the Dancer*, *The Lady of the Rose* and *Sybil* all became major West End hits, but these pieces had to share London's and Britain's favours with a veritable bevy of musical comedies and romantic musicals that were coming from across the Atlantic to feed stages, gramophones and dance bands that could scarcely get enough of what America had to offer. British producers – deprived of such stalwarts as Monckton and Jones, who had hung up their hats in the face of the "new" music – were soon seeking musicians from beyond the seas to provide the tunes for their new shows, and thus songwriters such as Jerome Kern, George Gershwin and Rodgers and Hart (and a good number very much less skilled) all provided sets of sometimes new, sometimes half-new numbers to decorate the London shows of the 1920s. In fact, so great was the fad and fashion for transatlantic tunes that, when one young producer set up the first of what would become a winning series of shows, he had his team of British songwriters hide their identities under what he fancied was an American-sounding pseudonym.

The British musical stage continued to turn out fine musical comedies – with sources from Feydeau and Desvallières (*A Night Out*) to Pinero (*Who's Hooper?*) – in the years after the war, but it wasn't until the later years of the 1920s that it produced the most interesting and the most durable shows of its own manufacture. By now the dancing craze was at its height, and a number of dancing stars had begun to appear at the tops of bills. One of these was little bespectacled Laddie Cliff. But Cliff didn't just do funny dances. In 1928 he initiated a series of dance-orientated musical comedies which featured himself, comedian Stanley Lupino and Australian dance couple Madge Elliott and Cyril Ritchard. Their first show was called *So This is Love*, and it not only scored a grand West End run, but achieved the unlikely distinction of being played alongside the choicest French musical comedies and *Mercenary Mary* in Budapest. Cliff continued as he had begun, with *Love Lies* (1929) and *Darling, I Love You* (1929), setting up a style and series of shows that would run very merrily till his premature death in the mid-1930s.

The year after *So This is Love* saw the production of what would be the most popular British musical comedy of this period, and it was a show with surprisingly little dancing in it. *Mr Cinders* was conceived by comedian Leslie Henson as a vehicle for himself, and so the emphasis was squarely on the fun. In the end, it was Bobby Howes who ended up creating the rôle of penniless, stepmothered Jim who meets and falls in love with his Jill, the heiress from up the road, when she has disguised herself as a maid to escape a driving charge. He gets to her ritzy birthday party unconvincingly disguised as an Amazonian explorer and then finds himself being chased round the countryside as a thief – on a motorbike – when her diamond necklace is stolen. The comedy was decorated by half a second-hand American score, but it was the other half, by local lad Vivian Ellis, that brought out the gems of the evening – the charming "Spread a Little Happiness", the fake explorer's crazy, revusical "On the Amazon" and the twinkling "Every Little Moment".

Mr Cinders was a first-class London hit, topping 500 nights before going out to visit the provinces, the colonies and – under the title *Jim und Jill* – Central Europe, with Europe's Nanette, Irene Palasty, taking top-billing as the "Princess Charming" of the piece. However, *Mr Cinders* won its most far-flung and frequent productions more than half a century on, after a 1982 London revival had outrun the original and relaunched the show on a second and much-loved life.

The British romantic musical proved it was still alive, as well, when *Bitter-Sweet* appeared in 1929. *Bitter-Sweet* was a surprise offering from Noël Coward, the author of so many whip-worded comedies and crisp songs and sketches, for it was a thoroughly sentimental piece in which its writer's known skills got little showing. Its tale told of a well-bred English girl's rejection of a conventional married life in favour of a runaway match with her romantic, Continental music-teacher. Sarah and Carl

Bitter-Sweet
The sword-unskilled Carl Linden (Georges Metaxa) fights for his wife (Peggy Wood) against the professional soldier, Lutte (Austin Trevor).

return to Vienna together, but when need forces her to go to work as a café dancing partner, Carl is killed protecting her from the lusts of one of her partners. Sarah goes on to be a successful singer, and settles for the comfortable, loveless life she'd once refused, kept alive only by memories of her great romance.

Coward's score was a fine one: romantic numbers, such as the evening's key love song "I'll See You Again" or Sarah's swirling conviction that she must answer "The Call of Life", were contrasted with some characterful fun from a group of Viennese "Ladies of the Town" or London aesthetes ("The Green Carnation"), with some stand-up material from a cabaret singer, Manon, whose piquancy and performance both contributed largely to the show's central act ("If Love Were All"), and some splendid ensembles – notably a lovely third-act sextet for a group of ageing married ladies ("Alas, the Time is Past") who had been Sarah's childhood companions and her accomplices in her rash first-act runaway.

Bitter-Sweet went on from its London success to be seen on Broadway, in Paris, and in Budapest, as well as becoming the source material for two films, but, although its favourite songs are still sung and although it was seen again in London as recently as 1988, it has not found the place it might have been expected to find in the international repertoire.

'Im weissen Rössl . . .'

The little Salzkammergut inn seems to be a touch
overstaffed with waiters. But for director Erik Charell
"bigger" was always synonymous with "better".

Depression Days

After the dazzling display of musical-theatre fireworks that had been showered across the stages of the world – a world that had never before been, and never again would be so theatrically busy and flourishing – in what seemed like a never-will-ending pyrotechnical display during that splendidly high-spirited and high-stepping decade that was the 1920s, the years that followed turned out to be rather less exciting. But you can't stop the wheel turning, even away from the winning slot.

There was still, of course, a regular supply of pleasant and even occasionally interesting new musicals produced in the years between the beginning of the Depression and the beginning of World War II, but very few shows appeared that could be favourably compared with the bubbling best of the years that had just danced by. Perhaps it was no coincidence that the most successful musical of the whole decade was actually brought out right at the very beginning of the 1930s. But it came from a slightly surprising place: not from New York, London, Vienna or Budapest, but from Berlin.

Im weissen Rössl premièred in Berlin just over two years after *Die Dreigroschenoper*, but in a house and under a management for whom the word "theatre" meant something

quite different to what it did for the likes of Hauptmann, Brecht and Weill. The Grosses Schauspielhaus and its resident producer, Erik Charell, specialized in Big Productions – the kind of Big Productions where production values and "concept" took precedence over everything else: stagefuls of moving scenery, dozens of costumes, acres of dancers and dancing – a sort of TV variety special tacked around a story and decorated with songs new, borrowed, remade or simply gathered together. Charell's shows weren't for discerning audiences. Yet it was he and his theatre that produced the piece that was for a very long time the most popular musical play to come out of Germany – or even, perhaps, of anywhere else. And it didn't have a single Grosses Schauspielhaus shimmy step or flamingo feather in it.

Im weissen Rössl

Im weissen Rössl *was based on a much-loved, much-revived 1897 German Schwank, a comic play which found end-to-end fun in the merry skein of intertwining love-and/or-marriage affairs that get themselves wound up and worked out during a summer holiday season at the Zum weissen Rössl inn. In this musical version, the romances were given rather more space than they had been in the original and the principal comedians' cavortings – which had been the most prominent part of the old play – rather less.*

Background: **Leopold (Max Hansen), the adorable and adoring head-waiter, has a mountainous crush on his boss.**

When city lawyer Otto Siedler checks in for his annual holiday in the Austrian Salzkammergut, the innkeeper Josefa Vogelhuber puts on her prettiest face. Her rather obvious tactics distress Josefa's adoring head-waiter, Leopold, horribly, but Siedler doesn't even notice his landlady's attentions. He's too busy romancing businessman's daughter Ottilie, who, in her turn, is supposed to be getting commercially allied to one Sigismund Giesecke, son of one of her father's underwear-manufacturing competitors and a baldly unbeautiful fellow who has, in any case, found himself a cute little biller-and-cooer of his own. It takes a visit, and some wise words, from the Emperor himself to

bring Josefa down to earth and transform the chain of awkward romances into one of happy marriages.

House composer Ralph Benatzky supplied the backbone of the merry, catchy score to the musical – Josefa's waltzing welcome "Im weissen Rössl am Wolfgangsee" and her rhythmically calf-slapping praises of what can be found "Im Salzkammergut", Leopold's mooning "Es muss was Wunderbares sein" and the Emperor's Sprechgesang philosophy "Es ist einmal in Leben so" – but other writers including Bruno Granichstädten, Robert Gilbert and most notably Robert Stolz, with two winning sentimental duos, "Mein Liebeslied muss ein Walzer sein" and "Die ganze Welt is himmelblau", also contributed to the typically (for the Schauspielhaus) patchworked musical part of the show.

The attractions of the favourite old tale and the charming music went far in helping the cosy, colourful, cheerful *Im weissen Rössl* to Depression-time success, but they were very materially aided by the vastly lavish, everything-that-moves-and-moos production designed by Ernst Stern and staged by Charell. One top critic, sated by Charell's earlier spangled extravagances, sighed happily: "Stern catches the gaiety of the country, and the Schuhplattler is a breath of fresh air after all that dreary revue dancing."

From Berlin, the show went first to London. The British *White Horse Inn* made the Salzkammergut holiday-makers into English tourists, titivated the plot, and topped up the ever-changing score with a second-hand Stolz song which would become famous as Leopold's "Goodbye". Remounted by Charell on the largest stage in the West End, it was a huge hit. The score remained a

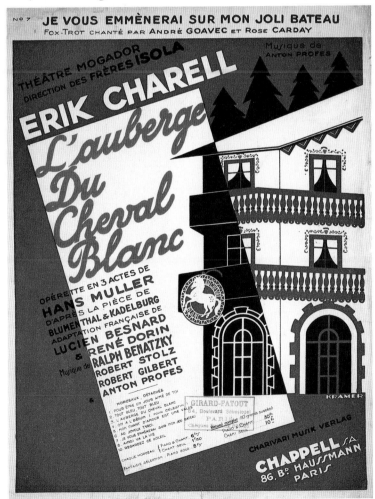

chimeric thing as the musical progressed from country to country and from success to success. In Australia an Ivor Novello song got stuck into the score, in Paris – where Charell again took charge, and the tourists became French – Anton Profès's "Je vous emmènerai dans mon joli bâteau" proved a pasted-in hit, in Vienna Anton Paulik and Granichstädten had new numbers featured in a version that spread itself scenically to all kinds of picturesque venues, whilst in New York (with small care for geography) a song called "In a Little Swiss Chalet" won an interpolated hearing.

After its first spectacular productions, *Im weissen Rössl* didn't fade away. Over the years that followed it was revived again and again in its various national versions. It was filmed three times, and it became, so it is said, the most oft-produced musical of all in English-speaking countries. Many of the show's later stagings were, necessarily, far from the original in size and splendour, but its charm and comedy have, through the years, proved themselves wholly capable of standing up alone, without the aid of the trains, boats, animals and real rain that featured in the original production.

Camilla Spira
Emil Orlik's sketch of *Im weissen Rössl*'s leading lady.

CREDITS

Im weissen Rössl

Singspiel (Revue-Operette) in 3 acts by Hans Müller, based on the play of the same name by Oscar Blumenthal and Gustav Kadelburg

LYRICS
by Robert Gilbert and others

MUSIC
by Ralph Benatzky and others

Produced at the Grosses Schauspielhaus, Berlin, 8 November 1930
UK: London Coliseum, 8 April 1931
Austria: Wiener Stadttheater, Vienna, 25 September 1931
Hungary: Király Színház, Budapest, 20 October 1931
France: Théâtre Mogador, Paris, 1 October 1932
USA: Center Theater, New York, 1 October 1936

CAST
Josefa Vogelhuber   Camilla Spira
Leopold   Max Hansen
Ottilie   Trude Lieske
Giesecke   Otto Wallburg
Emperor Franz Josef   Paul Hörbiger
Sigismund   Sig Arno
Otto Siedler   Walter Jankuhn

L'auberge du Cheval Blanc
The French version of the show proved to be the biggest hit ever to take the road from Berlin to Paris.

Viktória

Oszkár Dénes introduced the hit duo "Mausi" in Ábrahám's musical in both Budapest and Berlin. His partner in Berlin was Lizzi Waldmüller.

The other most attractive musicals to come out of Europe at this time were composed by a man who would undoubtedly have been the star of local 1930s theatre had his name not been Ábrahám. Pál Ábrahám was Hungarian, thoroughly musically educated and with a passion for American popular music. Like Granichstädten, he put bouncy American-rhythmed numbers into his scores alongside the more traditional music of the European stage, and between 1930 and 1932 – when he was still not yet thirty – he scored a trio of international hits: the wonderfully technicolored Russo-Japanese tale of *Viktória* and the lost hussar lover she refinds after she has resignedly wed an American diplomat; the trills and twangs of the southern-seas story of *Die Blume von Hawaii* (which featured an imitation of Al Jolson); and the naughtiness-in-Nice piece *Ball im Savoy*.

By the time these shows made their début, however, the great period of mid-European musicals was moving into its last years, sped on its way by the rise of National Socialism. A vast proportion of the people who were prominent in the musical theatre of Germany, Austria and Hungary were – like Ábrahám – Jewish, and in the coming years many, many composers, writers, producers and performers

– including virtually all the best – joined the exodus from Hitler's Germany, and often from Europe. A few stayed to be ruined or murdered, some – such as Eysler – stayed home, hidden, and survived, but the musical theatre tradition of Central Europe didn't. For all that Künneke, Stolz, Nico Dostal, Fred Raymond and others could do in the decades that were to come, the Central European musical was never again going to thrill the world as it had done so often and for so long. The heyday of the *Operette* was over.

In France, where the great era of jazz-age musical comedy was coming into its last and least productive stages, the situation was no better. Probably the best musical seen on French stages in the 1930s was one originally produced in Switzerland, with an Austrian book and a score made up two-thirds of second-hand music. *Drei Walzer* hadn't even been a success in Zürich. But, thanks to the friendship between Oscar Straus, who had arranged and composed the music, and Yvonne Printemps, the piece was made over for Paris as an I-get-to-sing-almost-all-the-score vehicle for the French actress and singer and for her non-singing boyfriend, Pierre Fresnay. And so, *Trois valses*, a charming three-generations love story like *Wie einst im Mai*,

Viktória

A happy ending, of course: Louis Treumann, Lizzi Waldmüller, Oszkár Dénes, Rita Georg and Otto Maran on the stage of the Theater an der Wien.

Die Blume von Hawaii
Annie Ahlers as the south seas princess of the show's title and Harald Paulsen (right) – Berlin's original Mackie Messer – as her unlucky-in-love American suitor.

but one with an infinitely more attractive heroine and with magnificently arranged music by Strauss sr, Strauss jr and Straus, went on to become a French musical-theatre classic, heading off to London, Broadway and a famous film version on the wings of its Paris success.

In the later 1940s, France raised its head for a while with a new run of musical theatre successes. But those successes were home-town ones only, and in the next half-century only two isolated French shows would again find fame on a wider scale.

So, with the European sources that had for so long provided so much to the musical theatres of the world now either fouled or dried up, only the English-language theatre was left with its nose and mouth at least half-above the devouring troubles of the 1930s. And that English-language musical theatre soon

found that it was on its own – it was going to have to rely almost wholly on the produce of the stages of England and America in its search for new entertainments for the new decade.

Dances for two ... laughs for all

The theatres of Britain, whose new product had been the least to the fore on international stages during the 1920s, still managed happily to provide much of their own musical theatre entertainment through the 1930s. The dance-and-laughter era of musicals that had been confirmed at the turn of the 1920s as the favourite amusement of the times continued energetically through the new decade, and star vehicles were the order of the day. Comedy favourites such as Leslie Henson, Bobby Howes, Stanley Lupino, Laddie Cliff and Cicely Courtneidge, and dance teams – Jack Buchanan and Elsie Randolph, Cyril

Right: ***The Millionaire Kid***
"Dance the polka again." The polka was only one of the dances displayed by Laddie Cliff, Vera Bryer and Co. in a show where the footwork and the fun were paramount.

Ritchard and Madge Elliott, Roy Royston and Louise Browne – were toplined in series of comedy musicals whose dance-based songs – sometimes delightful, sometimes too feebly copy-catted from good and not so good transatlantic writers to be believable – mostly didn't survive the end of their show's run except as momentary dance-band fodder.

The Gaiety Theatre mounted a run of successful musical shows with a sometimes winning touch of madness about them (*Seeing Stars, Swing Along, Going Greek, Running Riot*) which teamed top comic Henson with funnymen Fred Emney and Richard Hearne and with star dance pair Royston and Browne to fine effect. Jack Waller staged a series of musicalized plays (*For the Love of Mike, Tell Her the Truth, He Wanted Adventure*) for little-chap comic Howes, who also scored in the same producer's jolly *Yes, Madam?* and *Please, Teacher!,* Buchanan and Randolph followed their 1928 hit *That's a Good Girl* by dancing their way light-heartedly through *Stand Up and Sing, Mr Whittington,* and *This'll Make You Whistle,* whilst Laddie Cliff continued the happy dance-and-laughter series he had launched a few years back through *The Love*

Race, The Millionaire Kid, Blue Roses, Sporting Love, and *Over She Goes* before his early death, whilst still in his forties. And, alongside these years-long "sets" of shows, pieces such as the Courtneidge *Under Your Hat* or the charming *Jill Darling,* with its hit Vivian Ellis song "I'm on a See-saw", all added to the fleeting gaiety of the nation.

Only one 1930s London star-vehicle has survived into modern revival, and that one pulled off its great escape by rather special circumstances. *Me and my Girl* was written for Lupino Lane, an acrobatic comedy star who had had a first-rate success as a cheeky wee chappie called Bill Snibson in the musical *Twenty to One.* The new show gave him the same character and name, and put him into a different tale where he was an East-Ender who is discovered to be the heir to an earldom. The evening's comedy came from the upper class's hopeless efforts to make him a fit and proper person for his new post. The musical part of the show consisted of just a handful of Noel Gay numbers, including a lilting title-song and a thumping, repetitive dance piece called "The Lambeth Walk". Boosted by the promotion of "The Lambeth Walk" as a dance craze, by radio and young television showings of the entire musical, and then by wartime conditions which saw the dance tune become a troops song (and the show tack in "We're Going to Hang Out the Washing on the Siegfried Line"), *Me and my Girl* went on to run up a total of over 1,600 twice-daily performances. The show was later revived and filmed in Britain, but it had no life at all further afield until Gay's son mounted a revised version – with a full book of songs instead of the original half-dozen – in London in 1984. Its refreshing simplicity in a musical theatre world that had started to take itself awfully seriously won the public's enthusiasm in spades, and the new-style *Me and my Girl* went on to become a merry hit all round the world and in all sorts of languages.

Romance at old Drury

After his success with *Bitter-Sweet*, Noël Coward went on writing like-style romantic musicals. However, apart from the 1934 *Conversation Piece*, a vehicle for *Trois valses* star Yvonne Printemps, who introduced "I'll Follow my Secret Heart" in her rôle as a French lassie being trained as a courtesan in period Brighton, they often proved less than wonderful and/or less than successful. However, the romantic genre was well and truly kept alive on the British stage, and that thanks largely to another winningly versatile writer-performer, Ivor Novello.

The run of American romantic musical hits that had so long and so successfully filled the large auditorium of the Theatre Royal, Drury Lane, had finally and recently fizzled out, so Novello amiably took up his pen and wrote the made-to-the-Lane-sized *Glamorous Night* (1935) to help manager Harry Tennent solve his booking drought. With the ex-film star author/composer featured as its leading man, this amorous-dramatic tale of a young Englishman and a Continental prima donna mixed up in Ruritanian politics proved a great hit, and it launched Novello on a series of like-minded, self-starring musicals. *Careless Rapture*, *The Dancing Years*, *Perchance to Dream* and *King's Rhapsody* not only filled the larger theatres of Britain for many decades thereafter, but they also launched a whole

Below: *Jill Darling*
Song-and-dance partners Eddie Molloy and Teddie St Denis pose with the girls of the Saville Theatre chorus.

'JILL DARLING'

series of romantic theatre songs that would be sung by the sopranos and contraltos of the British Empire for longer than any similar body of music since the songs of Sullivan ("Waltz of my Heart", "Some Day my Heart Will Awake", "Love is my Reason for Living", "I Can Give You the Starlight", "Highwayman Love", "We'll Gather Lilacs"). Given that Novello himself did not sing, and all his rôles were thus virtually songless, the baritones and basses of the Empire didn't get the same service.

It is *The Dancing Years* (1939), with its topical wartime tale of a doomed romance between a Viennese-Jewish composer and his prima donna, that survives today as probably the best of Novello's works, although both *Perchance to Dream*, a dramatic three-generations piece following the amorous mishaps that beset the inheritors of the stately Huntersmoon, and *King's Rhapsody*, a Ruritanian tale of a foolishly proud young monarch and the women – mother, mistress and queen – who lead him to mess up his life and his career, have also stood the test of time and unspectacular revivals well.

Back on Broadway

Beyond the Atlantic, the romantic musical had now declined from its 1920s pinnacle. There were no new *Desert Songs* or *Student Princes* or *Show Boats* amongst the first-run shows of the 1930s. Friml and Romberg – although they were still working – had now given their best, and although the ever-fresh Jerome Kern supplied some fine songs for such pieces as *The Cat and the Fiddle*, *Music in the Air* and *Roberta* in the latter days of his long career, each of those shows was hamstrung by a preposterous libretto – dreary American-in-Parisisms or ersatz Vienneseries that made even Novello's extravagantly romantic stories look almost sophisticated. And so such well-known numbers as "She Didn't Say 'Yes'", "I've Told Every Little Star" and "Smoke Gets in your Eyes" have survived as concert, recording and nightclub standards, without their rather iffy settings, instead of as part of a theatrical whole.

The American songwriters' shows of this period proved to be altogether a happier lot than the romantic ones. But in spite of the fine and fashionable names attached to the best of them – names such as Rodgers and Hart, Cole Porter, George Gershwin or Kurt Weill - very

few Broadway musical plays of the 1930s have come down through the years as first-class revivable prospects. On the other hand, a good number of songs that were first heard in those works have survived healthily, divorced from their show, in a "single" existence sometimes made easier by the fact that a number of them weren't specifically written for the shows they appeared in anyhow. Thanks, very often, to having received the international showing they were denied on the stage through being reused in one or another of the hugely popular musical films of the time, these songs have won a continuing, worldwide popularity as recital items or even pasted into stage shows other and/or better liked than the ones in which they were first seen.

George Gershwin had his successes at the beginning of the decade – *Girl Crazy* in 1930 and *Of Thee I Sing* in 1931 – and then quit the regular musical theatre to compose the folk opera *Porgy and Bess* before his death in 1937. *Girl Crazy* was a toughly funny little piece of traditional musical comedy, decorated with a whole bundle of songs that would become stage, screen and singers' favourites ("I Got Rhythm", "Embraceable You", "But Not for Me"), but *Of Thee I Sing* was something both rather more appreciable and rather more unusual for its time – or any other. It was a

Above: **Glamorous Night**
Anthony (Ivor Novello) and Militza (Mary Ellis) flee the plotters of Ruritania by sea – until their ship gets sunk in the show's most spectacular moment.

Opposite: **Me and my Girl**
Lupino Lane is Bill Snibson – a right little cockney with just half-a-duet to sing.

The Dancing Years
Ivor Novello as Rudi and Roma
Beaumont as Grete.

genuine American *opéra-bouffe*. And, unlike the rest of the succession of unusually rather boring musical pieces of its period which tried to use the field of national politics as their playground, it was a deliciously clever one, imaginative and zany with the real zaniness of the great *opéras-bouffes*.

Of Thee I Sing dealt with the rise to power of a nice, everyday, muffin-loving American president, and above all with the problems he causes the men who "made" him when he decides to marry Mary the muffin-maker instead of the New Orleans belle who has won the nationwide contest for the post of Mrs President. When the crisis peaks, Mary saves the situation. How? By announcing "I'm about to be a mother". Motherhood is, of course, even more sacred than the Bill of Rights, so a happy ending is obligatory. With glorious logic, the belle of New Orleans is married off to the man who constitutionally fills in when the President is unavailable, that always forgotten creature called the Vice President.

Gershwin's score for this witty piece of burlesque was as joyously and smoothly spiky as George S. Kaufman and Moss Hart's text, ranging from a campaign song on love ("Love is Sweeping the Country") to Mary's *bouffe* trilling about her momentously impending motherhood, and all the time winking in the

direction of one musical tradition or convention or another as it made its melodiously pointed way to its Gilbertian end.

Of Thee I Sing had a good first run, but it failed utterly to travel beyond America. And even there it provoked no true imitators, unless you count an unfortunate and oddly dissimilar attempt at a sequel (*Let 'em Eat Cake*). It has also – even in these days when the Gershwin catalogue is being made to work hard for its living – been amazingly little seen around America. Whilst a frilly, girly remake of *Girl Crazy* (as *Crazy for You*) has happily done the rounds, George Gershwin's musical comedy masterpiece has stayed on the shelf.

Richard Rodgers and Lorenz Hart contributed no fewer than nine musical comedies to the Broadway stage in the 1930s, and those nine shows are a notable example of an opus which produced many, many more durable songs than it did revivable musicals. Their *Babes in Arms* must, in fact, remain some kind of a champion. Stymied as a remountable stage prospect by an asinine book about a bunch of pre-pubescents putting on a concert, it nevertheless contains more standards per square page of score than practically any other musical in recent stage history: "The Lady is a Tramp", "Where or When", "My Funny Valentine", "Johnny One Note", "I Wish I Were in Love Again".

The Rodgers and Hart show that survived the best from amongst their works of this period was *On Your Toes* (1936), a piece that mixed ballet and modern dance in an improbable plot about an ex-variety hoofer who masterminds the production of, and takes over the male lead alongside a sexually rapacious prima ballerina in, a contemporary dance piece. The songs included "There's a Small Hotel" and "Glad to Be Unhappy" for the non-dancer who got what was left of the hoofer at the end, but the ballerina – instead of singing – won her kudos performing feature-length dance numbers, peaking in the performance of the contemporary "Slaughter on Tenth Avenue", choreographed by former Russian ballet-man Georges Balanchine. Like the other eight Rodgers and Hart shows of the 1930s, *On Your Toes* failed to export successfully beyond Broadway first time round, but a later revival won it better coverage, and, as ballet companies start to follow operatic ones in looking to the makers for their repertoires, it may even end up more popular in the 1990s than in the 1930s.

By far the most successful amongst the newer men who arrived on the Broadway scene in the 1930s was songwriter Cole Porter. Like Rodgers and Hart, Porter provided the musical part for nine shows between 1930 and 1939, and like them his total of lasting songs far outweighed his total of lasting shows. However, it was Porter who – after firmly establishing his credentials with a lively show for dance star Fred Astaire (*Gay Divorce*, 1930, including "Night and Day") – turned out the numbers for the one American musical comedy of the era that has really and truly survived into the realm of revivals, the song-stuffed, sea-going saga called *Anything Goes*.

There were other Broadway hits in the 1930s that boasted a score of Porter songs, but there were even more Porter scores that boasted hit numbers. The in-jokey *Jubilee*, which the songwriter equipped with "Begin the Beguine" and "Just One of Those Things", and the low comic *Red, Hot and Blue*, which was the occasion for the launching of "It's De-Lovely", might have been less than hit shows, but they added materially to the songmaker's tally of top songs.

Porter had hit a low point, with a dreadful riding accident which disabled him for life, and a sad remake of the German musical *Bei Kerzenlicht*, before he hit the gong of success twice more, and twice in a row. *Anything Goes* stars Gaxton and Moore scored all over again in the jolly piece of Ruritanian nonsense called *Leave it to Me!* (1938, "My Heart Belongs to Daddy", "Most Gentlemen Don't Like Love"), and their co-star Ethel Merman found herself a fine rôle as another nightclub singer – one who inhabits the dreams of a lowly co-worker as Madame du Barry - through 408 nights of *Dubarry Was a Lady* (1939, "Friendship").

Again, neither *Leave it to Me!* nor *Dubarry Was a Lady* had any notable overseas success, but their in-the-black Broadway runs helped Porter come out as the most successful single songwriter of the decade on home stages. It was a record which looked fine enough at the time, but just a few years on down the line musical-theatre horizons would change dramatically, and once again, as in the 1920s, a home run would be only the very beginning of life for a winning Broadway show.

Left: **George Gershwin** switched from dance tunes to *opéra-bouffe* before ending his career with his best remembered stage work of all, *Porgy and Bess*.

Below: **Cole Porter** turned out a fat bookful of merry show songs throughout the 1930s and beyond.

Anything Goes

For an all-of-a-sudden musical, Anything Goes *has proved to be extraordinarily enduring. But it is not the only hurriedly made or remade show to have turned out to be a hundred times better and more successful than more carefully constructed contemporaries. The reason for the musical's "remake" was that, with the stars hired and the songs ready, producer Vinton Freedley decided to dump the show's Bolton/Wodehouse libretto.*

Background: Ethel Merman created the rôle of the holy-rolling nightclub singer Reno Sweeney. Here she poses with a quartet of be-ducked chorus men.

A new plot and new dialogue were carefully tacked around the existing cast, sets and musical material, and what had been the ocean-going musical *Bon Voyage* became instead the ocean-going musical *Anything Goes*.

Lovestruck Billy Crocker stows away on a Britain-bound liner in an attempt to chat the lovely Hope Harcourt out of the arms of her English Lord and into his own. Of course, the stowaway has to keep one step ahead of the pursuing purser, and so Billy is put through a series of disguises, helped both by a fondly friendly chanteuse called Reno, and by a minor criminal who has obligingly loaned him a much more successful criminal's ticket and berth. Billy and his crook pal end up exposed and in the brig, but they get out in time to tie up the happy ending.

The songs of the show were devoted largely to patented singing star Ethel Merman in the part of an evangelist-turned-vocalist, to the smoothly crooning leading man, as played by William Gaxton, and to legit soprano Bettina Hall as the girl for whose sake he floats across the ocean. Miss Merman had the bulk and the best of the action, hollering out her evangelical instructions to "Blow, Gabriel, Blow", ripping off the topics of the day in "Anything Goes", or flipping through a couple of typical Porter catalogue songs with Gaxton in "You're the Top" and "I Get a Kick out of You". Gaxton shared his quieter moments with his sweetheart ("All Through the Night"), and she turned surprisingly undemure for an ex-Gilbert and Sullivan soprano as she admitted to "The Gypsy in Me". Even the comical crook had a jolly musical moment as he advised, "Be Like the Bluebird".

Anything Goes had a fine 421 nights on Broadway and a good 261 in London, but it fizzled in Australia, and, like the rest of the product of 1930s New York and London, it didn't provoke too much attention beyond English-speaking stages. The top songs, however, survived, and years down the line, after Porter's death, when his stocks had risen to hagiographed heights, *Anything Goes* began – in variously patched-up versions – to be seen again. In 1987 a major New York revival of one of these versions was responsible for the show getting a second and wider whirl round the world, allowing audiences to see, half a century down the line, that back there in the 1930s, good musical-comedy fun had been there for the enjoying.

CREDITS

Anything Goes

Musical in 2 acts by Guy Bolton and P. G. Wodehouse. Revised version by Howard Lindsay and Russel Crouse.

MUSIC AND LYRICS

by Cole Porter

Produced at the Alvin Theater, New York, 21 November 1934
UK: Palace Theatre, London, 14 June 1935
Germany: Pfalztheater, Kaiserslautern, 10 February 1981

CAST

Billy Crocker William Gaxton
Hope Harcourt Bettina Hall
Reno Sweeney Ethel Merman
Sir Evelyn Oakleigh
  Leslie Barrie
Moon-Face Mooney
  Victor Moore

French singer Jeanne Aubert as London's Reno (obligingly rechristened "Lagrange" for her) and her backing group watch the birdie.

Bewitched, bothered and blackmailed

Pal Joey Vera Simpson (Vivienne Segal) finds that her lowlife fling with Joey (Gene Kelly) has hazards (June Havoc, Jack Durant). But none she can't cope with.

B'way OK!

The 1930s may have been a comparatively fallow period in the history of the musical theatre, but, like all fallow periods, it prepared the ground. And, in the years that followed, there was to be a superb crop of shows harvested from that ground. A crop of shows that would make their mark all across the world.

The 1940s was a decade when the centre of the world's musical theatre found itself a new home: in America. Or, as the expression goes, to the sad exclusion of such once important musical-theatre sources as Boston or Chicago, "on Broadway". London and Paris kept cheerfully on through those years during and after the war, but the great bulk of the action – and certainly the significant and wide-ranging action – of those years came from the left-hand side of the Atlantic ocean.

The most enduring American musical to come out of the early part of the war years was one with a score written by Rodgers and Hart. But although *Pal Joey* (1940) has become the most popular of all its songwriters' shows in modern times, it provoked some decidedly twitchy noses when it first appeared. The morning-after taste of its John O'Hara tale of a predatory dame and the medallion-man toyboy she picks up, and two acts later drops, didn't appeal overly to the 1940s, but the show's slice-of-sleazy-life air proved to be just the ticket for later and more jaded generations. *Pal Joey* – with singular help from such songs as "Bewitched", "I Could Write a Book" and "Take Him" – wins regular revivals half a century later, whilst longer-running Rodgers and Hart shows such as *By Jupiter* or *A Connecticut Yankee* are virtually forgotten.

Another interesting and effective musical show to come out of the early 1940s was Moss Hart's *Lady in the Dark*, a play which dissected and eventually sorted out the hidden emotions and fears of a seemingly successful, strong woman. The show's unusual musical part, composed by Kurt Weill to words by Ira Gershwin, was contained in a series of visits paid by this woman to a psychoanalyst and took the form of a series of on-the-couch 'dream sequences'. In those sometimes fantastical, through-composed scenas, which only occasionally stepped aside into conventional songs, the heroine delivered the tale of "Jenny", the girl who, fatally, would make up her mind, and a supporting character rattled off the speedy nonsense number "Tschaikowsky". The show's most attractive song, however, was the pretty "My Ship", the childhood melody that is the theme of and the key to the lady's hang-ups.

Unlike *Pal Joey*, *Lady in the Dark* hasn't worn well. In these self-knowing days, when a little bit of insecurity would scarcely seem to justify a whole lot of sessions with a deeply serious analyst, Hart's libretto seems naive, but in 1941 the show played 467 nights on a Broadway not yet sated with emotional vivisection.

Neither *Pal Joey* nor *Lady in the Dark* made any great impression beyond America. In that way, at least, the trend of the 1930s continued. But in 1943 there came along a show that would – a show that would go to all the corners of, at least, the English-speaking world, and go there with enormous success.

Oklahoma!

For a long time it used to be fashionable to label Oklahoma! *as some kind of "first", an "innovation" in the musical theatre. That hangover from a distinctly successful publicist's handout has now been cured, but the idea of* Oklahoma! *as somehow "significant" still hangs on. Why? What was so different about this show?*

Background: **One tease too far. The lustful Jud Fry (Howard Da Silva) gets heavy with Laurey (Joan Roberts).**

Right: **Joan Roberts as the evening's ingénue, backed by a chorus of Oklahoma country lasses.**

The answer is, nothing. It was a straightforward romantic period musical, shaped pretty much on the lines of author Hammerstein's earlier big hits – *The Desert Song* and *Rose Marie* – with a soprano heroine and a baritone hero, a comical soubrette and her jolly partners, an occasionally threatening villain, a sugary and smaller-than-usual story of love and pride and jealousy, and songs and dances to fit. To modern eyes, it was something of a mega-step back from the more adult and up-to-date *Pal Joey* or *Lady in the Dark*.

But there were two things about *Oklahoma!* that, if they weren't in any way capital-S Significant, were certainly notable. The first of these was that this fine, fresh, friendly bit of entertainment represented the first collaboration between librettist/lyricist Hammerstein and composer Richard Rodgers, a team which – having now come together after years working with other partners – would go on to turn out four of the most memorable musicals of the next two decades. The second was that their maiden musical was an enormously successful one. Like the 'victory musicals' of other wars, this good-old-daisical piece, with its winning mixture of romantic and

comic songs, and with pretty, balletic **scenas** replacing the one-to-one speciality-dances and the platooned choruses of the dancing-musical years, became a part of the worldwide rejoicings of the mid-1940s as it made its way to a warm reception and a long run wherever English was spoken and sung.

Flighty Laurey Williams is expecting her handsome cowhand Curly to invite her to the local dance, but she plays it all wrong and ends up spitedly partnering the dourly dangerous Jud Fry instead. Curly has to come to her rescue, and he wins himself a grateful and chastened bride, but the cheated Jud returns for revenge on the young couple's wedding night. In the ensuing fight, the villain falls on his own knife. This three-cornered love-tale was paralleled by a livelier triangle featuring not a knife but a shotgun. The gun belongs to the fond father of Ado Annie Carnes, and its aim is to get his quick-knickered daughter hooked up legal before she's gone and got herself altogether overcompromised. Annie's beaux are Ali Hakim, a Jewish pedlar who wants her, and Will Parker, a not very bright cowboy who wants to marry her. Fortunately for all concerned, he finally gets to.

The songwriters supplied their simple and staunchly singing hero and heroine with some delightful, ingenuous numbers ("Oh, What a Beautiful Mornin'", "People Will Say We're in Love", "The Surrey with the Fringe on Top", "Out of my Dreams"), and their soubrets with some top-notch comic pieces that ranged from Annie's wide-eyed justification for nearly-nymphomania ("I Cain't Say No!") to Will's period-topical description of the big city ("Kansas City") and his show-down with his girl ("All er Nuthin'"). "The Farmer and the Cowman" gave the excuse for a lively hoedown, whilst the massed hailing of the new state, "Oklahoma!", that was tacked on to the play's

happy end (on the excuse that the newly-weds will be living in a new United State) made a truly ringing climax to the evening.

Oklahoma! was produced by the Theatre Guild, and it gave both that group – an organization that had started out with deeply-serious-play intentions (yet had somewhy produced the little bucolic, song-studded play that served as a base for *Oklahoma!*) – its biggest ever hit, and Broadway its happiest romantic musical hit since *Show Boat*. The show smashed the Broadway long-run record with a first run of 2,212 performances, and the success that it won helped give a whole new impetus to a Broadway, and to a musical theatre much in need of such a booster. *Oklahoma!* raced through over 1,500 nights in postwar London and a fine run in end-of-the-decade Australia, and ultimately made its way to a more faithful than usual film version.

A round-the-world revival launched from Broadway in 1979, although keeping its runs to more modest proportions than the original, confirmed that the little tale of *Oklahoma!*'s chocolate-box cowboys and their girls and their now much-loved songs had lost none of their appeal over the years.

The farmer and the cowman, many a gingham gown and even a naughty out-west bar-room dancer.

CREDITS

Oklahoma!

Musical play in 2 acts by Oscar Hammerstein II, based on the play *Green Grow the Lilacs* by Lynn Riggs

MUSIC
by Richard Rodgers

Produced at St James Theater, New York, 31 March 1943
UK: Theatre Royal, Drury Lane, London, 29 April 1947
Germany: Berlin, 1951
France: Théâtre des Champs Elysées, Paris, 20 June 1955

CAST

Curly	Alfred Drake
Laurey Williams	Joan Roberts
Ado Annie Carnes	
	Celeste Holm
Will Parker	Lee Dixon
Ali Hakim	Joseph Buloff
Jud Fry	Howard Da Silva
Aunt Eller	Betty Garde

Annie Get Your Gun

Several popular musical stars had a shot as Annie following Ethel Merman's jolly original. Here's touring Annie, Mary Martin, in the traditional fringed skirt. But that hairdo doesn't look very frontier-like, does it?

Oklahoma! might have been first out of the blocks in America, but it had to share its 'victory' cavalcade around the world with a show that was written three years later. In fact, when all's said and totted up, *Annie Get Your Gun* really outgunned the older piece beyond American shores, running even-stevens with its rival in London, largely topping it in Australia, and even getting an admittedly disappointing showing as *Annie du Far-West* in Paris. But when successes are as big as these two were and are, counting up who nosed out whom is rather a useless exercise. Like *Oklahoma!*, *Annie Get Your Gun* was, quite simply, a big, big hit.

Annie Get Your Gun was the offspring of another first-time-together combination of experienced writers. Brother and sister Dorothy and Herbert Fields, who had turned out texts for several jolly Cole Porter shows during the earlier 1940s, made the showbiz love-story of sharpshooters Annie Oakley and Frank Butler into a libretto, and top popular songwriter Irving Berlin, whose three previous ventures into the world of musical comedy hadn't precisely produced any durable pieces of theatre, matched their text with a bookful of smiling songs which more than did its part in remedying that situation.

Annie's ingenuous description of frontier folk "Doin' What Comes Natur'lly", her frustrated wail that "You Can't Get a Man with a Gun" even when, as Frank admits, "My Defenses Are Down", his pink-and-white prototype of "The Girl That I Marry", their romantic "They Say It's Wonderful" and their rivalrous "Anything You Can Do (I Can Do Better)" made up the heart of a score that was severely devoted to its two stars. However, all those grand and good songs still left room for that thumpingly enduring paean to performing,"There's No Business Like Show Business", and a couple of pretty song-and-dance moments for a pair of supporting soubrets, as Annie Oakley went through the stages of learning just how you can get a man with a gun – if you don't shoot holes through his self-esteem.

Oklahoma! and *Annie Get Your Gun* might have led the post-war tidal wave of American musicals across the stages of the world's English-speaking lands, but it was left to another show successfully to carry Broadway's newest strain of musical theatre into Central Europe and that show was the 1948 *Kiss Me, Kate*. *Kiss Me, Kate* was written by the husband and wife team of Sam and Bella Spewack, a pair of journalists who'd made a successful start on the musical stage with the politician-prodding libretto to *Leave it to Me!* a decade earlier, and the songs were the work of their partner on that show, the man of the 1930s: Cole Porter.

Kiss Me, Kate

Like Annie Get Your Gun, *and like so many other musical shows and, particularly, musical films before – and after – it,* Kiss Me, Kate *was a show about people in showbusiness. The Kate who was supposed to do the kissing was an actress, Lilli Vanessi, who – for purely pecuniary reasons – is playing the part of Katharine in a musical version of Shakespeare's* The Taming of the Shrew.

Her director, producer and co-star is her ex-husband, Fred Graham. He has his eyes on the soubrette, she's having an affair with a high-up politician, but the old spark is still there and by the time the performance-within-the-performance and the piece itself – which have both been enlivened by the antics of two very plotworthy gangsters – come to an end, rewedding bells can be heard clanging merrily.

The songs of *Kiss Me, Kate* came in two varieties: those that were sung by the characters as part of the musical-seen-in-the-musical, and those that weren't. The first list included Petruchio's "Where is the Life That Late I Led", "I've Come to Wive It Wealthily in Padua" and "Were Thine That Special Face", Kate's "I Hate Men" and the finale "Kiss Me, Kate". The second took in the flowingly romantic "So in Love", a burlesque of Americo-Continental operetta, "Wunderbar", and Lois's admission to her partner that I'm "Always True to You in my Fashion" – a fashion that didn't seem to be much holier than Ado Annie's. Together, the two parts of the score

made up a particularly effective whole, and, since Porter for once kept his celebrity telephone-book firmly in his back pocket, making his comic songs comprehensible to all nations and all ages, it was a particularly and widely enduring one.

Kiss Me, Kate followed up a run of over a thousand Broadway nights with successful visits to London (400 performances) and Australia, but in 1955 it caused something of a breakthrough when it was successfully produced in Frankfurt. That success caused Central Europe – which hadn't paid too much attention to Broadway since the era of *No, No, Nanette* - to cast a fresh eye beyond the Atlantic, and thereafter a steady stream of the best produce of the American (and, occasionally, British) musical stage found its way into the theatres of Germany, Austria and Hungary. As for *Kiss Me, Kate* itself, in spite of all the memorable musical shows that succeeded it, it has remained one of the small handful of shows from Broadway's post-war heyday to be regularly repeated, during the last forty years, throughout Europe.

Background: Shrew-cure Petruchio (Alfred Drake), sweet Bianca (Lisa Kirk) and suitor Lucentio (Harold Lang) in their show-within-the-show.

CREDITS

Kiss Me, Kate

Musical comedy in 2 acts by Sam and Bella Spewack

MUSIC AND LYRICS
by Cole Porter

Produced at the New Century Theater, New York, 30 December 1948

UK: London Coliseum, 8 March 1951

Germany: Städtische Bühnen, Frankfurt, 19 February 1955

Hungary: Fövárosi Operettszinház, Budapest, 15 November 1963

Austria: Theater an der Wien, Vienna, 6 February 1973

France: Théâtre Mogador, Paris, 26 January 1993

CAST

Lilli Vanessi	Patricia Morison
Fred Graham	Alfred Drake
Lois Lane	Lisa Kirk
Bill Calhoun	Harold Lang
Gangsters	Harry Clark, Jack Diamond

Right: **Kiss Me, Kate**
Cole Porter poses with his film
Lilli-Kate (Kathryn Grayson) and
Fred-Petruchio (Howard Keel).

Below: **Carousel**
Gordon Macrae recreated Billy
Bigelow for the show's screen
version. Shirley Jones was his
Julie.

The shows of Rodgers and Hammerstein didn't find the same success in translation that *Kiss Me, Kate* did, but they more than made up for that with the successes won by their original English-language productions.

The partners followed up *Oklahoma!* with a musical version of another Theatre Guild play, Ferenc Molnár's international hit *Liliom*. If they'd stuck close to the play's original text, they would have turned out a piece nearer in flavour to *Pal Joey* than to their own first big hit, but Hammerstein (who had clearly seen which way theatrical box-offices were blowing) preferred to soften up the Hungarian author's characters and their motives and to sweeten the show's ending, so that *Carousel* (1945) was, again, a classic romantic musical. A classic American romantic musical – for Molnár's Hungarian wastrel here became Billy Bigelow from New England.

Out-of-work Bigelow marries a local mill-girl, and when she becomes pregnant he turns to thievery to support them. But he messes up his first job and is killed. Sixteen years later, the heavenly bureaucracy lets him briefly revisit earth and speak with his now-grown daughter. He messes that reunion up as well, but Hammerstein managed to turn things about a little, so that *Carousel* was able to end not in disappointment but on a note of hope.

Carousel had no place in its score for the more sparky comicalities of *Oklahoma!* (the secondary soubret pair here were a gentle couple who sang simply of "When the Children Are Asleep"), but instead featured one particularly lovely love song, "What's the Use of Wond'rin'", alongside a big, character-warming baritone monologue (Soliloquy) for the inherently unattractive hero and, most enduringly of all, the first example of a kind of number that would become a regular in Rodgers and Hammerstein shows: the big, rousing solo for a big, rousing female voice. Rather as if Aunt Eller had led the title-song in *Oklahoma!*. *Carousel*'s example was the rousing, gospel-tinted "You'll Never Walk Alone". It's a piece which has gone through a strange metamorphosis in modern-day Britain: it gets sung, *en masse*, every winter weekend (with terrible things done to its top notes) by thousands of spectators at soccer matches. But it started out as a staunchly soprano hymn of faith and hope.

The third big Rodgers and Hammerstein hit of the 1940s was a piece that deftly mixed full-blooded comedy and full-blooded tragedy. Like *Oklahoma!* and *Carousel*, *South Pacific* (1949) had its dead body – as in *Carousel*, it was the juvenile man – but this time the basic star line-up was different. It wasn't the soprano but the soubrette who was the central figure in this wartime tale of love in warm and dangerous places, and the male star was no juvenile, but – Lord forbid! – a middle-ageing operatic basso. This unlikely situation came about because the famous opera star Ezio Pinza had signed to do a musical, but his original producer couldn't find one for him to do. So Richard Rodgers stepped in and composed the rôle of the Frenchman Émile de Becque around Pinza and his glorious voice ("Some Enchanted Evening", "This Nearly Was Mine").

South Pacific's heroine was a nurse from Arkansas. Far from home, in the midst of the Pacific war, she falls in love with de Becque, but finds her small-town principles revolted at his past, miscegenous life and his mixed-race children. It is only when he, despairing of ever winning her, has gone dangerously into action, that Nellie Forbush realizes how foolish she has been. There is a happy ending for Nellie and de Becque, but the show's other, inter-racial, romance, between a young American lieutenant and an island girl, ends in tragedy and his death. The comic part of the show was in the hands of the chorus of GIs – most particularly one with clumsy ambitions to be a war profiteer – and of Bloody Mary, an island woman with altogether more profiteering skill.

It was Bloody Mary who garnered the "big" song of the evening with her glowing serenade to the island of "Bali H'ai", a song which went with de Becque's numbers, the tenor's "Younger Than Springtime" and a clutch of bouncy soubrette pieces for Nellie ("I'm Gonna Wash That Man Right out of my Hair", "Wonderful Guy", "Cockeyed Optimist") to make up the backbone of a score that would be heard on stage and exceedingly technicolor screen for decades to come.

One hit after another

Undoubtedly the most effective new team of musical playwriters to emerge in the wake of Rodgers and Hammerstein were Alan Jay Lerner and Fritz Loewe, and the show that launched their Broadway and international career was perhaps the most delightfully romantic of all the romantic musicals of the period, *Brigadoon* (1947).

In a fantastical new version of the favourite old hometowner-in-odd-places kind of libretto, Lerner's story followed what happens to two American hunters who stumble on a magical village in the highlands of Scotland. The one short day of each century that

South Pacific
Émile de Becque (Ezio Pinza) romances nurse Nellie (Mary Martin) with a brown, basso tale of falling in love "Some Enchanted Evening".

Background: **On the Town**
Taxi-driving Brunnhilde Esterhazy (Pat Carroll) keeps the party lively as she and her pals help Gabey (Harold Lang) track down true love in the show's 1959 revival.

Inset: **Leonard Bernstein**
The composer of five stage musicals which included some of the finest dance and orchestral music to have graced the musical stage.

Brigadoon is on earth is enough for one of them to have his pants purposefully removed by a determined soubrette, and for Tommy, the other, to fall deeply in love with soprano Fiona. But there is drama as well as romance in the village of Brigadoon. In revenge for his sweetheart's marriage to another lad, one villager is ready to quit Brigadoon, breaking the spell that binds it to earth and sending it forever into darkness. He is killed trying to leave. The foreigners depart before the witching hour, but in the final scene Tommy returns and the strength of his love makes Brigadoon reappear so that he can go to his Fiona.

Loewe decorated the pretty story with some deliciously tartan-tinted tunes – "The Heather on the Hill", "Come to Me, Bend to Me", "Waitin' for my Dearie", "I'll Go Home With Bonnie Jean" – that showed nothing of his German origins, as well as some lushly romantic pieces ("It's Almost Like Being in Love", "There, But for You, Go I"), some sparky soubrette bits and an overdose of the ballet music that had been made temporarily a musical-comedy must by the success of the romantic dances in *Oklahoma!* The result was a show that thoroughly and long charmed the English-speaking world both on stage and later on screen, and one which remains a classic of both its time and kind.

Not every musical of the new romantic wave had to have a death in it. There were still writers around who throve on comedy, and in the 1940s several finely funny musicals were brought to the stage. One of these was another piece with a fantasy libretto and a score by an ex-German composer. The brightly whimsical *One Touch of Venus* (1943) had a story – nearly a century down the road from *Die schöne Galathée* or *Adonis* – about a statue who comes to life and causes havoc in the modern world. The part of the statue was actually played by the same actress who, half a dozen years later, would be the Nellie Forbush of *South Pacific*, Mary Martin.

Miss Martin was Venus, let loose in contemporary New York and firmly attached to the rather gormless youth who has accidentally brought her to life rather than to his rich, handsome and yearning patron. She causes mayhem in the city, and in everyone's lives, until she realizes that, if she carries this thing through, she is going to end up as a suburban American housewife. Better to be a chunk of Anatolian marble any day.

Kurt Weill supplied the tunes to a book and lyrics by accredited humorists S. J. Perelman and Ogden Nash, and the team turned out as many attractive romantic numbers ("Speak Low", "West Wind", "I'm a Stranger Here Myself") as they did witty and wordful ones ("The Trouble With Women", "Way Out West in Jersey") for a show that notched up 567 performances in its Broadway run.

One Touch of Venus went from stage to screen, but (other than on celluloid) it didn't prove to be an export prospect. Another piece with a New York background did, however, travel a little better. The lively and likeable *On the Town* (1944) was the Broadway début of a group of young writers who were each to have a remarkable career – writers Adolph Green and Betty Comden and composer Leonard Bernstein – and their show was one that might once have been called a "revue", at that time when revue had stopped revueing anything, and almost had a plot. It was, in fact, a very near relation to the sort of show that the Gaiety Theatre had produced at the turn of the century with *A Runaway Girl* or *After the Girl*: a series of up-to-date songs and dances tacked onto the tiny framework of a travelling story. The runaway girl that the folk of this story were after was a Coney Island cooch dancer, for *On the Town* simply occupied itself with three sailors off on 24-hour leave and their search for 24-hour New York girls. Two of the guys get caught up in comical situations, but Gabey gets serious and so his pals and their partners join forces to help him go after his girl. They've only just caught her when the 24 hours are up.

What was, and always had been, important in this type of show was not so much the plot but what went into it, and the three young writers filled their show with a lively variety of comical sketch-scenes and musical numbers, ranging from the joyous "New York, New York", which marked the boys' arrival in town, to the comical "I Can Cook Too" and "I Get Carried Away", and the more moody "Lonely Town". There was also a large helping of very superior dance music to announce the arrival on Broadway of the man who was to be probably the most stunning composer of show dance music of all time.

Like *One Touch of Venus*, *On the Town* went from stage to screen, but although it progressed to revivals and a London showing it never, in later and perhaps more sophisticated days, took off again with the same joyousness that had characterized its first New York appearance.

Another musical with a fine, funny text was the musical comedy remake of Anita Loos's hilarious novella *Gentlemen Prefer Blondes* (1949), a piece so famously filmed with Marilyn Monroe in the rôle of its blonde moneybox of a heroine. The original stage representative of the singing Lorelei Lee was Carol Channing, who gambolled through the tongue-in-cheeks story of the little girl from Little Rock with a passion for diamonds (and the gentlemen who give them to her), equipped with a decidedly mixed bag of songs, for 740 Broadway nights. That mixed bag, however, included two numbers that both Miss Channing and Miss Monroe would mine very fruitfully – one for each of Lorelei's besetting characteristics ("A Little Girl from Little Rock", "Diamonds Are a Girl's Best Friend").

The Broadway 1940s also brought forth a variety of other successful shows. There was an Oscar Hammerstein Americanization of Bizet's opera *Carmen* as a musical called *Carmen Jones* (1943); there was the richly sung *Song of Norway* (1944), an operettic pasticcio on *Dreimäderlhaus* lines that did for Norwegian composer Edvard Grieg what had earlier been done to Schubert; there was yet another fantasy (but one which it seemed only Americans understood or liked) in the leprechauny tale of *Finian's Rainbow* (1947); and there was a curiously remade musical version of the famous farce *Charley's Aunt*, with its two lead male rôles rolled into one, under the title *Where's Charley?* (1948). There

was also a slightly larger than usual ration of interesting or adventurous failures, topped by a piece called *St Louis Woman*, which proved to be a bouquet of dazzling Harold Arlen songs in search of a libretto (it tried several times thereafter to find one). But the last couple of noteworthy contributions to the musical stage of the 1940s actually came from Europe: one from Britain, and one from France.

Britain's top show of this era was a slightly surprising romantic musical play. Surprising in that it came from the usually tub-thumping humorist A. P. Herbert and from Britain's most expert exponent of twixt-wars musical-theatre songwriting, the same Vivian Ellis who had been responsible for *Mr Cinders*. The show with which the two men made their hit was called *Bless the Bride*, and – like *Bitter-Sweet* –

Gentlemen Prefer Blondes
But the brunette didn't do badly in any case. Lorelei (Carol Channing) and friend Dorothy (Yvonne Adair) end the evening with a wealthy double-wedding.

Above: **Vivian Ellis**

The most important British musical-theatre songwriter of the 1930s and 1940s.

Opposite: ***The King and I***

The real Anna Leonowens went out lecturing on her Siamese experiences. Oscar Hammerstein gave his Anna and her King a more light-hearted relationship that would hardly have made up into a Victorian lecture!
Yul Brynner and Deborah Kerr in the film version of the show.

it followed the fortunes of a young British lady of some class who runs away to period Europe with a romantic foreigner. Lucy Willow, however, doesn't run away to tragedy. She runs, and her English family follow her, cavorting across beastly foreign France in mad pursuit. Then Lucy's Pierre is called up to fight in one of France's wars, so she returns sadly to England and the stiff-kneed fellow she was set to wed before romance came along. I'm happy to report that Pierre not only survives the fighting, but gets to England before Lucy has disposed of her hand.

Ellis's score was a delicious one, with the tenorious "Ma Belle Marguerite" and "A Table for Two", the idyllic duo "This is my Lovely Day" and the delicious waltz trio "I Was Never Kissed Before" seeing the composer stretch into a lyric vein that he had previously eschewed in favour of a more modern, dancing style with enormous success. *Bless the Bride* was played in London alongside *Oklahoma!* and *Annie Get Your Gun*, and it more than held its own with this great advance guard of the new wave of Broadway musicals until producer C. B. Cochran, in a rare and monumental error of judgement, decided to remove it and stage a successor. The successor flopped.

In Paris, little notice was taken of the new wave of Broadway musicals. For Paris had a new wave of its own, a wave launched by a piece that was (and is) considered by the French much as *Oklahoma!* is where English is spoke. France's 'victory musical' was called *La Belle de Cadix*, and it was about as different as was possible from the French "victory musical" of the last war. Whereas *Phi-Phi* had been pure dance-rhythmed sex comedy, the newer piece was a couldn't-be-more-classic romantic musical. The hero is a film star called Carlos Médina who goes to Spain to make a film, plays a wedding scene with a lovely local lass, and finds the ring-in actor who reads the wedding service is for real. This romantic plot – with its foreseeable development and ending – was paralleled by a lively soubret one (an assistant director and a perky Spaniard) in a libretto that neatly cocktailed up-to-date and glamorously screenic fun and music-filled romance.

That music was the work of a young songwriter called Francis Lopez, and he provided a whole throatful of royally ringing tenor numbers for his leading man ("La Belle de Cadix", "Maria-Luisa", etc), numbers which helped make a star of the young Luis Mariano, and which Mariano duly hoisted to nationwide popularity.

La Belle de Cadix set in motion an entire series of musicals on similar lines (many by Lopez and his librettist Raymond Vincy), a series that filled French theatres for long runs – including endless tours and provincial productions – for decades, and which provided a huge body of songs that would become French favourites, some of them to this day.

The first fine flush of the fifties

In the first part of the 1950s, Broadway went on to consolidate the new, sun-drenched place it had won in the 1940s at the centre of the musical theatre universe. Then, in the latter half of the decade, the American musical theatre went on to revel in perhaps its most outstanding years of all.

However, the "consolidating" period also yielded a very fine crop of new musicals, and many or most of them were the work of the men and women who had created the outstanding shows of the previous decade: Rodgers and Hammerstein, Lerner and Loewe, Leonard Bernstein, Adolph Green and Betty Comden, Irving Berlin, Cole Porter, Dorothy Fields, Frank Loesser. It was a list of names that, with very few additions in later years, would go down in history as the "royal family" of the greatest era of musical Broadway.

The Rodgers and Hammerstein team actually slipped a couple of flops into the first part of the 1950s, but, alongside the feeble *Me and Juliet* and the unattractive *Pipe Dream*, they also turned out one of their most satisfying hits: the based-a-little-on-fact Asian tale of *The King and I*. Nowadays, *The King and I* comes to us with the image of Yul Brynner's King stamped firmly across it – but that's not how the show started out. The idea for the musical came from actress Gertrude Lawrence, who had already inspired *Oh, Kay!* and launched *Lady in the Dark*, and the authors created her part of "I", otherwise the sometime Siamese royal governess Anna Leonowens, to be the show's starring rôle. The King whom Anna bullies out of his proud savagery and into a semblance of Western

La Belle de Cadix

"La Belle de Cadix a des yeux de velours…" Heartthrob tenor Luis Mariano and the sweetest of sopranos, Lina Dachary, in the show's 1949 revival.

ways was intended – as far as billing was concerned – only to be consort to the lady.

The songs that the partners gave their two slightly singing stars included some warming pieces – her "Getting to Know You", "Hello, Young Lovers" and "I Whistle a Happy Tune", their "Shall We Dance?" and his "Puzzlement" – but, of necessity, the lyric music of the score was sidewound into other parts. The slave Tuptim and her soldier lover sang two fine duos, and the King's chief wife was given perhaps the most beautiful of Rodgers and Hammerstein's big ladies' songs: the deeply devoted "Something Wonderful". A particularly successful dance portion included a stylized (and plotful) Asian retelling of "Uncle Tom's Cabin" and a winning kiddie display in "The March of the Siamese Children".

The King and I followed its predecessors to English-language stages and screens throughout the world, and it later proved a particular favourite for revival, both with Brynner – who made half a career out of repeating his most famous rôle in ever broadening versions – and later with other actors in the part he had hoisted to being the focus of the evening.

Lerner and Loewe followed *Brigadoon* with a show that was as far distant from the delicious fantasy of their Scots musical as could be. *Paint Your Wagon* was a lusty tale of gold-grabbers in the Wild West, a piece with a really vigorous

feel to it and hardly a chocolate-box cowboy or gingham gown in sight. It also sported some fine, masculine songs: the campfire "They Call the Wind Maria", the loping "Wand'rin' Star", the heartfelt "I Still See Elisa", and a rousing, rough-riding opening number ("Where Am I Goin'?") in which men from all over America are seen packing up what possessions they have and heading off into the unknown in the hope of finding those nuggets that will mean they'll never have to pack up again.

The virile *Paint Your Wagon* with its period, frontier settings was a far cry from the new show offered by the Comden, Green and Bernstein team. They stuck to the I-Love-New-York gaiety that had so illuminated their *On the Town*. *Wonderful Town* was, however, one up on the older show: it had a real broadbacked libretto as the setting for its winning songs and dances. Comden and Green used the hugely successful play *My Sister Eileen* as the starting point for a libretto that followed the cockeyed adventures of two sisters from Ohio who come to Greenwich Village in the hopes of making careers in the theatre and in writing. The Greenwich Village of *Wonderful Town* is about as real as the Montmartre garrets of *La Bohème*, but it served as the setting for a great deal of fun and for some grand musical numbers: the sisters glumly regretting "Ohio", blonde bazooka Eileen wondering intermittently if she might not be "A Little Bit in Love", and an intricate "Conversation Piece" at an embarrassed dinner-party.

Cole Porter wrote his last three musicals in the early 1950s. The mythological *Out of This World* bombed, but he scored a couple of Broadway successes with a couple of American-in-Paris musicals decorated with American-in-Paris songs: *Can-Can* and *Silk Stockings*. *Can-Can*, which was easily the better of the two and which didn't even have an American-in-Paris (except Porter) in it, gave the true story of the banning of that naughty dance in nineteenth-century Paris another whirl across the stage (Budapest, Vienna and even Madrid had all done musicals on the same topic soon after the event). Abe Burrows turned out a neat libretto about a dance-hall owner and the lawyer who, instead of prosecuting her, falls in love with her, in a combination of fun and romance which left plenty of places for the all-important songs and dances. The most famous of those songs were the Framerican "I Love Paris" and "C'est magnifique", perhaps the prettiest was a delicate "Allez-vous-en", and the most pointed was "Never Give Anything Away (That You Can Sell)".

Can-Can, with its spectacular staging – the highlight was the performance of a glamorous "Garden of Eden" ballet featuring the show's soubrette as its star – proved to have a little more overseas life to it that the more "real" and more thoroughly American Paint Your Wagon and Wonderful Town, but attempts to revive it in modern times have disappointed.

Irving Berlin's follow-up to Annie Get Your Gun was, not surprisingly, another vehicle for his "Annie", musical-comedy mega-star Ethel Merman. It was also another piece that, like Can-Can, picked up a nearly new idea, happily redecorated it with new twists and new songs, and turned it into a brass-bottomed hit. Cicely Courtneidge had not long been starring in London as Her Excellency, extravagant British Ambassador to somewhere in far-off South America, when Miss Merman stepped onto the Broadway stage as Mrs Sally Adams, brash, party-giving American Ambassador to the tiny far-off state of Lichtenburg and the leading lady of Call Me Madam. Sally spreads money and affection around her ditsy duchy with a liberality not quite in keeping with her official position, but, if she gets herself and Uncle Sam into the odd bit of diplomatic warm water, she also manages to get Lichtenburg on the wonderful way to being a "developing country" and organizes husbands for both its princess and, of course, herself. On the way, the star delivered a shillelagh-shower of numbers – declaring herself "The Hostess with the Mostes'", bludgeoning her man into romance with "Can You Use Any Money

Today?" and "The Best Thing for You Would Be Me" and, most memorably, providing her lovesick secretary with a motherly shoulder and some motherly advice in the counter-melodied duo "You're Just in Love".

Call Me Madam (1950) travelled well, following its Broadway run with fine seasons in Britain and Australia and making what was becoming the standard trip to the screen as well, but, for all its success, it didn't have anything like the length and breadth of career in those centres that the new musical from Where's Charley? songwriter Frank Loesser would. Then again, there weren't many shows that did.

Can-Can
Gwen Verdon was the sparkling soubrette of the show. She sparkled so much that the leading lady insisted that her part be reduced. But still she outsparkled everyone.

Far left: Howard Keel paddles Kathryn Grayson in *Kiss Me, Kate*.

Left: Marlon Brando milk-shakes Jean Simmons in *Guys and Dolls*.

Below: Audrey Hepburn goes Ascot in company with Wilfrid Hyde-White and Gladys Cooper in *My Fair Lady*.

Guys and Dolls

No one could possibly have guessed, on the evidence of the mostly primpingly pseudo-English songs that had decorated the English story of his awkward Charley's Aunt *musical,* Where's Charley? *or even from their writer's background as a multi-hitmaking popular songsmith, that Frank Loesser would, next time around, turn out one of Broadway's most memorable show scores of all time.*

There was nothing either primping or pseudo-English about the songs of *Guys and Dolls*. This one was all New York – and not even the New York that those shipboard or Ohio visitors had skated through in *On the Town* and *Wonderful Town*. The musical that the authors of *Guys and Dolls* drew from Damon Runyon's very personally styled stories of the New York heart-streets and their very characterful inhabitants seemed to get right round the ventricles of the city and its folk in a warmly funny and – for all its sometimes surreal craziness – real tale that was something altogether special.

It was the same Abe Burrows who had been responsible for the book to *Can-Can* who supplied the final text for a show which, amazingly, had to be constructed – as *Anything Goes* had been – around a set of songs written to be part of another, unsatisfactory libretto. He centred his story on an illegal gambling game called craps. When he has the funds and a venue, Nathan Detroit runs a Broadway crap game. One cashless and venue-less week, with a redhot game in prospect, he tries desperately to raise the wind by betting visiting gambling-man Sky

Masterson that the lad can't get local holy-roller girl Sarah Browne to partner him to Havana on a date. But Masterson promises Sarah to fill her ailing mission with "converts" if she goes, so she goes – and whilst she's

Background: "Roll 'em, roll 'em…" The Oldest Established Permanent Floating Crap-Game in New York is under way.

away Nathan sets up his crap game in the mission! But next day, as the evicted game goes on down in the sewers, Sky hits a winning streak, and before the mission is due to have its life-or-abolition inspection he's fulfilled his promise and crammed the place to the doors with his crapped-out victims. As for Sky, he himself falls victim to Sarah, and the evening ends with a reformed gambling-man banging the big drum in the mission band.

The richly individual collection of songs that illustrated the show gave its audiences a bit of just about everything. There was a regulation love duet ("I've Never Been in Love Before") for Sky and Sarah, a rattling and rolling "Luck Be a Lady" for the gambler, a tipsy little ditty for a Sarah who's tasted too many Havana-style "milkshakes" ("If I Were a Bell") and a burlesque of a revivalist song delivered by a not-very-repentant crap-player ("Sit Down, You're Rockin' the Boat"). Sky serenaded the streets of New York in "My Time of Day", Sarah serenaded her ideal man in "I'll Know (When my Love Comes Along)" and the gamblers serenaded "The Oldest-Established Permanent Floating Crap Game in New York". The guys swapped canonized racing tips in "Fugue for Tin Horns", and Nathan's always-fiancée-never-bride, Adelaide, led the girls of her Hot-Box Club in "Take Back your Mink" and "A Bushel and a Peck". Adelaide actually drew some of

the show's best musical moments, sniffling out an hilarious "Lament" over her interminably delayed nuptials (the very thought of which gives her raging, dripping hay-fever), tackling her ever-backsliding partner in "Sue Me" or joining Sarah in plotting matrimony in "Marry the Man Today".

Like many another fabulous and famous show, *Guys and Dolls* didn't pull a clean sheet of notices, but it did pull a hatful of the as yet not overlong or devalued list of awards up for grabs in its season, and moved on to run for 1,200 Broadway nights. That run was two and a half years old before Britain took a look at the show, and although its production was a fine success (555 nights) *Guys and Dolls* showed a strange reluctance to travel further. It toured, it was filmed, but although it was spoken of with enormous respect from early on, although it became quickly esteemed as a prize piece in the Broadway repertoire, it didn't seem to get performed a lot. The show's only return to Broadway in its first thirty years was in a badly beaten-about and racially restricted version that passed through in 1976. It was not until 1982 that a repeat was seen in London, and it was 1992 before Broadway finally welcomed back the musical. But when it did, *Guys and Dolls* was greeted with huge enthusiasm – more enthusiasm, in fact, than first time up. And it's a fair bet it won't ever stay away as long again.

CREDITS

Guys and Dolls

Musical fable of Broadway in 2 acts, based on a story and characters by Damon Runyon. Book by Abe Burrows and Jo Swerling

MUSIC AND LYRICS

by Frank Loesser

Produced at the 46th Street Theater, New York, 24 November 1950

UK: London Coliseum, 28 May 1953

Germany: Theater der Hansestadt, Bremen, 26 May 1968

CAST

Nathan Detroit	Sam Levene
Sarah Browne	Isobel Bigley
Sky Masterson	Robert Alda
Nicely Nicely Johnson	
	Stubby Kaye
Adelaide	Vivian Blaine
Arvide Abernethy	Pat Rooney

Left: Sky Masterson (Robert Alda) wins his bet by taking Sarah Browne on an Havana-awayday.

CHAPTER 10

Kismet
Ann Blyth adores 'Baubles, Bangles and Beads' in Hollywood's version of the show.

Of all the "royal family", only Dorothy Fields didn't manage to come up in these years with a success to parallel her best of the 1940s. But then her success of the 1940s had been *Annie Get Your Gun*. She did, however, produce two attractive, olde-America pieces with music by songwriter Arthur Schwartz, both of which featured one of Broadway's most endearing performers, Shirley Booth, in their lead rôle. Neither *A Tree Grows in Brooklyn* (1951) nor *By the Beautiful Sea* (1954) was a first-rate hit, but both won some fond followers during their life on the stage.

The writers of *Song of Norway* – Robert Wright and George Forrest – on the other hand, outdid their first big success with their second. Pasticcio shows have always been part and parcel of the musical theatre, even in its most sophisticated periods, and even those periods have brought forth big hits with musical scissors-and-paste scores. The Viennese Schubert story *Das Dreimäderlhaus* has probably been the biggest international success of the kind in the twentieth century, but Wright and Forrest's *Kismet* (1953) is

undoubtedly the best and most beautiful pasticcio show of recent times.

This time, instead of repeating the rather wanly fictional composer's-life-and-loves-and-reprocessed-tunes formula which the success of *Das Dreimäderlhaus* had encouraged, the authors took a fine, funny and colourful piece of forty-year-old theatre and gave it extra breadth, fun and colour with an exceptional piece of musical reworking that cleverly avoided the easy, and often inapposite, effects to be won by the reuse of very recognizable melodies. In fact, the score of *Kismet* rescued from virtual oblivion much of the music that it used.

The play that Wright and Forrest illustrated was Eddie Knoblock's extravagant oriental fantasy *Kismet* (1911), the story of a whip-witted Eastern beggar who – with the help of the kind of kismet or fate that helps him who helps himself – outwits a wicked Wazir and wins a Caliph for a son-in-law. The music they used was that of the Russian composer Alexsandr Borodin, most famous for his *Prince Igor* and its Polovtsian Dances. Several of those dances went into the score, notably in the making of the soaring love duo

"Stranger in Paradise" and the comic contralto description of the debaucheries of Baghdad, "Not Since Nineveh", but other pieces ironed together melodies and sections from various works in a hugely effective score, from which the baritone solo "The Olive Tree", the quartet "And This is my Beloved" and the pretty "Baubles, Bangles and Beads" have all remained favourites.

Of the new writers who surfaced on Broadway in the first years of the 1950s, the quickest and most certain success went to another twosome: Jerry Ross and Richard Adler. Ross and Adler wrote two musicals in two years, scoring two international hits that made up into two Hollywood films, and then it was over. Ross died of bronchiectasis at the age of 29, and Adler never ever found the same success without his partner.

The first of their musicals together was *The Pajama Game*, an odd show with a strangely unsympathetic leading lady. Babe is a tart little dollybird who has become a factory union rep and who wiggles her advantages at her foreman as part of a plan to score points in a wages dispute. The poor man actually gets stuck with her at the end of the show, but in some kind of compensation he also gets the hit song of the night. A bit taken aback by his own rotten taste in women, he sings baffledly to his dictaphone, "Hey There! (You with the Stars in your Eyes)". Other catchy musical moments included Babe's scornful waltz-time insistence "I'm Not at All in Love", and the description of the passion pit "Hernando's Hideaway" and the dance spot "Steam Heat", both of which fell to the star dancer of the piece.

Ross and Adler's second show, *Damn Yankees*, was another case altogether. This one had a libretto that rustled with warm fun and enjoyable people. Middle-ageing baseball fan Joe Hardy would give anything for his favourite team to win the Pennant. Anything? The Devil takes him up on it, and Joe is transformed into a home-run-hitting hero who turns the fortunes of his straggling team around – until the time comes to pay his promise. The songs, again, were a fine collection, from the rallying of the team coach trying to instil some "Heart" (since talent is clearly out of reach) into his pre-Joe team, to the sexy prowlings of the devil's mantrap assistant, Lola, declaring dangerously "Whatever Lola Wants (Lola Gets)".

Damn Yankees
The Hell-sent Lola (Gwen Verdon) explains to Joe Hardy (Stephen Douglass) why he has to give in to her. She's irresistible.

Every day in every way they're getting better and better

The second half of the 1950s was a remarkable time on Broadway. Once more, a good number of that "royal family" of musical theatre writers who had so lavishly supplied the post-war stage with musicals came up with the goods, and, with the help of a handful of newer-comers to musical-theatre success, in just a handful of years they turned out some of the most famous, the most enduring, the just plain best musicals of the English-language stage: *My Fair Lady, The Sound of Music, West Side Story, The Music Man*.

CHAPTER 10

My Fair Lady

You would never have thought that a show with a title like My Fair Lady *would have become one of the biggest hits in musical theatre history. After all, if you forget "London bridge is falling down . . .", it doesn't really mean anything. Other shows (including* The Desert Song, *no less) had actually tried similar titles and – even in the days when meaningless titles were all the rage – dumped them. Whoever said "what's in a name?" had a point.*

Background: "Wouldn't it be Loverly…" Eliza Doolittle (Julie Andrews) shares her dream of 'warm face, warm hands, warm feet' with her friends.

My Fair Lady was – four and a half years down the line – Lerner and Loewe's successor to *Paint Your Wagon*, but, unlike it and unlike *Brigadoon*, it was a musical edition of an existing play: G. B. Shaw's *Pygmalion*. *Pygmalion* was the story of a cockney flower-girl called Eliza Doolittle who manages to pass for a princess at a society ball after having had her rude vowels ironed out by a tetchy linguist and swapping her grubby native outfit for a new frock bought for her from the Army and Navy Stores by the linguist's chum.

Lerner took just a few liberties with Shaw's story. When the playwright published his work, he specifically added an epilogue in which he described what happened to the made-over Eliza when the transformation from ahhhwing cockney to perfectly vowelled lady was effected and the experiment for which Professor Higgins had used her as raw material was done. According to Shaw, she married Freddie Eynsford-Hill, a useless if adoring member of the upper-middle classes, and tried to run a flower shop. She did not move back in with Professor Higgins. Lerner stopped short of having Eliza and Higgins walk down to the footlights in wedding outfits, but when *My Fair Lady* ended you were clearly supposed to see the beginnings of real romance.

However, had Lerner not introduced this note of tenderness in his adaptation of the work of a playwright who didn't know what tenderness was, one of the most successful songs of the show would never have seen the light of stage. For Higgins's half-bewildered reaction to the (temporary) walk-out staged by Eliza, when she feels her efforts in carrying off the challenge haven't been appreciated, was expressed in song: the lovely "I've Grown Accustomed to her Face". Higgins's other songs were each in a rather more rattling vein: his intolerant railing at accented speech ("Why Can't the English?"), his misogynistic "Hymn to Him", and his self-deluding and self-centred "An Ordinary Man". Eliza, on the other hand, ran the gamut, from her early dreamingly cockney "Wouldn't it be Loverly"

170

to the furious, hurt "Just You Wait, 'Enry 'Iggins" and its later counterpart, the equally furious but more hurtfully refined "Without You", and the longingly romantic "I Could Have Danced All Night". There were also two knees-uppish pieces for Eliza's dustman father ("A Little Bit o' Luck", "Get Me to the Church on Time") and a starry-eyed serenade for the hopeless Freddie ("On the Street Where You Live") in a score where nearly every number was to become a well-known favourite.

My Fair Lady became the biggest musical hit that Broadway had ever seen. It ran for 2,717 nights, establishing a New York theatre record that would hold for nearly ten years, and, more than that, it went round the world in a manner that no American musical had ever done before. The stars of the Broadway production repeated their triumph in London, and other English-speaking venues soon

followed where America and Britain had succumbed. But then the show not only went into Central Europe – via an enormously successful production at Berlin's Theater des Westens – but also to Scandinavia, to Italy, to Israel and to South America, from the top of the world to the bottom, from the stage to the screen, round and back again, and even, eventually, to France – which had by this time completely isolated itself from the outside world as it wallowed about in the remnants of its own, decaying musical theatre tradition.

My Fair Lady quite simply covered the world in a manner that no musical had done since goodness knows when. And, wherever it went, it won approval and popularity. *Kiss Me, Kate* might have opened the door to the rest of the world for the new wave of Broadway musicals, but it was *My Fair Lady* that marched triumphantly through that door.

CREDITS

My Fair Lady

Musical in 2 acts by Alan Jay Lerner, based on the play *Pygmalion* by George Bernard Shaw

MUSIC

by Frederick Loewe

Produced at the Mark Hellinger Theater, New York, 15 March 1956

UK: Theatre Royal, Drury Lane, London, 30 April 1958

Germany: Theater des Westens, Berlin, 25 October 1961

Austria: Theater an der Wien, Vienna, 19 September 1963

Hungary: Fővárosi Operettszinház, Budapest, 11 February 1966

France: Théâtre Sebastopol, Lille, 8 October 1977

CAST

Professor Henry Higgins
　　　　　Rex Harrison

Eliza Doolittle　Julie Andrews

Alfred Doolittle
　　　　　Stanley Holloway

Freddie Eynsford-Hill
　　　　　John Michael King

Colonel Pickering
　　　　　Robert Coote

Professor Higgins (Rex Harrison) gets the beer-browned breath of Alfie Doolittle (Stanley Holloway) right between the nostrils. But he doesn't flinch.

The Sound of Music

The Sound of Music *was the last of the five great romantic musicals with which the partnership of lyricicst Oscar Hammerstein II (here seeing the production of his 40th show in 40 years) and composer Richard Rodgers put their mark on the musical stage of the 1940s and the 1950s. And it was in several ways the greatest and the most successful of them all.*

The ex-nun wins both the von Trapp children and their father. Mary Martin (far right) as the stage Maria and Julie Andrews (background) as her screen counterpart.

The musical was based on the real-life history of the Trapp Family Singers, an Austrian singing group which escaped from the German invasion of their country, and when a stage musical version of their story was originally envisaged the idea was to illustrate it with music that the singing group had actually performed. However, as the project advanced, Rodgers and Hammerstein became involved, and by the time the show reached the stage there were none of the pretty, but rather straight-backed harmony pieces of the Trapp repertoire in the score, but instead a full book of Rodgers and Hammerstein numbers, numbers that would become standards around the English-speaking world.

Vivacious nunlette Maria Rainer, sent from Nonnberg Abbey to be governess to the seven children of the widowed Baron von Trapp, brings music back into his home, and joy back into the hearts of his growing-up family. She also innocently routs the worldly Viennese aristocrat who was to have been the Baron's new wife, and ends up herself becoming the Baroness von Trapp. When the invasion takes place, and von Trapp refuses to cooperate with the German régime, the family has to flee. With the help of the nuns of Maria's former abbey, they escape over the mountains to freedom.

The star soubrette rôle of Maria was endowed with the bulk of the show's music, ranging from a rhapsodic hymn to the hills, "The Sound of Music", to a series of songs for and with the seven children – "The Lonely Goatherd", "My Favourite Things", "Do-Re-Mi" – and a more sentimental moment with their father ("An Ordinary Couple"). This rather simple star music was contrasted with spikier songs for the more sophisticated characters, von Trapp's Viennese lady and a conniving concert agent ("There's No Way To Stop It", "How Can Love Survive"), and with some full-blooded lyrical material for the sub-operatic inmates of the abbey. From this more substantial part of the music came Rodgers and Hammerstein's last and perhaps most famous big lady's song, the Mother Abbess's soaring homily, "Climb Every Mountain".

When it was first produced, *The Sound of Music* was found by the super-sophisticated to be rather too ingenuous to be satisfying, but there were plenty of large audiences more than willing to revel in its charm and its attractive songs, and the show went on to a fine Broadway run (1,443 nights) before going on to take London by storm. By the time its West End production closed, *The Sound of Music* had knocked *My Fair Lady, Oklahoma!, Annie Get Your Gun* and all the rest right off their top spots, and become simply the longest-running Broadway musical ever to have played London (2,395 performances). If the London run was a triumph, there was nevertheless still better to come. Not beyond the English-language stage, for Rodgers and Hammerstein's musicals were never to put up much of a show in that area,

but on the screen. For the film version of *The Sound of Music* was nothing short of a phenomenon. In real terms, the screenic *The Sound of Music* must be the most successful celluloid version of a stage musical ever made – and the best known. The image of Julie Andrews as Maria running along, arms aflung, through the glorious alpine meadows up above Salzburg is engraved in the popular consciousness like no other image in the stage-to-screen canon. And those mountains . . .

The vast success of the filmed *Sound of Music* did, however, put a mighty mortgage on its stage future. How could any subsequent stage production reproduce those mountains? Not to mention Julie Andrews. But in 1981 London's Ross Taylor took up the challenge, and, with a neatly adapted text and design that managed to take in more elements of the film than might have been thought possible, he relaunched *The Sound of Music* for a fine new West End run and for generations of theatregoers to come. In the meanwhile, you can still take a *Sound of Music* coach-tour from Salzburg through the locations used in the film. The only trouble is that so many of those alpine meadows are now no longer runnable through – they're crammed with the chalets of this "developing" world.

CREDITS

The Sound of Music

Musical in 2 acts by Russel Crouse and Howard Lindsay

LYRICS
by Oscar Hammerstein II

MUSIC
by Richard Rodgers

Produced at the Lunt-Fontanne Theater, New York, 16 November 1959
UK: Palace Theatre, London, 18 May 1961
Germany: Stadttheater, Hildesheim, 9 March 1982
Austria: Schauspielhaus, Vienna, 27 February 1993

CAST

Maria Rainer	Mary Martin
Captain von Trapp	Theodore Bikel
Mother Abbess	Patricia Neway
Elsa Schräder	Marion Marlowe
Liesl	Lauri Peters
Rolf	Brian Davies
Max Detweiler	Kurt Kasznar

West Side Story

Both My Fair Lady *and* The Sound of Music *were great and instant successes in the theatres of Broadway and Britain, but the third mega-hit of the later 1950s took decidedly longer to take off. Nowadays, there doesn't seem too much that's outlandish about Arthur Laurents's New Yorkish update of the Romeo and Juliet story, nor about his show's large and youthful dance content. But, back in the 1950s, the urgent, contemporary* West Side Story *was a bit harder for audiences to take than Eliza Doolittle's amusing old English antics or the sweet story of the singing nun of Salzburg.*

Tony (Larry Kert) and Maria (Carol Lawrence) dream of a life together "Somewhere" that's greener than the slums of New York.

So paying public reaction was a bit slower, and it took altogether longer – and again the boost of a particularly fine film version – to turn the show into the classic it now is.

West Side Story is set in urban New York, against a background of what the youngsters who take part in it, with a deadly childish seriousness, would like to think is "gang warfare". The Romeo of the story is Tony, once the leader of the Jets, a juvenile "gang" exclusive to the children of immigrants from Europe; his Juliet is Maria, the sister of the big boss of the Sharks, a gang made up of youngsters from Puerto Rico. The tragedy of their story is launched when the Sharks' leader resorts to a knife to beat a Jet in a fight. Both boys end up dead, and Tony – who has murdered Maria's brother – is on the run. Before the final curtain, he too is dead, the third victim of the foolish, wasteful children's games that have, in this day and age, taken the place of Harrigan's brawnier, more honest German-versus-Irishman-versus-negro barneys.

In spite of any initial reticence there might have been about *West Side Story* as a show, its songs quickly became favourites: Maria's falling-in-love "I Feel Pretty", Tony's deliriously happy "Maria", their starry-hearted anticipation of their next meeting "Tonight", their longing sigh for a happier, less factioned world "Somewhere" and the rousing, clear-eyed view of "America" sung and danced by the Puerto Rican girls and boys. However, some of the highest-lights of the *West Side Story* score came not in its extractable songs but in its dance music – exciting, vibrant dance music such as the musical stage had rarely if ever heard before – and in its ensembles ("Tonight", the duo "A Boy Like That"), which joined the more obvious "numbers" in making up a score of a rare and rich variety.

West Side Story ran for 732 performances on Broadway, toured, and even returned to New York, but the other main centres were very backward in taking up this show that was so unlike the usual Broadway fare. In the end, the show's publishers had themselves to sponsor a London showing that no established producer was willing to risk. Their faith was justified when the West End production firmly outran the Broadway one, playing for 1,039 nights. It was, however, the film version of the show, a stormingly effective screenic remake by original stager Jerome Robbins which appeared some four years after the stage première, that finally confirmed the international reputation of *West Side Story* and its songs and helped largely to put the seal on its status.

Regularly revived on English-language stages in the last couple of decades, *West Side Story* has also found more favour than most of its contemporaries in theatres further afield, and whatever reticences the public of 1957 might have felt are now well and truly forgotten.

CREDITS

West Side Story

Musical in 2 acts by Arthur Laurents

LYRICS

by Stephen Sondheim

MUSIC

by Leonard Bernstein

Produced at the Winter Garden Theater, New York, 26 September 1957

UK: Her Majesty's Theatre, London, 12 December 1958

France: Alhambra, Paris, 30 March 1961

Austria: Volksoper, Vienna, 25 February 1968

Hungary: Parkszínpad, Budapest, 3 July 1969

CAST

Tony	Larry Kert
Maria	Carol Lawrence
Riff	Mickey Calin
Bernardo	Kenn LeRoy
Anita	Chita Rivera

Jets and Sharks watch their "champions" square up for a fair fight, but the fairness soon gives way to cowardice and knives.

Candide
Robert Rounseville as Voltaire's pretty but passive hero and Max Adrian as the philosophical Pangloss in the show's original and unsuccessful version.

The year before the production of *West Side Story*, Leonard Bernstein had suffered his first Broadway flop. Now, in the musical theatre (and probably elsewhere in life too) a flop is normally a flop for very good reasons. And very, very rarely has a show that has been a flop on its first metropolitan showing ever been reworked into a second-time-round hit. But just exceptionally it does happen. *Candide* was that rare exception. Thank goodness. For in its revised version (the one that was seen in New York in 1973, and not the re-re-revised versions seen since) it proved to be one of the most brilliantly funny, piercingly pointed bits of *opéra-bouffe* heard in decades.

Candide is a picaresque philosophical saga based on Voltaire's celebrated novel, and it follows its exhaustingly optimistic hero and his nearest and (occasionally) dearest through the kind of multi-coloured series of episodes of death, destruction, disembowelment and variegated molestations that might happen to

any nice Westphalian bastard who insists on believing that, like the philosopher said, all is for the best in this best of all possible worlds. Naivety turns out to be its own reward (plus a little death, disembowelment and molestation).

The colourfully extravagant adventures of Candide, his beloved Cunégonde and their dogmatic, expedient tutor Dr Pangloss were given a suitably colourful, extravagant musical accompaniment from which the take-away treat was the coloratura explosion "Glitter and Be Gay", a burlesque of the operatic Jewel Song convention, in which Cunégonde bewailed her temporary but boring occupation as a repeatedly ravished Spanish courtesan.

Although made in the 1950s, *Candide* didn't become a hit till the 1970s. By the 1990s it had vanished from the commercial stage into the opera-house repertoire where, along with several other suitable classics of the musical stage, it helps palliate the purseholes left by expensively unpatronized operas.

Following up *Guys and Dolls* wasn't going

to be easy for anyone involved, but Frank Loesser found the good way. He changed register and wrote – book, lyrics and music – a show that was wholly different in tone and in style to his last big hit. He swapped the Runyonesque New Yorkers of *Guys and Dolls* for another but very different set of warm, wonderful and wholly realistic American characters, the characters created by Sidney Howard in his play *They Knew What They Wanted*, and he gave those characters not the sort of merrily characterful songs that had been the joy of the earlier show, but a full-blown romantic musical-play score.

The Most Happy Fella (1956) was a classic combination of eyelid-tugging sentiment and country comedy, but its heart was the tale of a middle-aged rural winegrower and his penfriend bride. He sends her his handsome foreman's photo instead of his own plumply ageing one, and when she arrives for the proposed-by-post wedding she is devastated to find out the truth. But love grows, as the best love does, and when Tony and Rosabella finally get their love duet it is one of the most blooming love duets in the musical theatre, "My Heart is So Full of You". Elsewhere the score turned out lively snip-outable numbers such as the loungers' anthem "Standing on the Corner (Watching all the Girls Go By)", the comical "Ooh, my Feet" and "Big D", the gentle "Somebody Somewhere", the windblown "Joey, Joey, Joey" and some truly bristling ensemble music. None of this was easily recognizable as being the work of the man who just a few years back had penned such hit-parade pieces as "Baby, it's Cold Outside" and "On a Slow Boat to China".

Another great show of this period was also a one-man job – book, lyrics and music. The one man on this occasion was a man new to Broadway, for Meredith Willson was first and foremost a flautist and film composer. He was also a friend of Frank Loesser, and Loesser encouraged him through the years and years that he spent trying to turn his memories of his Iowa childhood into a musical. The years were well spent, though, for the result was *The Music Man* (1957).

"If *Guys and Dolls* is the most New York of Broadway musicals, *The Music Man* is surely the most American. There is more heart-warming truth in the Iowa folk of this tale of a tricky travelling salesman shamed out of his shenanigans for the love of a good but difficult woman than in all the Ruritanian farmers and cowboys of *Oklahoma!* put together." Who wrote that? Well, actually, I did. Quite a few years ago. And I wouldn't change a word of it. *The Music Man* is a truly special show.

Super-salesman "Professor" Harold Hill travels in musical instruments. By the time folks realize they're no use if you can't play them, he's moved on to the next state. But he meets his Nemesis in River City, Iowa. The local ladies are charmed, the school board harmonized, the inimical mayor stalemated, and the instruments for the new boys' band ordered and paid for, but Harold lingers, falling in love, and he is caught. His patent untaught method of music-making is a sham. But his charming, his harmonizing, and his falling in

The Most Happy Fella
"Rosabella" (Jo Sullivan) gives in to the man (Art Lund) she thought she was to wed, but she comes to love her generous and less picturesque penfriend.

West Side Story (far left) and *The Sound of Music* (background) were given fine, faithful film remakes and are two of the greatest stage-to-screen successes. *The Boy Friend* (above) wasn't and didn't.

179

love all add up to much more good than a little bit of gentle fibbing does in the way of bad, so Harold Hill is allowed his happy ending.

Willson's score flowed from the salesman's pattering "Trouble" to the wistful "Goodnight, my Someone", the romantic "Till There Was You" and the ringing, marching description of the day that "Seventy-Six Trombones" came to town, in an evening that was winning, warmhearted and wonderful, from end to end. And it played end to end 1,375 times in New York and another 395 in London.

Winning, warmhearted and wonderful weren't quite the adjectives that one would stick on *Gypsy* (1959). This piece, from the pens of *West Side Story*'s Laurents and Sondheim, was a *grande-dame* musical: one of those usually brash and brassy shows that sport as their central character a lady of a certain age, often overdressed and/or overpainted and/or overtinselled and/or overloud – the kind of character that sometimes recalls the female impersonators of burlesque days. But in a *grande-dame* musical the rôle is for real. *Gypsy* was also a part of what became a trend around this time towards shows that came across more harshly than before – in story and/or music and/or playing. They were vigorous and slick, professional, effective and even well written, but they lacked the heart and the carefree fun of a piece like *The Music Man*. But there was no doubt that this kind of show had its fans, perhaps as many fans as the merrier kind of musical, and *Gypsy* was only one show of many to follow this particular path.

Its story didn't centre so much on the titular Gypsy – historical stripper Gypsy Rose Lee – but rather on her grotesquely ambitious stage mother, a self-centred harridan who shoved her children into performing in a quest for some vicarious stardust. Baby June became actress June Havoc, quiet Louise accidentally turned into a popular peeler. The rôle of mother Rose was tailored to the measure of end-of-career Ethel Merman, the Annie who once got her gun and the Ambassadress who demanded she be called Madam. She whacked out the eternally optimistic "Everything's Coming up Roses", and the climax of her performance was an extended item called "Rose's Turn", in which all the adulation-starved woman's ambitions were poured crazily over the stage in a top-of-the-bill

eleven-o'clock number that brought the show to its star-celebrating peak.

Gypsy had a fair run of 702 nights, and was filmed with very limited success, without provoking much attention anywhere else. But the show came back. A 1973 London production launched a Broadway revival, an Australian production and further repeats, and *Gypsy* started to win some very fervent fans, especially amongst those with a fondness for the *grande-dame* kind of musical and the "Rose's Turn" kind of performance. Not to mention star actresses of a certain age with an eye for a big, showy part. So *Gypsy* lives on in the 1990s with perhaps rather more vigour that might have been expected in the 1950s.

There were and are, of course, big, loud ladies' rôles to suit all tastes and all kinds of musicals. They didn't come much bigger and louder, for example, than the part of Princess Winnifred the Woebegone in the fairytale burlesque *Once Upon a Mattress*. But Princess Winnifred, as inaugurated by comedienne Carol Burnett in a voice that could strip the britches off a bricklayer, wasn't interested in chewing up her spangles in middle-aged-crisis agony, she was too busy being a brass-bottomed hoot. She was also part of a small-scale musical which had a small-scale life, even though it won representations in several countries and languages beyond America.

The late 1950s produced all kinds of fine shows, successful shows, and fine and successful shows in the shadow of the greats, but on the whole it was the bigger Broadway shows, rather than the *Once Upon a Mattress*-sized pieces, that went forth to dominate the musical stages of the English-speaking world. As a result of this domination, writers in Britain found the only outlet available for their work was in smaller venues, and the bulk of what was best in the British musical of these years was nurtured in club, regional and suburban theatres.

London's club theatres were what would now be called "fringe" venues and the pieces that were produced there were scaled to size. Amongst the most popular such houses were the New Lindsay, the Watergate and the one that still exists today, the Players'. It was from the Players' Theatre that came forth the most widely and lastingly successful British musical of the era.

The Boy Friend

Before it became small, The Boy Friend *was very small. It started out as one of the three "halves" of a Players' Theatre programme – a one-act musical comedy fondly remembering the shows of* No, No, Nanette *days. But its success soon led to its growing to fuller proportions and taking a place as the main attraction on the bill at its little theatre.*

The scene is the Côte d'Azur, France, and the finishing school run by Mme Dubonnet. Pretty pupil Polly Browne is without a partner for the carnival ball. Why? Because she is so rich that any budding beau has always been seen as just another fortune hunter. But then she meets Tony. He's nothing but a messenger boy, he thinks she's a secretary, and soon they are planning a blissful, penny-pinched future together. Alas, Tony vanishes before the carnival fairylights are even lit, and it seems that Polly's dream of love has flown. But no! With the finale looming, he comes back and the truth tumbles out. Tony is no messenger, but a real live British lordling. Polly Browne will have her blissful future after all, even though she'll have to whistle for the penny-pinching.

Wilson's songs caught the flavour of the period delightfully. The pupils of Mme Dubonnet's school cooed flapperishly over that *sine qua non* "The Boy Friend", Polly and Tony dreamed of romance in "A Room in Bloomsbury" and promised each other "I Could Be Happy with You", and madcap Maisie squeaked out her belief in "Safety in Numbers" where men are concerned and dance-duoed with her Bobby to "Won't You Charleston With Me?". The adults, too, were blessed with fine and funny numbers: Madame Dubonnet wooing her old admirer – Polly's papa – with "Fancy Forgetting" and the pouting "You Don't Want to Play With Me Blues", and Tony's father – a lascivious Lord off-the-leash – baiting a soubrette with the assertion that "It's Never too Late to Fall in Love".

The Boy Friend progressed by stages to Wyndham's Theatre in the West End, and there it settled down for a run of no fewer than 2,084 performances, establishing itself as one of Britain's longest-ever running musicals. Thereafter, it kept up an almost permanent presence in the British provinces and colonies for many, many years, as well as being seen on Broadway (the only British musical at the height of the Broadway boom) and in a number of productions throughout Europe. It has returned twice to the West End of London as well as fêting its fortieth anniversary in a revival back at the Players', but wherever *The Boy Friend* has gone it has always scored its greatest successes when played as it was written – as a fondly written "new 1920s musical", rather than as a campy parody.

CREDITS

The Boy Friend

Musical comedy in 2 acts (originally 1 act) by Sandy Wilson

Produced at the Players' Theatre, London, 14 April 1953, and Wyndham's Theatre, London, 14 January 1954
USA: Royale Theater, New York, 30 September 1954
Germany: Nordmark Landestheater, Schleswig, 29 January 1960
France: Théâtre Antoine, Paris, 18 September 1965

CAST

Polly Browne	Anne Rogers
Tony	Anthony Hayes
Maisie	Denise Hirst
Dulcie	Maria Charles
Bobby	Larry Drew
Lord Brockhurst	John Rutland
Madame Dubonnet	Totti Truman Taylor
Percival Browne	Fred Stone

Whilst *The Boy Friend* was teasing the London long-run record, another little show was actually on its way to breaking it. *Salad Days* came out of the regional "repertory" theatre system. This wasn't really a repertory system at all, just a system where a theatre employed a more or less permanent company through a season of plays. And they didn't really do musicals. Not until *Salad Days*, anyway. *Salad Days* was produced at the Bristol Old Vic as a sort of end-of-season jaunt, in the same way that the serious theatres of Paris used to follow their seasons of classic plays by playing a topical revue at Christmas. The show was put together by two company members, Julian Slade and Dorothy Reynolds, in a revusical way that allowed all the actors to have a jolly time and to show off any special talents they might have. Its story was really less important than its scenes.

But a story there was: a little tale about what happens to Tim and Jane when they've finished at Bristol Uni, and have to go out into real life. What happens is that, whilst he's looking for a job for himself and her mother is looking for a husband for her, they meet this tramp in a park, and the tramp has a magical piano that makes people dance. Things get more improbable from there on (a flying saucer arrives later) but at the end Tim has a job and Jane a husband: Tim.

The songs of *Salad Days* were written to the pretty narrow measure of the company's voices, with only Jane – who pulled the best sing-y numbers as she assured us she was having "The Time of my Life" or mulled over her marriage prospects in "I Sit in the Sun" – being required to sing above the stave. But pieces such as "We're Looking for a Piano", "Find Yourself Something to Do", "We Don't Understand our Children" and the nightclubby tale of "Cleopatra" all proved merry musical moments in the show's revusical style.

At the end of its short, predestined Old Vic run, *Salad Days* moved from Bristol to

Salad Days

Eleven actors (but many more characters) and a piano that makes people dance, act out Dorothy Reynolds' and Julian Slade's Bristolian entertainment.

London's Vaudeville Theatre. It proved a perfect alternative to what *The Times* called "the hard-hitting, hard-boiled American musical" that was dominating the main musical houses of the West End, and it stayed there for a record 2,283 performances before heading back to the provinces. Over the years that followed, the show must have been played at least once at almost every British regional house – and even some further afield – and Slade and Miss Reynolds were launched on a series of like-tasting shows (*Free as Air*, *Hooray for Daisy*, *Follow that Girl*, *Wildest Dreams*) over the next half-dozen years.

Needless to say, after the hits made by *The Boy Friend* and *Salad Days*, club and regional theatres produced plenty more new musicals. A film-festival spoof called *Grab Me a Gondola* came to town from Windsor, the New Lindsay Theatre Club turned out a delicious parody of the 1910s musical stage called *Chrysanthemum*, and the Stratford East Theatre Royal mounted a fine musical play called *Make Me an Offer* set in the street markets of London, but the small handful of most interesting local musicals on the West End stage in the last years of the 1950s were shows that had been custom-built for town.

In the late 1950s there was a brief fashion amongst British writers for the "realistic" musical. Soho usually came into it somewhere, as being representative of ever-so-adult London lowish-life. Of course the bulk of these pieces were about as realistic as a red rabbit – even embarrassing in their attempts to be "adult". But amongst them there was one really superb musical play. It was called *Expresso Bongo* (1958), it was written by novelist Wolf Mankowitz and by Julian More of *Grab Me a Gondola*, and it was loosely based on the story of a young singer then on the up and up, Britain's first rock star, Tommy Steele. The play was taut and tough, as were its songs – by More, David Heneker and Monty Norman – spot-on parodies of current trends in pop music playing alongside classy character numbers such as an ageing actress's worries about the ravages of "Time" or her revusical shopping spree "We Bought It".

Lock Up Your Daughters (1959) was as "antique" as *Expresso Bongo* was of-the-moment. It was a musical version of an eighteenth-century piece by Henry Fielding of

Tom Jones fame, and it was the initial production at the new Mermaid Theatre. The old tale of lechery in high and low places was given a rousing set of songs, with lyrics by a young man named Lionel Bart ("When Does the Ravishing Begin?", "I'll Be There", "On a Sunny Sunday Morning"), and the show proved to be roisteringly bawdy fun, as near the knuckle as it might be in those days when the stage was still subject to the censor – which did its prospects no harm at all. *Lock Up Your Daughters* had a fine success in Britain, was found too rude for America, and didn't go anywhere else, but it provoked a rash of attempts at musicals with "bawdy" Restoration books in years to follow. Not one succeeded.

Sandy Wilson's *Valmouth* (1958) wasn't like either *Expresso Bongo* or *Lock Up Your Daughters*. In fact, it wasn't like anything else the British musical stage had ever seen or ever would see again. It also wasn't a commercial success, for this musical redaction of the work of the esoteric novella-ist Ronald Firbank was caviar of the most rarefied kind – caviar which provoked both outrage and hurrahs when the show first appeared. Wilson somehow brought a cavalcade of Firbank's most greenly glorious characters – his nymphomaniacal centenarians, his mysterious massaging negress, his appalling clerics and his ambisextrous sailor boys – onto the stage in a svelte and startling story, with songs ranging from the high comic ("Only a Passing Phase", "Just Once More") to the almost genuinely affecting ("When All the Girls Were Pretty"), and the results were amazing. But not commercial. Fans of *Valmouth* talked of it for years after, to the annoyance of younger (and often disbelieving) folk who had not had the chance to see it. But a superior 1982 revival at the Chichester Festival showed that the oldies hadn't lied, and a new generation of caviar-eaters was armed with the wherewithal to persecute their youngers: the story of this show that wasn't commercial, but was superb.

Every now and then, a show pops up from an utterly unlikely source and becomes a one-off hit. In the 1950s, such a show came out of a secondary theatre in Paris. *Irma la Douce* was a curious, argot-filled, half-fantastical musical by Paris journalist Alexandre Breffort and Edith Piaf's preferred songwriter, Marguerite Monnot. Its story told how a law student falls for a tart, becomes her lover, then jealously disguises himself and books her working hours for himself alone. Its not an arrangement that works very well financially, and it's also a bit exhausting, so he finally decides to bop off the "customer" – and finds himself sent to Devil's Island for murder! Fantasy allows him to paddle home across the seas for Christmas and the birth of Irma's twins – one per father. The songs of *Irma la Douce* included several that still get sung – in French or English – today: "Avec les anges" ("Our Language of Love"), "Dis-donc", "Y'a que Paris pour ça". An important part of the charm of the original show was the cheeky argot, or slang, in which it was written – a translator's nightmare. But the English adaptation done by the songwriters of *Expresso Bongo* – Heneker, More and Norman – hit the tone to a nicety, and *Irma la Douce* went on to triumph in the West End, on Broadway, and round the world, a little French show afloat, all alone, amidst the dreadnoughts of Broadway and the busy little wherries of Britain.

Above: **Lionel Bart** One of the brightest songwriting stars of the British fifties musical theatre.

Below: *Lock Up Your Daughters* Simultaneous 18th-century sex – Hy Hazell and Frederick Jaeger on top, Richard Wordsworth and Stephanie Voss underneath.

'The Simple Joys of Maidenhood . . .'

Camelot: Guenevere (Julie Andrews) isn't really going to miss them now she's discovered that maidenhood ends with Arthur (Richard Burton).

American Dream

The 1960s dawned fine and sunny on Broadway. The God of musical comedy was in his Manhattan heaven – probably taking his ease somewhere up on the top of the tallest building in Times Square and surveying all that he lorded over – and all was right with the world. World? There was no other musical-comedy world but right here.

In the decade and a bit since the end of the war, every musical staged on Broadway bar one had been of home manufacture, and a whole list of those home-made shows had been exported north, south and east to fill English-language theatres around the world. Small wonder that 1960s theatregoers started to believe that writing musicals was something only Americans really did. Small wonder that when a couple of American musicians went down in print referring to the musical as "this specifically American art form" half the world actually fell for it. Broadway did, quite simply, dominate the musical stages of the world.

The early 1960s produced a handful of blockbuster shows fit to challenge even the works of the famous 1950s. This was the time of *Fiddler on the Roof*, of *Hello, Dolly!*, of *How to Succeed in Business Without Really Trying*, *Camelot*, *A Funny Thing Happened on the Way to the Forum*, *Bye Bye Birdie*, *Little Me* and *Funny Girl*. For all those memorable and well-remembered shows made their début on Broadway between 1960 and 1964.

Oscar Hammerstein II died in 1960, and the only contribution that Richard Rodgers made to the musical stage in the years that immediately followed was a trendy bit of American-in-Parissery called *No Strings*. But if Rodgers and Hammerstein were absent from the roll-call of hits, Lerner and Loewe certainly were not. In 1960 they turned out the gorgeous *Camelot*, a merry and occasionally moving musical comedy version of the Arthurian legend which – like the novel from which it was drawn – never allowed its serious historico-mythological background to get in the way of the fun. Richard Burton played a boyish Arthur, puzzling over how best to be king, Julie Andrews was a pouting Guenevere, the physical production was spectacular in the

Above: **Fritz Loewe**
Four outstanding stage musicals
and then … nothing. Loewe quite
simply retired from Broadway.

Right: *A Funny Thing Happened
on the Way to the Forum*
The conniving Pseudolus (Zero
Mostel) up to his Ancient Roman
antics with the maiden-merchant
Marcus Lycus (John Carradine).

extreme, and a list of songs such as "I Loved You Once in Silence", "If Ever I Would Leave You", "Take Me to the Fair", "How to Handle a Woman" and "Camelot" ensured that the successor to *My Fair Lady* on Broadway and in Britain would be a triumph.

Frank Loesser had his first misfire in 1960 with the oddly unimpressive *Greenwillow*, but he was back the very next year, sparking on all cylinders, riding high with his *Guys and Dolls* librettist Abe Burrows and a couple of pals on another major hit. This time it was a red-blooded contemporary musical comedy. *How to Succeed in Business Without Really Trying* is the title of the book that window-cleaner Ponty Finch uses as his bible as he climbs faster than sound from the depths of

the mailroom to the very top of the corporate tree, blithely using other people's rumps as rungs on the ladder of success. The ins and outs of Big Business provided the cues for a number of funny songs on the way – the frantic importance of the "Coffee Break", the oft-battered maxim that "A Secretary is not a Toy", "The Company Way" – alongside Ponty's hymn to himself ("I Believe in You"), his beloved's admission that she'd be "Happy to Keep his Dinner Warm" as he strides onwards to chairmanship, and the winning pre-sexual-harassment-days song of mutual attraction in the office, "Been a Long Day".

How to Succeed lived up to its title. Not only did it triumph on Broadway and in the West End, but France got a lesson on *Comment réussir dans les affaires sans vraiment se fatiguer*, Austria and later Germany were instructed *Wie man was wird im Leben, ohne sich anzustrengen*, and Hollywood put out its version under the original all-in-one-breath title.

Comedy really received its due, and duly really came up trumps, in the early 1960s, but not all of that comedy was as contemporary-coloured as *How to Succeed*. When Stephen Sondheim, who had written the lyrics for *West Side Story* and *Gypsy*, supplied his first Broadway score as a composer, it was as an accompaniment to one of the cleverest and funniest libretti to have been seen around in years – but one that was far from modern. *A Funny Thing Happened on the Way to the Forum* was Larry Gelbart and Burt Shevelove's reduction into one hilarious piece of farcical musical theatre of all those Plautus and Terence plays that once made up an obligatory part of one's Classical education. As in those Ancient Roman plays, the central character was the wily servant, the subject matter was love (or sex, anyhow) and money, and there were seemingly insoluble situations galore in a plot which followed slave Pseudolus's attempt to earn his freedom by satisfying the wants of his burstingly pubescent master. The burstingly pubescent master and his lecherous old pater both have their eyes on the same virgin, but she's already been sold to a very baritonic captain . . . well, life isn't ever easy for a slave who needs to please everyone at once. The brilliance of the book didn't blind out the songs, and such pieces as the opening declaration that it's "Comedy Tonight", the dirty old "Everybody Ought to Have a Maid", the heroine's admission that she has no talent except "Lovely" and a memorably funny sub-operatic bit ("Bring Me my Bride"/Funeral Sequence) for the frustrated captain all added to the fun. Like *How to Succeed, Funny Thing* took its fun to further fields, and after scoring resoundingly in New York and London it went on to be *Sur le chemin du forum, Ein verrückter Tag auf dem Forum* and a rather song-denuded film.

There was fun of a different, and again more up-to-date kind to be found in another show that introduced a new band of names to Broadway with a bang. Michael Stewart wrote the book for Broadway's first musical to touch on the craze for rock 'n' roll music – even though it didn't use that music for its score. *Bye Bye Birdie* had a story that was set in the rock music business world, but Lee Adams and Charles Strouse's songs were pure traditional musical comedy. The leading man of *Bye Bye Birdie* is actually an agent, the agent for the Birdie of the title. The Elvis-Presleyish Birdie is actually a he, his first name is Conrad, and he's got a problem. Or, rather, his agent's got a problem. Just as he's about to start repaying all the money that's been lavished in building him up to stardom by making some really big bucks for everyone around him, Conrad's gone and got drafted. Bye bye. A publicity junket is arranged whereby Conrad will kiss goodbye to young America in the person of one teenage fan, but that big event – broadcast countrywide on TV – goes horribly wrong. So there was plenty of crazy action going on in among such songs as "Put on a Happy Face", "A Lot of Livin' to Do" and "Kids".

Adams and Strouse had to wait a decade to find once more the success of *Bye Bye Birdie*, but Michael Stewart launched pell-mell into a career as one of Broadway's top bookwriters. In 1961 he followed up *Birdie* with a winning adaptation of the screenplay *Lili* as the libretto to the musical *Carnival*. This time the songs were written by Bob Merrill, the writer of more 1950s novelty pop-hits (from "How Much is that Doggie in the Window?" to "If I Knew You Were Comin' I'd've Baked a Cake") than you'd think possible. He didn't put pop-chart novelties into *Carnival*. Instead, he caught the simple charm of the story of an orphan girl and the crippled circus puppeteer who loves her delightfully in such pieces as "Love Makes the World Go Round" and "Yes, my Heart!".

Carnival was a success only in America, but Stewart's next show turned out to be a record-breaker, a show that travelled from one end of the earth to the other.

How to Succeed in Business Without Really Trying
Co-workers like these can be the downfall of a man with his mind on a higher position. Billy de Wolfe is the executive with a yen to harass simply glinting off his spectacles.

Hello, Dolly!

Hello, Dolly! *was a musical version of the Thornton Wilder play* The Matchmaker, *which was a descendant of a famous Viennese comedy* Einen Jux will er sich machen *which had itself originally been taken from an elderly English play. Thornton Wilder's version made Mrs Dolly Levi, the matchmaker, the central character of what had previously been principally a story about a couple of small-town lads out for a day in the big town, and the musical compounded what he'd done in spades.* Hello, Dolly! *was a pretty grande-ish dame musical.*

Matchmaker Dolly Levi has decided that widowhood has palled and that her next client will be herself. Her target is Yonkers merchant Horace Vandergelder. In the course of a day that Horace spends in New York to look over the ladies on Dolly's books (and march in a parade), the conniving lady manages to put him off everyone else, get herself treated to a flash supper, and by the time they get back to Yonkers the protesting Horace has been tamed into a proposal. Also out on the town that same day are Vandergelder's clerks, Cornelius and Barnaby. They spend half their day avoiding their boss, who turns up everywhere they go, but they go home with a pretty pair of New York conquests on their arms and the prospect of less of a dogsbody life. All thanks of course to the ubiquitously interfering Mrs Levi-Vandergelder.

Songwriter Jerry Herman, who had not long since scored his first Broadway success

with an enjoyable musical about middle-aged love in warm places (novelly, the warm place was Israel) called *Milk and Honey*, wrote the numbers of *Hello, Dolly!* and he came up with a whole row of soon-to-be-standards. The biggest success of all was the title-song which – with a little help from an idiosyncratic recording by Louis Armstrong – became one of the most popular show songs of the era. "Hello, Dolly!" happened when Dolly arrived for her flash supper at a restaurant where she'd been a regular during her first marriage. As she came regally down a staircase that Cinderella might have envied, Dolly was greeted in roaring chorus and whirling dance by the entire staff of the establishment, all flinging themselves into a routine that gave a new meaning to the words Production Number.

Elsewhere the star strummed out a bewildering march in praise of "Motherhood, America and a hot lunch for orphans", got

Background: **Dolly is still Dol-lee in French. Or even Belgian. And no Horace Vandergelder on earth could resist Belgium's Annie Cordy.**

CREDITS

Hello, Dolly!

Musical in 2 acts by Michael Stewart, based on Thornton Wilder's play *The Matchmaker*

MUSIC AND LYRICS

by Jerry Herman

Produced at the St James Theater, New York, 16 January 1964

UK: Theatre Royal, Drury Lane, London, 2 December 1965

Germany: Schauspielhaus, Düsseldorf, 26 November 1966

Hungary: Fövárosi Operettszinház, Budapest, 23 February 1968

Austria: Theater an der Wien, Vienna, 10 September 1968

France: Théâtre Mogador, Paris, 29 September 1972

CAST

Mrs Dolly Levi	Carol Channing
Horace Vandergelder	David Burns
Cornelius	Charles Nelson Reilly
Barnaby	Jerry Dodge
Irene Molloy	Eileen Brennan
Minnie Fay	Sondra Lee

*grande-dame*ish as she whacked out her determination to make the most of life "Before the Parade Passes By", and toyed with a "Goodbye, Dearie" that meant just the opposite as she turned the marital thumbscrews on the resisting Horace. The lads had a lively "Put on your Sunday Clothes" and joined their girls to sing of what they imagine is "Elegance", whilst the ballad of the night went to Cornelius's pretty Irish Irene with her anticipatory "Ribbons Down my Back".

Broadway's *Hello, Dolly!* was a raging success, and before Dolly – who was played during the run by a bevy of stars, from Carol Channing, Ginger Rogers and Martha Raye to Betty Grable, Pearl Bailey, Ethel Merman and Phyllis Diller – said goodbye to the St James Theater she'd knocked *My Fair Lady* off its top spot with the longest run of any Broadway musical: 2,844 performances.

But *Hello, Dolly!* didn't follow that first famous run with the same kind of worldwide success that Lerner and Loewe's show had had. London only took to the piece – after a very sticky start – when favourite comedienne Dora Bryan was brought in to play Dolly; a Parisian production featuring perhaps the most delightful Dolly of them all, Annie Cordy, did only fairly; and although the show fared well enough in its German-language productions, return engagements in the main centres were greeted only with short runs. Even a film version, with Barbra Streisand starred as a younger and more likely Dolly than is sometimes the case (the rôle sometimes seems to encourage rather distasteful granny-casting), didn't really take off. But *Hello, Dolly!* remains a perennial and perennially produced favourite, and doubtless sometime and somewhere the flaming success of that first, great production will come its way again.

Fiddler on the Roof

Hello, Dolly! *didn't keep its Broadway long-run record for very long. Eight months after the première of Stewart and Herman's show,* Fiddler on the Roof *opened, and by the time its Broadway billboards came down, it had turned out to be an even longer-running hit.* Fiddler on the Roof *was a very different kind of musical to the brashly and brilliantly comical* Hello, Dolly!. *There was plenty of humour in the newer show, particularly in the character of its leading man, the wryly human Russian-Jewish milkman Tevye, but it was humour of wholly another kind.*

Background: **Tevye and his daughters have even made their way into the world's opera houses in recent years. Max Gillies, Georgina Ciot and Rochelle Whyte in Australian Opera's production.**

The characteristic that came over most strongly in both the libretto and the songs of *Fiddler on the Roof* was truthfulness. The writers succeeded in making the audience really feel for the people acting out their little truer-than-life story up there on the stage. And you can't feel for people who aren't true and real. You can't actually feel for gimme-a-greenbacked-future Dolly Levi, much as you may roar with laughter at her bossy antics, but it is very difficult to resist getting your sentiments into gear in the face of a jolly little milkman who, after 25 years of an arranged marriage, suddenly needs to have his wife tell him "I love you".

Tevye, Golde and their daughters live their lives in the small Russian village of Anatevka in the traditional way that the Jewish folk of the area have always lived – until the younger generation starts to buck at those traditions. One beloved daughter refuses the arranged marriage her father has promised and insists on marrying for love, a second runs off with a dogma-spouting "student", a third goes furthest of all and weds outside the religion. And whilst every law and belief that Tevye has lived by is being torn asunder at home, the world outside is changing too. Soon he and what is left of his family are chased from Anatevka by the pogroms. They will go to America, taking their tattered traditions with them, and try again there to live their lives as God has commanded them.

The songs of *Fiddler on the Roof* were written by Sheldon Harnick and Jerry Bock, a team who had previously had a Broadway success with a bright but conventional singing-politician musical called *Fiorello!* Their numbers for *Fiddler on the Roof* came from a wholly different register – a rich mixture of the warmly sentimental and the warmly funny. Tevye put God on the spot, asking shyly for a little relief from the troubles of everyday in "If I Were a Rich Man", Motel the tailor burst out with incredible happiness in "Miracle of Miracles", daughter Hodel went into self-imposed exile with her man "Far from the Home I Love", and the older folk looked back through the "Sunrise, Sunset" of the years, whilst in merrier moments the girls warded off the uncontrollable "Matchmaker, Matchmaker" and the folk of Anatevka joined in such lively ensembles as "To Life" and "Tradition".

The songs and music included a sufficient, characterful tinge of Jewishness without that tinge ever becoming intrusive, and neither the staging nor the dances of the piece ever left the little world of Anatevka to go "out-front" in old-fashioned musical-theatre style. The featured dance routine in a show about a time and place where women were not permitted to dance was a memorable re-creation of the all-male Bottle Dance.

Fiddler on the Roof's 3,242 Broadway performances were the preface to a fine career further afield. London took to the show with all the unbridled enthusiasm it hadn't evinced for the previous "record-holder" and welcomed it in the West End for 2,030 performances, *Anatevka* was a full-scale hit in Germany and Austria, *Un violon sur le toit* visited Paris and *Hegedüs a háztetön* made itself a place in the enduring repertoire in Hungary. Sydney, Helsinki, Tokyo, Amsterdam and many other cities also gave an enthusiastic welcome welcome to versions of *Fiddler on the Roof* as it made its way round the world, establishing itself on the way, through a whole series of revivals on the commercial stage and even productions (thankfully ungimmicky ones, so far) in opera houses, as one of the greatest and most frequently played musicals of all time.

CREDITS

Fiddler on the Roof

Musical in 2 acts by Joseph Stein, based on the stories of Sholom Aleichem

LYRICS
by Sheldon Harnick

MUSIC
by Jerry Bock

Produced at the Imperial Theater, New York, 22 September 1964

UK: Her Majesty's Theatre, London, 16 February 1967

Germany: Operettenhaus, Hamburg, 1 February 1968

Austria: Theater an der Wien, Vienna, 15 February 1969

France: Théâtre Marigny, Paris, 1972

Hungary: Fövárosi Operettszinház, Budapest, 9 February 1973

CAST

Tevye	Zero Mostel
Golde	Maria Karnilova
Tzeitel	Joanna Merlin
Motel	Austin Pendelton
Hodel	Julia Migenes
Lazar Wolf	Michael Granger
Yente	Beatrice Arthur
Perchik	Bert Convy

When God and your wife both seem to be having a go at you, what's a man to do? Maria Karnilova (Golde) and Zero Mostel (Tevye).

The 1960s brought to the Broadway stage for the first time a songwriter who – without ever provoking any wild fashions or fan-clubs – was, in the decades that followed, to forge himself perhaps the most important place on the musical stage of any of his compatriots. Cy Coleman has composed the songs for nine musicals since 1960, those shows have brought to the fore even more hit songs, and – in a reversal of the usual procedure which sees a writer putting out his most praised work near the beginning of his career – he has picked up Broadway "Best Musical" awards for his two most recent shows.

Coleman made his Broadway bow with *Wildcat*, a work built round the talents of TV-star Lucille Ball. She played a tough little lady on the trail of an oil well (and a man), and Coleman and lyricist Carolyn Leigh gave her a top-notch hit number to sing: "Hey! Look Me Over". It was a pretty good hit to be starting your stage career with. But Coleman and Miss Leigh then came up with a very different piece that put in evidence talents of a kind that hadn't got a showing in the straightforward *Wildcat*: a special sense of

songwriting humour that would serve Coleman enormously effectively over the years and shows to come.

Once upon a time, Patrick Dennis, the author of *Auntie Mame*, invented another amazing lady. She was called Belle Poitrine and she told her story in an hilarious book of memoirs called *Little Me*. ` Playwright Neil Simon turned *Little Me* into an equally hilarious stage piece, and the *Wildcat* pair supplied the numbers ("Real, Live Girl", "The Other Side of the Tracks") that made it a musical. *Little Me* didn't turn out one of Broadway's longest-running musicals, but it was certainly one of its funniest, and it had a fine career – particularly in Britain.

There's many a show that's made a star, but equally there's been many a star that's made a show. Sometimes it even works both ways at once – as in *Funny Girl*. Barbra Streisand was 21 years old when she created the part of Fanny Brice in Isobel Lennart's fictionalized story of the life and love of the favourite musical-comedienne of yesteryear. She played it on Broadway and briefly in London, and then filmed it for posterity. For which posterity

Funny Girl

Barbra Streisand made a memorable Fanny Brice in the biomusical based on the comedienne's life.

should be duly grateful, because rôle and star don't often come together in such a choice fashion. The star hoisted a couple of Bob Merrill and Jule Styne's taut-heartstringed songs to popularity ("People", "Don't Rain on my Parade"), but there were plenty of other less out-front numbers that supported these breastbusters ("If a Girl Isn't Pretty", "You Are Woman", "Who Taught Her Everything She Knows?") in a score that more than did its part towards the success of the show.

Keeping it up

The second part of the Broadway 1960s didn't bring out any *My Fair Lady* or *Fiddler on the Roof*, but three or four solid new international winners arrived to add themselves to the impressive parade of post-war American-bred hits. At the head of this little list was the latest piece from the man who had signalled his coming with *Wildcat* and *Little Me*. On this occasion, Cy Coleman allied himself with one of the few remaining members of that post-war "royal family" who was still active, lyricist Dorothy Fields, and together they provided the songs to Neil Simon's touchingly comical adaptation of an Italian screenplay as *Sweet Charity* (1966). The part of Charity, an accident-prone, not very good-time girl on the eternal lookout for true love, was created by Gwen Verdon, the Lola of *Damn Yankees* and probably the greatest singing-dancing-actress of her Broadway era. She delivered "Where Am I Going?", "I'm a Brass Band" and "If my Friends Could See Me Now" on her way to Charity's husbandless final curtain, but the real hits of the night went to supporting characters – a group of dance-hall girls encouraging a "Big Spender" to spend on them, and a schlock-religion messiah spouting his creed in "The Rhythm of Life".

Two other "royal family" members were also involved in new musicals in the late 1960s, but neither of those shows got anywhere near *Sweet Charity* in success. There's little doubt, though, that Richard Rodgers was unlucky. He allied himself with the best of the newer talent about – *West Side Story* writers Laurents and Sondheim – on a musical play called *Do I Hear a Waltz?*, which failed. Some of Rodgers and Sondheim's finest work went down with a show whose producers and director couldn't quite work out what it was they'd created.

Fritz Loewe went into retirement after *Camelot*, suffering from what he insisted was ill-health, but Alan Jay Lerner remained on the Broadway scene for another quarter of a century. During that time he wrote seven more musicals, but without ever again finding the success of his earlier shows. The 1965 "dream sequence" piece *On a Clear Day You Can See Forever* ("On a Clear Day", "Come Back to Me") did the best of the seven, but that best wasn't good enough.

Jerry Herman followed up his mega-hit, *Hello, Dolly!*, with rather more success than the Hammerstein-less Rodgers and the Loewe-less Lerner. After shooting a singing Dolly Levi to superstardom, he launched another *grande dame* of literature on a Broadway musical career: Patrick Dennis's Auntie Mame. *Mame* didn't dress herself in the same kind of tongue-in-cheeks garb that the *Little Me* of a few seasons back had done. She was rousingly madcap rather than sophisticatedly *bouffe*, and, given the long runs she totted up, it seems the public of the time preferred its over-the-moon ladies that way. *Mame* had an excellent career on Broadway and in Britain.

Herman then turned to another *grande dame* of fiction, *The Madwoman of Chaillot*, and produced what has claims to be his best score. But theatregoers preferred Dolly and Mame to the dottier and less out-front Aurélia, and *Dear World* was a failure.

The biggest hit of the later 1960s came from a team new to Broadway. Dale Wassermann (book), Joe Darion (lyrics) and Mitch Leigh (music) combined on the umpteenth musical version of the Don Quixote tale to have reached the stage over the centuries. It remains to be seen whether *Man of La Mancha* will last better than Massenet's operatic *Don Quixote*, but it has undoubtedly already had more performances than its illustrious ancestor. The 1965 *Man of La Mancha* sent Quixote out on his quest accompanied by a little Jewish Sancho Panza and equipped with a musical creed that would become almost a symbol of the 1960s and its sensibilities: "The Impossible Dream". A run of 2,328 Broadway performances hoisted the show into the top league before it went forth on a quest of its own – to all the major musical-theatre centres. It found, like Quixote, mixed fortunes on its

Background: **Hair!**
Fancy these nice, clean young people saying all those naughty words. Paul Jabara, Steve Garnet, Leata Galloway and Suzannah Norstrand flaunt their microphone cords.

Half a Sixpence
"Hold it! Flash, bang, wallop! What a picture!…" Tommy Steele (Artie) and Marti Webb (Ann) get wedding-photographed.

travels: London didn't take to it, but a French version with celebrated *chanteur* Jacques Brel starring did well, and a German adaptation did even better. Hollywood's Quixote – as portrayed by Peter O'Toole – had the best fortune of another kind, though – the "fair Dulcinea" that he encountered on his quest was none other than Sophia Loren.

1960s sensibilities were also rife in another long-running show of the period. *Hair* undoubtedly is a musical. Its creators called it "the American tribal love-rock musical". But this was the 1960s and it wasn't considered pathetic to say or write such things; it was even considered to be daring. And *Hair* did everything it could to be seen or thought daring: lots of naughty words; song titles such as "Hashish", "Sodomy", "Coloured Spade" and even "Manchester"; mockery of religion. And for those who weren't bothered by naughty words or what people said about God, there was a well-publicized flashlet of then unaccustomed nudity. It's history now that it all worked. *Hair* became a long-running hit, and its principal song "Aquarius" a sort of spooked-out anthem for the aimless of the age.

If there was one show that you'd have thought was guaranteed to die with the 1960s, it was *Hair*. But it is actually still around, touring middle-Europe's one-night stands for the nostalgic pleasure of the now middle-aged children of the era, and of those who've just caught up with the 1960s. Little glimpse of nudity and all. And, of course, in English. Well, who listened to the words anyhow?

Another show from the mid-1960s that is still with us today, though in altogether rather better health and venues, is *Cabaret*. But there couldn't have been too many folk about to bet that this show would survive thirty years as a favourite when it had its first round of productions from 1966 on. Joe Masteroff, John Kander and Fred Ebb's musical version of Christopher Isherwood's tales of pre-war Berlin did well. It ran for 1,166 performances on Broadway, 336 in London, 59 in Vienna and got cancelled in Sydney. By all normal laws, that could and should have been it. Only in 1972 a film version – quite considerably altered – was made. It starred Liza Minnelli as Sally Bowles, that brainless little lass from Chelsea, London, who is out to have a desperately decadent time in naughty 1930s Germany. Miss Minnelli and the film both scored triumphs, and in the wake of the triumph of *Cabaret* the movie, *Cabaret* the stage show was given a second life. And Sally Bowles, the rôle, became a vehicle for many a Minnelli "wannabe" – striving starlets who set out to copy the star's stinging singing, but rarely had the talent to reproduce her delicately tremulous acting performance. And so, *Cabaret* and Sally underwent a bit of a sea-change: nowadays when the show is staged Sally Bowles is more often than not portrayed as a nonsensically nightclubby vamp.

Writer Cliff Bradshaw meets striving club-singer Sally when he comes to lodge in the Berlin house of Fräulein Schneider, and she quickly moves in on him. But it soon becomes evident that Nazi-clouds are gathering: middle-aged Frln Schneider has to break off her last-hope engagement because her affianced is a Jew, Cliff discovers he has been fooled into couriering Nazi funds and is beaten up when he won't go on. Frln Schneider has no option but to stay in Berlin, but Cliff will leave. And Sally? With what she imagines is decadent flair, the sorry, self-deluded girl has the child she is carrying aborted and announces that she, of course, will stay in Berlin. She is far too extraordinary a person to be at home anywhere less extraordinary.

Kander and Ebb's songs included some that were the kind of performance material they would show themselves to be such dab hands at over the years, and some that related to the story itself, but it was the numbers performed at the Kit-Kat Club ("Don't Tell Mama", "Cabaret", "Willkommen", "Three Ladies", The Money Song, "If You Could See Her Through my Eyes") by Sally, the club's master of ceremonies and his Walkürian "girls" that proved to be the show's big winners.

Meanwhile, over in Britain . . .

The later 1950s had seen the British musical coming back out from the club and regional theatres that had produced its winners at the beginning of the decade, as producers once again found that there was plenty of profit to be made from home-grown shows. And so, during the 1960s a handful of fine new British musicals followed *Expresso Bongo*, *Lock up Your Daughters* and *Make Me an Offer* onto the London stage.

David Heneker, who had collaborated on *Expresso Bongo*, found himself in an unusual position when he was commissioned to write a musical as a vehicle for Tommy Steele – the very rock star on whose rise to fame the earlier show had been sort of based. As it eventuated, the show for the star was a very much greater hit than the show about the star, for *Half a Sixpence* (1963) not only turned out to be the most successful show with which the songwriter and the star would be involved (and each of them had more fine shows to come), but both the musical and its merry songs became favourites throughout the English-speaking world.

Steele played Kipps, H. G. Wells's shop-boy in the novel of that title, who inherits a fortune and finds that it brings him all sorts of oversized ambitions and unappetizing hangers-on and almost loses him the girl he loves. He loses the money, gets himself back into order and refuses a second fortune when it comes along. Heneker's songs included two pieces for the star that would become standards, his exchange of lovers' tokens with his Ann in "Half a Sixpence", and the crazy wedding-day photo "Flash, Bang, Wallop!".

There were two further London musicals from the early 1960s that made themselves a mark beyond Britain, and the two were wholly unalike in character. One is a piece that doesn't survive too well today because it is imbued with those so-very-datable 1960s attitudes which now seem so tamely quaint. *Stop the World – I Want to Get Off* (1961) was a kind of 1960s harlequinade written by pop-singer and actor Anthony Newley as a vehicle for himself. You followed Newley – with very occasional interruptions from other folk – from cradle to grave, via ambition, accomplishment, marriage, infidelity, fatherhood and disillusion and a set of songs including a couple of heartstring-savaging ballads that made a beeline for the hit parades ("Once in a Lifetime", "What Kind of Fool Am I?").

The other and better-wearing hit was *Oliver!* (1960), Lionel Bart's musical version of Dickens's *Oliver Twist*. Much of Dickens's tale was sugared up in the neatly filleted remaking of the famous novel as a musical: the vicious Fagin became a lovable, low-comic rogue, his band of thieves was transformed into a pack of dancing imps, and a bunch of starving orphans dreamed of food in sweet soprano unison. But there were other moments where Bart held back no punches at all, and the most effective of those were contained in the love story between East End Nancy, the tart who befriends the strayed Oliver, and her brutish man, Bill Sikes.

It was that part of the tale that brought forth the choice number of the score, a torch song such as the British musical stage hadn't heard in a very long time – "As Long as He Needs Me". But alongside that strong-feeling piece there were a whole heap of others that became well known and well loved, as *Oliver!* established itself as internationally the most successful British musical since *The Boy Friend*. Little Oliver sighed sadly "Where is Love?" and was inducted into Fagin's band by the Artful Dodger to the strains of "Consider Yourself (at Home)", Nancy whopped out the pub song "Oom-pah-pah" and her conviction that "It's a Fine Life", gross Mrs Corney simpered "I Shall Scream" as she cosied up to the local Beadle, and Fagin pattered out a set of character songs ("You've Got to Pick a Pocket or Two", "Be Back Soon", "Reviewing the Situation") that confirmed his chirpy character.

Background: *Oliver!* Nancy (Vivienne Martin) shares jolly, thieving, pot-ever-full poverty with Oliver (Colin Page) and the Artful Dodger (Michael Goodman).

Ron Moody (as Fagin in *Oliver!*, top left) and Topol (as Tevye in *Fiddler on the Roof*, left) repeated their stage performances on film. The celluloid version of *Camelot* (bottom left) featured Richard Harris and Vanessa Redgrave in roles new to them.

Above: **Ron Grainer**
Composer of the fiendish
soprano music that helped make
Robert and Elizabeth's heroine an
almost uncastable rôle.

Opposite: ***Robert and Elizabeth***
Browning (Keith Michell) and
Barrett (June Bronhill) lived out
their passionate love affair to the
light-opera score of its
generation.

Oliver! played for no fewer than 2,618 West End performances, and it has returned regularly to London ever since that first run. It also put up a score of 774 Broadway nights, at the time the longest run ever achieved by a British musical in New York, was made into a highly successful film, and eventually – a quarter of a century after its first showing – even made its way into Europe on the new wave of appreciation of English-language musicals – old and new – that arose in the 1980s.

Oliver! was the most widely successful British musical of the 1960s, but had it not been for a gentleman from New York with sufficient connection with the law to send out his scripts accompanied by letters written encouragingly on New York Supreme Court headed paper, *Robert and Elizabeth* might have given it a run for its money. *Robert and Elizabeth* was a musical remake of the play *The Barretts of Wimpole Street*. I say "a", because there had been another. It was called *The Third Kiss* and it was written by the New York gentleman in question. The gentleman got a British film company interested in his show, and they found a young stage producer to test its possibilities. He saw straight away that *The Third Kiss* was unproduceable and approached a playwright, who approached a director, who approached a composer, and by the time the show opened there wasn't a word or a note of the original left. But what there was instead was probably the best romantic musical to have come out of the British theatre in something like half a century.

Elizabeth Barrett has been an invalid since her brother's death, encouraged by her almost incestuously attached father to remain languishing in her room, believing that she was responsible for the boy's drowning. She has whiled away her unmoving days writing poetry and that poetry has caught the attention of Robert Browning. Suddenly he leaps into her life, full of vigour and fire, and a battle begins between Browning and Mr Barrett for the love and the life of the young woman. Browning encourages her to walk, Barrett destroys her confidence, dreading that he might lose her. But finally, with the support of Elizabeth's tyrannized brothers and sisters, the lovers escape to the sunshine of Italy: the long night in the life of Elizabeth Barrett is over.

The score to *Robert and Elizabeth* was composed by Australian Ron Grainer and the part of Elizabeth tailored to the voice of June Bronhill, the most remarkable English light opera soprano of her era. It was hard, long, strong and high, high, high: right up to top D in alt. But the high notes were not just high notes – they were there for dramatic effect, and pieces such as Elizabeth's Soliloquy, her longing for "The World Outside" and her passionate defence of the right of "Woman and Man" to love were remarkable numbers. Robert ("The Moon in my Pocket", the duet "I Know Now") and Barrett (two parlando pieces) also had solos, but the other musical gem of the night came in a gentle ensemble for the shuttered-in young Barretts, dreaming of "The Girls That Boys Dream About".

Robert and Elizabeth ran for nearly a thousand nights in London, but when Broadway time came it was banned. The gentleman of *The Third Kiss* used his legal position to prevent the show opening in New York. And so *Robert and Elizabeth* had to be content with showings in Australia and South Africa and in the British provinces, and what might have been remains a might have been.

Success in the West End was, of course, no guarantee of success in America. Another long-running London piece, *Canterbury Tales* (1968), found little more joy on the other side of the sea than its fellow bit of censor-days "bawdy", *Lock Up Your Daughters*, had done. But, then, the strains of the medievalish "I Have a Noble Cock" must have seemed pretty coy to the kind of sensations-seeker who had already been to see *Hair*.

In the same year of 1968, however, three weeks before *Canterbury Tales* opened its more than 2,000-performance run at the Phoenix Theatre, a much more important and far-reaching production of a new musical took place in London. It took place on the stage at Colet Court School, and it was the pupils' performance of a 15-minute cantata written by a couple of friends of the school's music-master. A quarter of a century later, a much expanded *Joseph and the Amazing Technicolor Dreamcoat* would be playing on the vast stage of the London Palladium, and Tim Rice and Andrew Lloyd Webber would be Sir Tim and Sir Andrew, and two of the most famous musical-theatre writers of the century.

'As if we never said Goodbye'

Sunset Boulevard
Patti LuPone was Norma
Desmond.

I Can't Stop Singing

During the something like a a quarter of a century that had passed since Annie Get Your Gun, Oklahoma! *and* Kiss Me, Kate *had gone into action as the advance guard of the invasion of the world's stages by the made-on-Broadway musical, the kind of musical play they represented had dominated the scene.*

But at the start of the 1970s, a breath of fresh air swept through the musical theatre – *Jesus Christ Superstar*. The lively, up-to-date colloquialism of its lines, the oh-so-accessible mixture of the classical and the youthfully modern that was its music, and even its form – the sung-through "rock opera" set-up that replaced the songs-and-scenes layout of the kind of musical play that had been standard since the war – the Prussian war – all combined to make up a show that was something new, something different and something definitely fresh.

There had already been all kinds of attempts – some of them well received – to break away from the classic musical play format. Pieces ranging from the Broadway opera type of nearly-musical – *Street Scene, The Consul* and their kind – to the virtually formless and textually trendy *Hair*, but *Jesus Christ Superstar*, unlike those experiments, didn't turn out to be a short-lived novelty or one-off affair. It was, indeed, a hit in its own right, but it was also just the beginning of what would be a series of hits for 26-year-old Tim Rice and 22-year-old Andrew Lloyd Webber, and for the style of writing that, very largely, they initiated.

Jesus Christ Superstar

Jesus Christ Superstar followed the last days of the life on earth of the son of God who was known to man as Jesus Christ. However, instead of telling the greatest story ever told in the traditional way, Rice gave one man's version of the famous "facts": the end of Christ's mortal days as seen through the eyes of his disciple Judas, the man who was responsible for giving his leader up to the Roman rulers of Jerusalem, and thus earned himself forever the image of the archetypal betrayer.

Inset: **Tim Rice and Andrew Lloyd Webber.** Two young men who would go on to be Sir Tim and Sir Andrew and two of the outstanding names in their era's musical theatre.

Background: **Jeff Fenholt** in the title-rôle of the show's original Broadway production.

Judas sees Jesus Christ's personality cult, and the hysteria it engenders, as endangering their whole crusade on behalf of Christianity, and that is why he sacrifices his leader to what he believes is the greater good. Only too late does he realize, suicidally, that he has undoubtedly been just a pawn in God's larger design.

The music of *Jesus Christ Superstar* was written-through. The whole show, from start to finish, was sung, without any dialogue intervening, just as the score of the much smaller *Joseph* had been. However, within that sung-through, cantata-style format there were passages that were equivalent to conversation and to songs, and several of the featured song-sections proved extractable and popular beyond the confines of the show, notably Mary Magdalene's plangent "I Don't Know How to Love Him" and the paean to the

"Superstar". The most impressive pieces of the score, however, didn't fit into a handy half-a-45rpm disc, and Jesus's monologue in the Gardens of "Gethsemane", the menacing basso profondo cum counter-tenor music given to the plotting priests and the tearing pop tenor phrases that accompanied Judas's night-long dilemma were the most important parts of a score that was both distinctly unusual and distinctly effective.

Superstar actually began its life as a recording, a double-disc album containing the full score of the show, but the remarkable sales achieved by that recording – particularly in America, where it several times topped the LP charts – soon led first to concert performances and then to a full-scale theatre staging. The first, Broadway mounting was an extravagantly gimmicky one: part-*Hair*, part-*Godspell*, part-kitchen sink. But by the time the show finally opened in London, it had been realized that this old-fashioned, 1960s-ish kind of production wasn't the way to go at all. London received a strong, sinewy and sincere staging of *Superstar*, and its reward was the longest run ever for a musical in the West End theatre (3,358 performances).

The show travelled the world with the kind of speed and ease that only the very most outstanding musicals do: Australia had its *Superstar* on show only six months after the Broadway opening, and Germany, France and Scandinavia all followed closely behind. Japan, Brazil, Mexico, Spain, Hungary – one by one other likely and less likely countries welcomed the show (though South Africa banned it as irreligious!) – and, two decades and more on, as big, new mountings circle countries from America to Australia, it maintains its popularity in repeat productions all round the globe.

Rice and Lloyd Weber's rock opera travelled the world. Left: A poster for a Japanese version of the show. Below: Daniel Balavoine as Christ in its Paris production.

CREDITS

Jesus Christ Superstar

Rock opera in 2 acts

LYRICS
by Tim Rice

MUSIC
by Andrew Lloyd Webber

Produced at the Mark Hellinger Theater, New York, 12 October 1971
Germany: Munsterhalle, Munster, 18 February 1972
France: Théâtre National du Palais de Chaillot, Paris, 1972
UK: Palace Theatre, London, 9 August 1972
Hungary: Open Air Theatre, Szeged, 25 June 1986

CAST

Jesus	Jeff Fenholt
Judas	Ben Vereen
Mary Magdelene	Yvonne Elliman
Pontius Pilate	Barry Dennen
Caiaphas	Bob Bingham
Annas	Phil Jethro
King Herod	Paul Ainsley

The appearance of the novel, sung-through *Jesus Christ Superstar* didn't, of course, mean that the songs-and-scenes musical became outdated overnight. Quite the contrary. If anything, it was – certainly for the present – to stay the norm, and definitely for anything that whiffed of the comical. And in the hands of men such as Cy Coleman (aged 41), Neil Simon (43), Arthur Laurents (52), Stephen Sondheim (40), Michael Stewart (41) and Jerry Herman (37) the musical with humour wasn't yet about to die of old age. However, in the early 1970s a number of the top talents of Broadway did rather mark time.

A Little Night Music
All kinds of things can happen during "A Weekend in the Country".

Pieces such as Stewart and Coleman's *See-Saw* and Stewart and Herman's *Mack and Mabel* turned out popular songs, but didn't turn into popular shows. But there was one man in that group who certainly didn't mark time: Stephen Sondheim. In the four years from 1970 to 1973 he wrote the songs – words and music – for no fewer than three new musicals, and the results moved him from an established place as one of Broadway's top lyricists to a perch on the very top of the musical-theatre heap.

The first two of his three shows, although they were indeed made up of scenes and songs, both moved away somewhat from the normal musical comedy format, for neither George Furth's text to *Company* nor James Goldman's libretto to *Follies* sported what might properly be called a plot. In each case, the audience was presented with a set of characters who had come together for a party, and having come together were then paraded revusically across the stage, each doing his often flashbacked bit in sketch and/or song, until the parade was rounded off and everyone went home – with little, if anything, actually having happened. This kind of layout gave Sondheim the opportunity for plenty of stand-up and stand-out songs, and numbers such as "Getting Married Today", "Another Hundred People", "Barcelona", "You Could Drive a Person Crazy", "The Ladies Who Lunch", "The Little Things You Do Together", "Losing my Mind" and that mega-*grande-dame* number, "I'm Still Here", all found themselves places in the already bulging Sondheim songbook.

It was the third Sondheim musical of this period, however, that brought its writer to his peak as a composer. *A Little Night Music* was a dazzling piece of musical theatre with all the shape that the earlier two shows hadn't bothered about. Its libretto was Hugh Wheeler's adaptation of the Ingmar Bergman screenplay *Smiles of a Summer Night*, and it told the story of two middle-ageing folk – a provincial lawyer and a touring actress – both trying unsuccessfully to prolong their youth in relationships with much younger partners. If that sounds a bit like a pre-war operetta plot – the rich old Marquis and the young countess he's about to wed until true young love comes along and he has to drop out – it couldn't have been less so. Wheeler told his story, in which the older pair were the evening's most sympathetic characters, in a dry, warm, sophisticated manner which was carried over into a stunning and witty score, highlighted by such pieces as the ensemble "A Weekend in the Country", the three-part scena "Soon"/"Now"/"Later", and the show's surprise hit "Send in the Clowns", and the sum total was a show of very special delights that duly delighted wherever it went.

The early 1970s produced several shows from writers who weren't, or didn't become, a regular part of the musical-theatre scene, and one of those turned out to be the longest-running hit of its era. *Grease* was the latest example of what might be called the college musical, a piece in line of descent from shows such as the 1920s *Good News* with its merry tale of the growing generation, its pains and its preoccupations. But this college musical was a tongue-in-cheek one, a loving burlesque of the 1950s years of ponytails, ducks'-arses, Vaseline tonic, hoop-earrings, chewing gum and what's good for acne. As early as the 1970s, when the show first came out, the 1950s were already the good old days. In the 1990s, when *Grease*, having broken American records in both the theatre and then in the cinema, not only returned to the scene of its triumph on Broadway for a second bite but also, finally, became a hit in London, "good" just isn't a strong enough adjective. Groovy. Whatever the adjective, the schooldays love story of Danny and Sandy, accompanied by Warren Casey and Jim Jacobs's endearing set of pastiche songs – the teenage disaster number "It's Raining on Prom Night", the good advice crooned to a "Beauty School Dropout", the defensive "There Are Worse Things I Could Do" – has become a classic of the musical theatre stage.

Another one-off hit of these years was *The Wiz*, a whooped up version of *The Wizard of Oz* with lively new songs by Charlie Small and an all-Black cast. Very politically incorrect. But racism, like many such other modern-isms, hadn't become fashionable in the 1970s, and *The Wiz* gave lots of people a lot of high-octane fun through a splendid Broadway run. It also cornered rather more attention than another musical with a largely black cast which actually had much more substantial qualities. *Purlie* was a joyously funny play-turned-musical with a score by songwriters Gary Geld and Peter Udell of "Sealed with a Kiss" and "Ginny Come Lately" fame. *Purlie*, of course, didn't sound like those. Its music was, in turn, an exciting and wryly humorous accompaniment to the story of a preacher called Purlie Victorious, who is out to hornswoggle some cash he is sort of owed out of the double-hornswoggling old Cap'n Cotchipee. He wants the money to rebuild Big Bethel Chapel and start preaching there, so that makes all his cheating OK. What was even more than OK was the music, from the ingenue's soaring "I Got Love" to the thrilling massed funeral music ("Walk Him up the Stairs") that formed the farewell for the hated Cap'n.

Neither *The Wiz* nor *Purlie* made a mark beyond America, but another show from these Broadway years certainly did. Rice and Lloyd Webber were not the only young writers to get amongst the hits in the 1970s. Stephen Schwartz, just a couple of weeks Lloyd Webber's elder, was but 22 when his *Godspell* took off, and by the time he was 25 he had a second hit, *Pippin*, running on Broadway in tandem with the first. The merrily biblical little *Godspell* with its very youth-orientated recounting of a handful of gospel tales and parables and its bouncy little now-flavoured songs has proved more enduring by far than the very 1960s-ish *Pippin*, and it has run through production after production, all around the world, for two decades.

London, too, launched a one-off novelty hit when Richard O'Brien's endearing little *The Rocky Horror Show* (1973), a comical piece of sci-fi parody with a transvestite hero, some pastichey songs and a message of "don't dream it, be it", emerged from a tiny off-West End venue to begin a long cavalcade around the world's stages and screens. But, as the 1970s progressed, pieces of the *Godspell* and *Rocky Horror* kind and size were succeeded as the long-runners of the era by more conventionally shaped and sized musicals.

Below: *Godspell*
Bouncy bits of Bible stories from David Essex, (left) and friends.

A Chorus Line

A Chorus Line *was another show about people in showbusiness, but it was one that wasn't quite like any of its predecessors. When the word first filtered through in 1970s theatrical circles that there was this group of dancers who were going to do a musical about auditions, the news was greeted with incredulity. Auditions were just job-hunting. And ... a Broadway show with no costumes and no scenery and just dancing?*

Of course, that wasn't what *A Chorus Line* was at all. It was the next show in the line of *Company* and *Follies*. Bring a group of people together for an occasion, and then have a look at their insides. On this occasion the show was based on real life, many of its characters being built around the personalities and experiences of a '"working group" of dancers (not all of whom ended up playing "themselves") who had taken part in a series of sessions under the aegis of director/choreographer Michael Bennett.

A Chorus Line had several advantages over *Company* and *Follies*. Firstly, it and its characters had a goal, and the action had a result. At the end of the evening, when everyone went away, something had happened. The successful dancers had a job. But most importantly of all, much more than the two earlier shows had done, the piece showed its audience characters that they could like, and like a lot. All those young performers out there on the stage, dancing their hearts out, striving for a job in the chorus – you wanted them all to get it. Even bitchy Sheila. Especially poor Kristine who danced so beautifully but couldn't sing in tune. And when willowy, camp

"One ... singular sensation ..." The auditionees give their best to the music, the mirror and the man in the stalls.

Paul – the best dancer of the lot – fell to the ground with the kind of injury that meant he'd never dance again, it was worse – far worse – than Billy Bigelow or Joe Cable getting killed, or even Polly Browne losing her gold bracelet. *A Chorus Line* was a moving experience, a never-to-be-forgotten couple of hours in the theatre.

The scene is the final audition for a Broadway chorus line. The dancers on stage perform the set routines, the director in the stalls weeds them down, and then gets the last survivors to talk about themselves. Their different preoccupations and problems come to light in speech or in song-and-dance. When the dancing is resumed, one dancer is badly injured, and the audition continues with a different feeling behind it. The careers – the lives – of these young people are so fragile, so easily ended, and they know it. Finally the director chooses his dancers, and the curtain comes down.

The songs of the show – the audition number, "One", and the hymn to a dancer's life, "What I Did for Love", apart – were devoted mostly to the personal or professional life of one character or another: Mike's tale of how he started dancing after seeing his sister's efforts ("I Can Do That"), Diana's story of how a pretentious drama teacher put her off acting ("Nothing"), Val's description ("Dance: Ten, Looks: Three") of how a bit of plastic surgery on her "tits and ass" helped her to success, Cassie's overwhelming devotion to the "The Music and the Mirror" or the all-too-frequent story of ballet classes that were an escape from unpleasant homes ("At the Ballet").

A Chorus Line transferred to Broadway from its original venue in Central Park, and there became an immense hit. Fifteen years later when it closed, after 6,137 performances, it had become Broadway's new long-run record holder. Curiously, though, unlike *My Fair Lady* and *Fiddler on the Roof*, it didn't carry its triumph to other countries and media. A competent but unexciting London production failed to set the show alight in Britain, a Continental tour proved unexceptional, and even a much-discussed film version didn't provoke anything like the enthusiasm of the original show. But *A Chorus Line* nevertheless remains a phenomenon of and a landmark in the history of both the Broadway and the worldwide musical stages.

CREDITS

A Chorus Line

Musical by James Kirkwood and
    Nicholas Dante

LYRICS
by Edward Kleban

MUSIC
by Marvin Hamlisch

Produced at the Public
    (Newman) Theater, New
    York, 15 April 1975 and at
    the Shubert Theater, New
    York, 25 July 1975
UK: Theatre Royal, Drury Lane,
    London, 22 July 1976
Austria: Raimundtheater,
    Vienna, 16 October 1987
France: Théâtre du Châtelet,
    Paris, 16 December 1987

CAST
Paul	Sammy Williams
Diana Morales	Priscilla Lopez
Mike	Wayne Cilento
Val	Pam Blair
Cassie	Donna McKechnie
Zach	Robert LuPone

In the giant shadow of *A Chorus Line*, a number of other fine musicals made their bow on the Broadway of the mid- and later 1970s, and many of them came yet again from the hands of the hit-makers of the past years.

Chicago (1975) was the work of Kander and Ebb and of director-choreographer Bob Fosse, and it followed the style set in the club-scenes of their *Cabaret* – frilly and feathery and funny, and rotten to the roots. *Chicago* was a sourly satirical look at the ways and, more to the point, byways of Justice as fleetingly witnessed in the story of Roxie Hart, murderess. Gwen Verdon played noxiously blonde Roxie alongside another outstanding dancer, Chita Rivera, as her jailbird rival for the newspaper headlines and for the service of plum defence lawyer Billy Flynn. The story of how the maximumly insincere Flynn manipulates the press and the court into letting Roxie off (whilst an incoherent but innocent woman hangs) was told as a "musical vaudeville", a series of razzly nightclubby turns that included numbers such as Billy's barefaced "All I Care About (is Love)", his bow to "Razzle Dazzle", the period piece "All That Jazz", and a Cell-Block Tango by the singing-dancing Murderesses of the Cook County Jail. Directed and played with sizzling style, *Chicago* was a first-rate hit on Broadway before going further afield.

Another writing team that held good for another hit was that of Geld and Udell, who followed up the bristling *Purlie* with *Shenandoah* (1975), a musical version of the old James Stewart movie about the Civil War, set with country-style songs. This one wasn't as OK with the critics as the more sophisticated *A Chorus Line* or *Chicago*, for it was as splendidly old-fashioned as all get out. Warm, sincere, wholesome, and full of musical numbers that worked a treat as a part of the throat-tugging story of Charlie Anderson, the Shenandoah Valley farmer who refuses to get involved in this war of other folk's making until his own family is made to suffer by it. Some splendid baritone monologues for Charlie ("I've Heard it All Before", "Meditation") were contrasted with some kiddie numbers, some lilting romantic pieces ("We Make a Beautiful Pair") and some moments that were truly touching ("The Only Home I Know"), in a show that, for all that some sneered at it as sentimental, stayed on Broadway for over a thousand performances.

If, however, there had been prizes going for sentimentality down there in the 1970s, it wouldn't have been the rather masculine *Shenandoah* that topped the poll, but Broadway's very biggest hit of 1977. *Annie* had a get out, though: it was based on a cartoon, the famous, half-century-old "Little Orphan Annie", and it didn't really aspire to a third dimension for its characters. Sentimentality in strips – no matter how ingenuous – was more all right in the 1970s than sentimentality in real, proper people. And Little Orphan Annie was all right anywhere and anyhow.

Little Orphan Annie is let out of her orphanage and taken to stay at the home of filthy-rich Daddy Warbucks as a Christmas treat. But she acts so cute over the holiday period that he decides he wants to keep her. Only Annie insists he can't, because she really isn't an orphan – one day, she knows, her family will come back for her. Daddy keeps his upper-lip stiff, and he calls in the President of the United States and even NBC to help find Annie's parents. But all the applicants, including the disguised brother of orphanage madame Miss Hannigan, turn out to be phonies, so Annie settles happily for the new Daddy who's offering.

Annie's wide-eyed, optimistic hopes for "Tomorrow", Miss Hannigan's petrified, vituperous attack on "Little Girls", and her dreams, with her brother and his moll, of the "Easy Street" they could live on with Warbucks's reward money were amongst the most winning numbers in the comic-strip score that Martin Charnin and Charles Strouse concocted for their comic-strip characters, and they and others of the songs all became popular favourites as *Annie* triumphed on Broadway (2,377 performance), in London (1,485 performances) and in other houses from Mexico and Australia to Denmark, Spain, South Africa and Japan.

Strouse had had to wait quite a while and quite a few shows between the hits of *Bye Bye Birdie* and *Annie*, but Neil Simon's record in the musical theatre was, at this stage, made up of nothing but success: *Little Me*, *Sweet Charity*, the 1968 remake of the screenplay *The Apartment* as the amusing *Promises, Promises*, and now perhaps most successfully

of all, *They're Playing our Song* (1979).

They're Playing our Song was a conventionally sized musical only in that it was produced in a large house, had large scenery and sported a full-sized band, but its cast was certainly not large. It consisted of just two leads and a half dozen supporting players representing their alter egos, who never spoke, but who provided the backing to their songs. The songs for *They're Playing our Song* were written by *A Chorus Line*'s Marvin Hamlisch and his ex-girlfriend Carole Bayer Sager, and it was generally bruited about that the show – which was about a composer and the klutzy girl who comes to write his lyrics and stays to run his life – was an autobiomusical. If that really was so, it would seem to be a famous first. But whether it was or wasn't, it was an hilariously funny piece, and if Hamlisch and Bayer Sager really had lived through anything approaching the events of Simon's plot, it was fairly amazing that they had survived, sane, till opening night.

The songs they wrote were mostly presented as the work of the two characters in the show ("I Still Believe in Love", "Fallin'", "Workin' it Out"), but some – like the everybody-shut-up title-song, or the wistful "If He/She Really Knew Me" – illustrated the progress of the nerve-wracking romance between Sonia Walsk and Vernon Gersh.

Above: **Annie**
A flock of jolly little orphans strut their stuff in Broadway's champion children-and-animal musical. The dog comes on later.

Opposite: **Chicago**
Velma Kelly (Chita Rivera) and Roxie Hart (Gwen Verdon), the merry murderesses of the Cook County Jail.

They're Playing our Song totted up tidy runs on Broadway and in the West End, but then – helped undoubtedly by its size (and the size of its two star rôles) – it went on to be seen all over the world: *Están tocando nuestra canción, Sie spielen unser Lied, Stanno suonando la nostra canzone, A mi dalunk szól* – and so forth.

The Michael Stewart–Cy Coleman *I Love my Wife* – a comical piece about abortive wife-swapping plans in New Jersey – was another show that didn't have a large cast (four principals, four on-stage bandplayers) but managed a large number of productions. Coleman's most remarkable work of the 1970s, however, was not this jolly romp but a piece turned out in partnership with no less a pair than the still sparking Betty Comden and Adolph Green. The most durable team of the American musical stage and its most versatile composer adapted the successful old play *Twentieth Century* in burlesque-operettic style, and the result was quite simply one of the cleverest, funniest, most musically witty musicals of all time. The only trouble was that *On the Twentieth Century* was so darned witty that, even though it picked up Broadway's Best Musical award for its year, it ran out of witty audiences well before it had racked up the fine totals won by other, less witful shows. Broadway kept its wits for 460 nights; London managed only 165.

If *On the Twentieth Century* rated unchallengeably as the cleverest musical of its era, there was equally little doubt as to which show raised the biggest belly laughs. It was *The Best Little Whorehouse in Texas*, and those laughs didn't come, as they so often do, from low-comic fooling, but from exactly the same place that the witty laughs had come in the other show: the words. *The Best Little Whorehouse in Texas* told the story of a nice, comfy little down-south brothel, the extermination of which becomes the target of an up-himself broadcasting "personality", but it told it in dialogue like no one surely ever heard outside of Texas: scatological oaths and earth-scraping expressions to which the musical stage was undeniably virgin. It was filthy – but it was hugely funny. It was also decorated by some winning country-style songs, ranging from the brothel-keeper's encouragement to a shy new recruit ("Girl,

You're a Woman") to a plain girl's wish for a bit more feminine daring ("Doatsey Mae") and the soft-shoeing finagling of the local Governor, out to "Sidestep" the issues he's being unwillingly forced to face by the full-of-shit little runt from the telly.

Perhaps the Texan oaths didn't export as well as they might, perhaps this was just one set of prostitutes too many on the musical stage, but in spite of a fine 1,584 performances on Broadway, *The Best Little Whorehouse in Texas* failed to travel, and both its foreign and its screen versions stayed far from the original production in success.

Stephen Sondheim had followed the shimmering *A Little Night Music* with a curiously (and purposely) hobble-paced 1976 musical called *Pacific Overtures*, a musical which featured two-dimensional characters that were of a different kind from *Annie*'s. These ones were stylized Japanese characters, set loose in a kind of masque about the American "invasion" of once happily isolated Japan. The piece was a puzzlement to *A Little Night Music* devotees, but Sondheim had here taken his first step away from the musical-theatre mainstream on a path that he would follow, deliberately and in the main uncommercially, for the next two decades.

His next show, however, seemed in some ways to take a U-turn from this very personal path. *Sweeney Todd* was a broad, British melodrama – a musical based on the old *String of Pearls* tale of the butchering barber of Fleet Street, EC4, and full of the tuppence-coloured characters and near-burlesque effects of its melodrama genre – and it was produced on Broadway with all the lavish, traditional accoutrements of spectacular theatre. That Broadway production did fairly well (557 performances), but *Sweeney Todd* eventually found its future not in large-scale mountings like this first one, but in small-theatre productions that emphasized the gory melodrama of the original play and the equally strong-stuff mixture of the gloomily powerful and the parody that the composer had provided as a musical accompaniment, instead of stacks of scenery.

It was another powerful musical, a musical that actually took power and the people who make use of it as its subject, which proved to be the outstanding show of the 1970s.

Stephen Sondheim. The composer/lyricist of *A Little Night Music* followed his outstanding show with an idiosyncratic set of musicals that won an idiosyncratic following.

Opposite: **Sweeney Todd** The demon barber (Denis Quilley) at his grisly game.

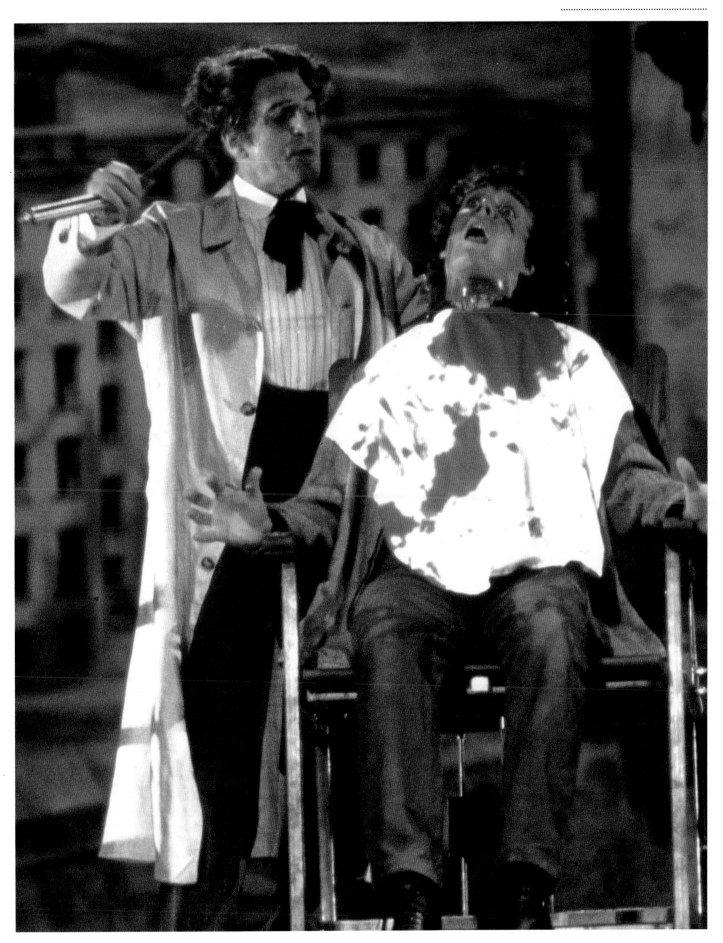

Evita

Eva Peron (Elaine Paige) on the balcony of the Casa Rosada.

Having made their first big hit with a musical about religion, Rice and Lloyd Webber went on to take what was in those days almost the only touchier subject around (later days have managed to dream up a few still more touchy) as the background to their next show: politics. Worse, unfashionably un-trendy-liberal politics.

The story of *Jesus Christ Superstar* was succeeded by *Evita*, a show telling the tale of Eva Peron, wife to Argentinian President Juan Peron and the "guardian angel" of the people of her country during her short but very visible time in the sun.

The story of the rise of Eva Duarte from small-town girl to so-so actress to mistress and then wife of one of the most forceful men of her country, to power as the president's wife, and finally to semi-sainthood in the eyes of the peasant folk of Argentina, whom she won to her cause with the eternally saint-making promise of a robbed-from-the-rich something-for-nothing, was dramatic stuff. Her death from cancer at the height of her popularity, and before her naive and revengeful schemes fell apart, was a custom-made final curtain. The life and character of Eva Peron were truly the material of which libretti are made.

Rice and Lloyd Webber wrote *Evita* in the same sung-through style as *Jesus Christ Superstar*, telling their tale in a series of musical scenes that followed the rise of Evita from her lowly beginnings to her place as Madame President and to her premature death. Only four other principal characters shared those scenes: Juan Peron, the military man Evita urges into power, the teenaged mistress she replaces in his bed, the tango-singer Magaldi, "the first man to be of use to Eva Peron", whom she uses to get her to the city in the first place, and a narrating, commenting, but mostly sneering and jeering character called Che, who was used to represent generally the opposition – from all sorts of diverse quarters, and mostly impotent – to Eva and to her ambitions.

Evita was first heard, like *Superstar* had been, as a double LP recording, from which Eva's post-election speech "Don't Cry for Me, Argentina" and the ejected mistress's ballad "Another Suitcase in Another Hall" emerged to power their way into the upper reaches of the hit parades in a manner that no show's music had done for many years – especially an unproduced show. But when the triumphant stage version of *Evita* took its place on the West End stage there was a whole string of other musical pieces that proved equally notable – Eva's scalding "Rainbow High", Che's mocking "What a Circus", the stalking, challenging Waltz for Eva and Che, the political musical-chairs of the grimly staged "Dice are Rolling" and a flaming first-act finale in which the hopeful people acclaim "A New Argentina".

Evita was one of the greatest successes ever to have been seen on the London stage. To the fury of those whose political persuasions made them go purple at what they saw as the glorification of a lady whom they had over the years taken great pains to paint as the devil incarnate (and of whom the world's perception was forever changed – by a musical!), *Evita* went on to a first run of 2,900 London performances, to a tenancy of nearly four years on Broadway, and to productions in every corner of the theatrical world – except Argentina. There, it was banned.

CREDITS

Evita

Musical in 2 acts by Tim Rice

LYRICS
by Tim Rice

MUSIC
by Andrew Lloyd Webber

Produced at the Prince Edward Theatre, London, 21 June 1978
USA: Broadway Theater, New York, 25 September 1979
Hungary: Margitszigeti Vörösmarty Színpad, Budapest, 14 August 1980
Austria: Theater an der Wien, Vienna, 20 January 1981
Germany: Theater des Westens, Berlin, 10 September 1982
France: Palais de Congrès, Paris, 20 December 1989

CAST

Eva Peron	Elaine Paige
Che	David Essex
Juan Peron	Joss Ackland
Peron's Mistress	
	Siobhan McCarthy
Magaldi	Mark Ryan

CHAPTER 12

Cats

The early 1980s saw the continuing rise of composer Andrew Lloyd Webber as the single most successful writer in the musical theatre. It was a remarkable rise, but it was also one that was completely understandable, for he hit the musical mentality of the time bang in the bullseye.

Background: **A circle of Cats.**

Right: **Little white Victoria (Finola Hughes) leads the felines of the local rubbish dump in a dance under a bulbous moon.**

Lloyd Webber provided just the kind of music that the theatregoing public, from one side of the world to the other, wanted to hear: tuneful, substantial without being operatically hefty, a blend of the traditional and the modern that allowed lovers of both kinds of music to ease into what sounded as if it might be the opposite field without ever feeling uncomfortable. In an age where show tunes had almost entirely slipped from their old place in the hit parades Lloyd Webber got them back there, and he finally ended up as the first musical-theatre composer since Ivan Caryll in 1903 (when conditions were somewhat different) to have five musicals playing in the West End at one and the same time.

In the early 1980s, there were no fewer than three new Lloyd Webber shows given their première, and the first and the most vastly successful of these was *Cats*, a dance musical based on T. S. Eliot's cat poems. If the musical-theatre world had thought that the folk who created *A Chorus Line* were a touch crazy in their choice of a subject, what did it think of this one – a show full of dancing, poetry-singing cats cavorting about in Gillian Lynne dance routines all over a revolving rubbish tip? Religion, OK. Politics, fair enough. But choreographed cats? Well, it's history now: *Cats* is the most successful musical of all time – so far, anyhow.

Cats started out being just a handful of songs: a handful of songs composed by Lloyd Webber to the not-quite-for-children words

of T. S. Eliot's jolly, whimsical feline poems. Only bit by bit did that set of songs get expanded into a larger set of songs, and ultimately into a full-length stage musical. The cat characters and their numbers – some of them taken from unpublished pieces of Eliot's work supplied to the production team by his widow – were threaded onto a wafer-

214

thin framework that was nothing like a conventional plot. For *Cats* was a piece on the revusical *Company* or *A Chorus Line* format: the cats who stalked and leaped and danced in and out of the vast almost-in-the-round tip which was the setting of the show were seen getting together for something called a Jellicle Ball, and at that ball, which brought the evening to its climax, one cat was to be chosen to have an extra life, an extra chance to make good. But the fact that the bedraggled Grizabella, the fallen glamour cat, got the brass ring and ascended radiant and redeemed to the Heaviside layer on an old inner-tube was altogether less important than the entertaining series of songs, and most particularly of dances, that had gone before.

Its dance element was what made *Cats* a

most unusual show. We had had sung-through shows before (and, indeed, there was no spoken dialogue in this one), but this was – to all intents and purposes – a danced-through show. With the exception of the venerable, basso Old Deuteronomy, the paterfamilias of the proceedings and MC of the ball, and of Grizabella (both of whom nevertheless tripped a step or two during the night), the whole cast of *Cats* was made up of skilled dancers. And the entire show was choreographed. The comical Gumbie Cat instructed cockroaches in tap-dance, Mr Mistoffelees tapped and *fouettéd* himself show-offishly catatonic, kitten-burglars Mungojerrie and Rumpleteazer bounced out a thieving little *pas de deux*, a pair of posy pussies vamped out the tale of "Macavity", and a little white kitten danced alone in the moonlight in some of the top-cat-spots of the entertainment.

Not quite all the highlights of the evening came in dance. For, like the previous Lloyd Webber shows, *Cats* also had its hit-parade song. That hit song wasn't, however, one of Eliot's poems, but a number put together from fragments and ideas taken from the poet's work and attached to a nearly new Lloyd Webber tune to make up a longing solo for the despised Grizabella, "Memory".

Cats opened in London 14 years ago, and on Broadway – in a slightly revised version – more than 12 years back. As I write, both these productions of a show which has been restaged (both in its original three-sided version and one adapted to a proscenium arch stage) all round the world, are still running.

Left: Rumpleteazer (Bonnie Langford), Grizabella (Elaine Paige) and Victoria (Finola Hughes).

CREDITS

Cats

Musical in 2 acts, based on T. S. Eliot's *Old Possum's Book of Practical Cats*

MUSIC

by Andrew Lloyd Webber

Produced at the New London Theatre, London, 11 May 1981
USA: Winter Garden Theater, New York, 7 October 1982
Hungary: Madach Színház, Budapest, 25 March 1983
Austria: Theater an der Wien, Vienna, 24 September 1983
Germany: Operettenhaus, Hamburg, 18 April 1986
France: Théâtre de Paris, Paris, 23 February 1989

CAST

Old Deuteronomy	Brian Blessed
Gus	Stephen Tate
Grizabella	Elaine Paige
Griddlebone	Susan Jane Tanner
Rum Tum Tugger	Paul Nicholas
Gumbie Cat	Myra Sands
Mister Mistoffelees	Wayne Sleep
Skimbleshanks	Kenn Wells

When *Cats* was still just that first handful of songs, all sorts of ideas were put forward as to what might be done with it. One idea mooted was that the numbers might make up into a kind of song-cycle that could be presented as half of an evening's entertainment, along with a version of the Variations on a Theme of Paganini that Lloyd Webber had composed for his 'cellist brother, Julian. When *Cats* went on to bigger and better things, the germ of that idea lingered, and eventually that other show did happen. An entertainment choreographed to the Paganini Variations was teamed with a song-cycle, *Tell Me on a Sunday,* a piece recounting the details of the unfortunate love-life of an English girl in New York that Lloyd Webber had written with lyricist Don Black, and the show was called *Song and Dance.* Intended just for a limited run at London's Palace Theatre, it proved a full-sized hit, ran for two years, and went on to other performances – often in nationally reorientated versions – in a number of other countries.

Lloyd Webber's third hit of the early 1980s

came with *Starlight Express.* This time round, after the more sophisticated and up-to-date tones of *Tell Me on a Sunday,* the composer expressly went for a kind of show and a kind of score that would have an appeal for younger audiences – and, of course, for all those grown-up children who have as much of a thing about trains as their wives have about cats. Oddly enough, *Starlight Express* didn't throw up hit-parade material in the way that *Jesus Christ Superstar, Evita, Cats* and even *Tell Me on a Sunday* had done, but it didn't need to. Its fascination didn't lie in its songs but in its staging: high-tech scenery and roller-skated train races. For the excessively slim plot line that allowed a series of anthropomorphic trains to fill the stage with their songs and skated dances was a kind of far-out fable about a dear little steam train who, through having faith in the "Starlight Express", gets to beat all the horrid, modern diesel and electric engines in a speed race. Nevertheless, amongst the pounding, piston-rhythmed pop-music that accompanied the trains in their carefully timed and choreographed races up and around the

Starlight Express
Rusty (Ray Shell), the good little steam-engine, with a trio of well-built young carriages.

auditorium, across a piece of hydraulic bridge-work, to their finish centre-stage, the composer still found place for some enjoyable songs: a jilted dining-car bewailing in Tammy Wynettish tones that she's been "U.N.C.O.U.P.L.E.D" and two smashed-up bits of rolling-stock regretting "One Rock and Roll Too Many".

Starlight Express proved to be all that it was intended to be and more. Like *Cats*, it is still a fixture of the West End stage, more than three thousand nights after its première – but in a rather different shape to the one it sported on opening night. For the show ran so long that its purposeful "modern-ness" eventually became nothing of the kind and, in a kind of exercise not attempted since the Victorian days of musical-comedy "second editions", it was revised, reorganized and rechoreographed – without ever closing down – so that, as the show rolled on towards its first decade on the West End stage, it is a 1990s *Starlight Express* rather than a 1980s one that holds the stage at the Apollo Victoria Theatre.

Whilst Lloyd Webber was beginning what was starting to look like a takeover of London's less favoured theatres (*Evita, Cats* and *Starlight Express* all went into unpopular houses and turned their fortunes round), the more usual musical theatres failed to turn up any exciting newly minted shows to set alongside his successes. What was being talked about as a revival of the British musical stage actually wasn't anything of the kind. A remake of the 1930s *Me and my Girl* and a splendid but scarcely original stage version of the classic film *Singin' in the Rain* couldn't count either as "new" shows or indeed as any kind of "revival" of musical-theatre writing. What was being seen wasn't too far off being a one-man effort. For other new and exciting musical-playwriters were very thin on the ground. But Britain wasn't alone in that spot: the same was true also on the other side of the Atlantic. The hits that came from America in the first part of the 1980s came not from new talents but from the tried and proven Michael Stewart, Cy Coleman and Jerry Herman.

Stewart and Coleman scored a first-rate hit with a biomusical that took for its hero the nineteenth-century circus proprietor Phineas Taylor Barnum. A relatively small group of multi-talented performers acted out episodes from Barnum's life, from his beginnings

exhibiting Joice Heth, the oldest woman in the world, General Tom Thumb, and the far-too-attractive vocalist Jenny Lind, via his wife-provoked attempts at more legitimate business and politics, to his flaming return to the world of showbusiness with Barnum and Bailey's circus. The telling of the tale took place in a stylized circus ring, and the performers – including the actor playing Barnum himself – illustrated each turn of the story with feats of balancing, juggling, acrobatism and a fiesta of other circus arts in a vastly colourful display of songs, dance, music and feats. The music that accompanied the action wasn't eclipsed in all this. Coleman provided some of the grandest march music in musical-theatre years for his circus folk ("Come Follow the Band", "Join the Circus"), as well as some clattering pieces for the star ("Museum Song", "Prince of Humbug"), some smoother ones with and for his wife ("The Colors of my Life") and characteristic numbers for several of the "attractions". The combination of all the elements – at the centre of which Barnum and his wife remained firmly fixed throughout – made *Barnum* into an international hit.

Barnum had its very biggest success in Britain, where the star rôle was magnetically taken by Michael Crawford, but it probably travelled to more countries during the 1980s than any other new Broadway musical. If it had any kind of a competitor for that honour, though, that competitor would undoubtedly have been Jerry Herman's newest work, *La Cage aux folles*. *La Cage aux folles* was the latest member of a grand old tradition (*I Love my Wife* had been another recent one) – the fine French farce turned into a fine Broadway musical. This French farce had been a particularly huge success, with a seven-year run in Paris and a stormingly successful film being its chief qualifications until the musical version put in its appearance.

Barnum
Actor Michael Crawford learned a whole register of circus skills in order to play "The Prince of Humbug".

Cy Coleman: Broadway's most versatile and successful composer of recent decades gets manhandled by *Barnum* take-over Tony Orlando.

Saint Tropez nightclub owner Georges finds himself in a quandary when his son gets engaged. The trouble is that the boy's future in-laws, a particularly rednecked local politico and his mousy wife, want to meet his parents, and Georges' "wife" is a man: officially Albin, but by night the one-and-only Zaza, the in-drag star of the entertainment at the Cage aux folles. Georges tries to do the best by everyone, but feelings invariably get dented, and the farce rides highest when Albin decides that he will be a proper mother, and doffs a frock and wig to entertain his prospective "in-laws". The wig comes off at just the wrong moment, but "maman" triumphs in the end.

Herman turned out some charming songs – a Trenet-ish love song ("Song on the Sand") for Georges, a pretty "Anne on my Arm" for the youngsters, a singalong "The Best of Times", and a pair of the grandest-dame numbers possible for Zaza, the grandest-dame of them all: a morale-boosting "A Little More Mascara" and a tempestuous "I Am What I Am", which quickly found its way out of the show and into the repertoire of the very blowtorch-singers of whom Albin was the sweet, grotesque mimicry.

La Cage aux folles notched up 1,761 nights on Broadway. Oddly, it failed to catch on in its other English-language productions, but in Central Europe the curiously literally titled Ein Käfig voller Närren proved extremely popular, and the show found its way into a good number of Continental houses.

Stewart followed Barnum with a second fine hit when he contributed to a stage remaking of the famous musical film 42nd Street. Little Peggy Sawyer tapped and squeaked-to-sang her way from a last-minute job in the chorus of a Broadway-bound show to fame as the stand-in star of its première on the Great White Way; loomingly impressive producer Julian Marsh uttered the showbiz mega-phrase about going out there a youngster but coming back a star; and a squadron of jailbait-young dancers (a larger

Blood Brothers
Robert Locke and Con O'Neil as the tragic twins of Willy Russell's Liverpudlian tale.

squadron – or so it seemed – than any that had appeared since the heyday of the tap-shoe and a free wages market) tapped themselves into a frenetic heap, in the course of an evening that was as fine a bit of nostalgia as any that had ever been seen on the Broadway stage. Or on the many others that this live, young and healthy version of 42nd Street went on to visit after its nearly 3,500 performances on the New York stage.

Alongside this trio of well-travelling Broadway hits, there was also a handful which limited their success to America. One of the most enjoyable of these was Dreamgirls, a showbiz musical about a girl-group which – depending whether you were a theatregoer or a theatrical lawyer – either was or wasn't based on the Supremes. The main character of the show was Effie, a great singer who gets dumped from fronting the group as it rises to stardom because she doesn't have the Barbie-doll look that's a sine qua non for the job. Henry Krieger supplied a razzling Motown-type score for this gotta-make-it-good-in-showbiz show, a score topped by Effie's searing don't-you-dare-dump-me monologue "And I'm Telling You I'm Not Going" and a bouncy pop-song-within-the-show, "One Night Only".

America actually tried harder than Britain did, during these years, to bring out good new musicals, but without turning up too many winners. Stephen Sondheim went determinedly further out on the opaque limb he'd clambered onto with Pacific Overtures with an awkwardly two-halved piece called Sunday in the Park with George, Peter Udell's musically uplifting Amen Corner went under quickly, and a wandering, ineffectual piece called Nine, based on the film 8 1/2, although it won some favour, was consigned by most to pseud's corner. Even Liza Minnelli and Chita Rivera, two of the most loved stars of Broadway, couldn't make a hit out of the new Kander and Ebb show, The Rink. It seemed that almost everyone had lost the knack of writing what the public wanted to hear. But Andrew Lloyd Webber could obviously do it. So what was the recipe?

Whilst murder, mayhem and woundingly large losses hit many of the big houses and their big shows, there was still, fortunately, some happy smaller-scale musical theatre entertainment going on, on both sides of the Atlantic. In Britain, Willy Russell's tragic tale of a

pair of Liverpudlian *Blood Brothers* was one that – after a short first run and an opportune revival – eventually went on to long-running success. The show told the tale of twins, separated at birth, who become bosom friends as youngsters, but, after time and unequal talents have taken them to opposite ends of life's success scale, end up at the heart of a fatal drama. The central character of the show was neither of the twins, but their mother, and it was she who drew the bulk of the show's small score of plangent, folksy songs.

In America, the big winner amongst the smaller shows was a delicious parody of old horror movies, *Little Shop of Horrors*. Its hero was nerdy Seymour Krelbourne, a Skid Row shop-assistant who finds a strange and interesting plant during a total eclipse. He tends it, feeds it his own blood when it turns out to be bloodiverous, and is its last pre-curtain victim as the hungry chunk of flora – which is nothing less than an alien from outer space with flowers on – heads onwards to world domination. Alan Menken and Howard Ashman's songs caught the burlesque mode delightfully, with a girl-group booping out the

title-song, Seymour's wan beloved getting lyrical over suburban housewifery "Somewhere That's Green" and the plant howling out its demand "Feed Me!". *Little Shop of Horrors* went on to run for over 2,000 off-Broadway performances, and sallied forth from the back streets of New York in its own attempt at world domination. Menken and Ashman did even better – they went forth from off-Broadway to write songs for the triumphant new wave of Disney cartoon musicals.

The early 1980s did, in fact, start one more major musical on its career. But this one really took its time about becoming an international hit. The musical version of Victor Hugo's celebrated *Les Misérables* first saw the light of stage in Paris in 1980, for a limited season at the Palais des Sports. It played 105 times, and that would have been it had not the show's pre-production recording come to the attention of London producer Cameron Mackintosh. Five years later *Les Misérables* opened in London. But the show that Londoners – and eventually the rest of the world – saw was a *Les Misérables* much altered from the one that had originally played in Paris.

42nd Street

The venerable stage of London's Theatre Royal, Drury Lane, rang with the sound of endlessly dancing feet. Claire Leach (centre) was the show's instant star.

Les Misérables

In the years that followed Jesus Christ Superstar *a number of other writers attempted to imitate the dramatic, sung-through nature of Rice and Lloyd Webber's hit show. None had much success. But the French pair of Schönberg and Boublil turned out a merry, cartoon-like potted version of what happened during* La Révolution française *before going on, seven years later, to tackle another mighty subject in* Les Misérables. *This one had nothing of the cartoon about it, though; it was no less than a full-strength musical version of Hugo's dramatic tale.*

Jean Valjean has spent a long time in prison and has now, at last, been released on a ticket of leave. But he breaks the terms of his parole, and the dour policeman Javert sets out to bring him back to justice. The fugitive has become a prosperous provincial factory-owner and small town mayor, and has pledged to take under his wing the orphaned child of an ill-treated employee when, years later, Javert finally finds him. Valjean and the young Cosette escape to Paris. There the grown girl falls in love with the student Marius, but Marius becomes involved in the era's anti-government street fighting, so Valjean takes to the barricades to preserve the boy from harm. There he meets Javert, a government spy, but when his dogged tormentor is this time put into his power, Valjean lets him go, and the policeman – his beliefs in right and wrong now irreparably confused – commits a tortured suicide. Valjean delivers the wounded Marius to Cosette and, happy that his mission is done, dies in peace.

This vast, twenty-years-and-more story was peopled by a whole panoply of characters: the rapacious Thénardiers, foster parents to Cosette and then Parisian petty thieves, their sad daughter Eponine who gives her life for the Marius she loves and their cheeky son Gavroche who falls under the bullets of the foolishly hopeless fighting, the sacked Fantine who falls into prostitution and an early death, and the merry students whose pitiful idealism costs them their lives on the barricades. All these folk and more took part in the skilfully slimmed version of the great tale that passed across the stage in the musicalized *Les Misérables* and in the end-to-end tidal wave of music which – particularly in its remade version – featured a whole line of excisable single numbers: Eponine's longing "On my Own", Javert's "Stars" and his desperate dilemma "Who is This Man?", the students' rallying cry "Red and Black" and Marius's broken "Empty Chairs and Empty Tables", a crude innkeeper's number for the Thénardiers

Background: **Jean Valjean finds the maltreated child, Cosette, in the hands of the worthless Thénardier and his wife.**

("Master of the House") and a series of dramatic pieces for Valjean and for the soon gone Fantine.

London's revamped and anglicized *Les Misérables* was not greeted with unalloyed praise. The vast, complex panorama of the show seemed too much for many people in its early audiences to cope with, and at one stage there was question of closing the show after its season at the Barbican Theatre. But producer Mackintosh took his courage in his hands and transferred the production to the West End, and thereafter *Les Misérables* never looked back. Nine years on, after a vast array of other productions from Poland, Iceland, Denmark, Norway and Sweden in the north to New Zealand and Australia in the south, and many, many others in the middle it is still not looking back, as that production runs steadily on, in parallel with an equally successful Broadway version.

Left: The students prepare to die on the barricades.

Below: "A little drop of rain…" Eponine (Frances Ruffelle) dies in the arms of Marius (Michael Ball).

CREDITS

Les Misérables

Musical in 2 acts by Alain Boublil and Jean-Marc Natel, adapted from the novel by Victor Hugo.

New version adapted by Trevor Nunn and John Caird, translated by Herbert Kretzmer with additional material by James Fenton

MUSIC

by Claude-Michel Schönberg

Original version produced at the Palais des Sports, Paris, 17 September 1980

UK: revised, English version, Barbican Theatre, London, 8 October 1985

USA: Broadway Theater, New York, 12 March 1987

Austria: Raimundtheater, Vienna, 15 September 1988

Hungary: Rock Színház, Szeged, 14 August 1987

France: Théâtre Mogador, Paris, 12 October 1991

CAST

Jean Valjean	Colm Wilkinson
Javert	Roger Allam
Marius	Michael Ball
Cosette	Rebecca Caine
Thénadier	Alun Armstrong
Mme Thénadier	
	Susan Jane Tanner
Enjolras	David Burt
Eponine	Frances Ruffelle

The biggest hits that came to the stage in the early 1980s have turned out to be long-lasting favourites indeed. They have run longer in their first productions than the greatest musicals of earlier days could have dreamed of running, they have permeated parts of the world where the mainstream of Western musical theatre had never or hardly ever gone before, and they have attracted people to the theatre – in all sorts of countries and in many languages – who ten, twenty years ago never went near one. The musical theatre, in the 1980s, was prospering hugely. There was only one hitch – one that wasn't perhaps obvious to the twice- or thrice-a-year theatregoer: these great big, glorious hits – they were so few. So desperately few. And underneath them was – what? In the years that were to follow, the same thing would hold true: big hits – very big, but fewer and fewer shows – fewer and fewer good shows for the dying-to-be-regular theatregoer, that still thriving species that seemed rapidly to be becoming the forgotten race of the musical-theatre world, to go to see.

But was and is this shrinkage so surprising? Musicals had, even by the early 1980s, become such grandiose and expensive things to mount. The days of the £2,000 production of *Stop the World* seemed a million years away. The financial risk involved in mounting a show had become enormous – particularly for a brand new musical. How many producers could afford to take such a risk? And having taken the risk and won, was it so odd that a producer would need and want to maximise the paying attractions of his show with as long runs as possible in the main centres.

Nostalgia is, of course, always safer. Big revivals of old favourites, or "new" shows made up from sticking old and well-known songs and stories together just like they did two centuries ago, are a less wild punt in money-worrisome days and circumstances. And those days were, already, in the 1980s, clearly upon us. But fortunately the hardy regulars were still there – Andrew Lloyd Webber and Cy Coleman, Cameron Mackintosh and Stephen Sondheim – supported by an occasionally on-the-target group of less regular or new writers and producers

It was Andrew Lloyd Webber and Cameron Mackintosh who were the pair of producing powerhouses that launched what turned out to be the biggest hit of the last decade, *The Phantom of the Opéra*.

Cameron Mackintosh
The producer of a number of the world's biggest musical-theatre hits of the 1980s.

The Phantom of the Opéra

With what would Andrew Lloyd Webber follow the religion and politics, the dancing cats and the skating trains of his previous shows? What new bit of unexpected musical theatricality did the man who was, already, supplying not only the West End but the world's stages with an unprecedentedly significant part of its musicals (and whose last work had been, for heaven's sake, a requiem mass!) have on his menu for the next course?

The Phantom (Michael Crawford) and his protégée (Sarah Brightman).

The answer, when it came, might have been unexpected, but the show itself was one that stepped less distance from the romantic musical stage of the grandest days of the songs-and-scenes show than almost any of the composer's previous musicals. *The Phantom of the Opéra* was a straightforward romantic musical melodrama: a version of a French novel that had made up, most famously, into a memorable Lon Chaney movie. Of course, this was a virtually sung-through romantic melodrama, but it was also one that, in its composer's now well-established style, took plenty of time out for what stood up as separate musical numbers – romantic pieces for the show's benighted heroine and her aristocratic lover ("All I Ask"), pieces insidious ("Music of the Night") and dramatic ("The Phantom of the Opéra", "The Point of No Return") for the Phantom and his singing prey, operatic pastiche of all kinds for the stars of the opera house where the action takes place, and, in particular, some exciting

ensemble work ("Prima Donna") which took the show and its score that extra step on from a simple songs-and-recit format towards something more ambitious and exciting.

The "Phantom" of the Paris Opéra is not a ghost, but a brilliant and horribly disfigured man who lives in the sewers beneath the great building. Secretly, he has been training the voice of the pretty chorine Christine Daäé, and his powers as a teacher are so great that when, by the use of his seemingly paranormal powers, he frightens the management into giving her a lead rôle, she triumphs. But the Phantom has fallen in love with Christine and, jealous of her attachment to the Vicomte Raoul de Chagny, he kidnaps the girl and carries her off to his quarters in the depths of the Paris underground. Raoul must go to find her down there, at the risk of his life.

As well as its powerful and passionate story and its sweepingly romantic music, *The Phantom of the Opéra* was given the third traditional element of the romantic musical play and, indeed, of the classical opera: a stunning physical production. The stage of the Opéra, with its great chandelier whose fall brought the first act to its close, the dark heights and depths of the stair-filled theatre edifice, the sewers with their forest of surreal candelabra through which the Phantom and Christine float on their way to his home, the colourful masquerade of the *bal de l'Opéra* – all these eye-catching scenes did their breath-baiting bit towards producing a piece of romantic musical theatre such as the musical stage had not seen in years – if ever.

The musical theatre duly showed its thanks, for *The Phantom of the Opéra* proved a triumph, not only in London and on Broadway, but wherever it travelled. Such a triumph, indeed, that – in a manner that had virtually died out with the old days of theatrical piracy – it provoked a number of copy-cat shows, pieces that retheatricalized the out-of-copyright French novel and embroidered their own musical scores upon it in a sad attempt to edge in on the glory (and, of course, the money) generated by what is already one of the biggest hits to have come out of the modern musical theatre, and may – who knows – even go on to prove itself the very biggest of all.

CREDITS

The Phantom of the Opéra

Musical in a prologue and 2 acts by Andrew Lloyd Webber and Richard Stilgoe, based on *Le Fantôme de l'Opéra* by Gaston Leroux.

LYRICS
by Charles Hart

MUSIC
by Andrew Lloyd Webber

Produced at Her Majesty's Theatre, London, 9 October 1986
USA: Majestic Theater, New York, 26 January 1988
Austria: Theater an der Wien, Vienna, 20 December 1988
Germany: Neue Flora-Theater, Hamburg, 29 June 1990

CAST

The Phantom	Michael Crawford
Christine Daäé	Sarah Brightman
Raoul de Chagny	Steve Barton
Carlotta	Rosemary Ashe
Firmin	John Savident
André	David Firth
Ubaldo Piangi	John Aaron

Opposite: A half satirical wink at the scenic excesses of the operatic stage.
Left: Raoul (Steve Barton) tracks the captured Christine (Sarah Brightman) to the Phantom's home in the Paris underground.

Since the started-small days of *Joseph and the Amazing Technicolor Dreamcoat*, Lloyd Webber musicals had been getting bigger and bigger. But after the vibrantly romantic and swingeingly spectacular *The Phantom of the Opéra*, the composer took a purposeful hitch in this galloping expansion. In *Aspects of Love* he helped himself to a comparatively intimate and unspectacular story of love in warm places and set it with a score that curled itself around that story to winning effect. The half-century old tale of a French actress who prefers the comfortable love of an ageing roué to the urgent passion of his young nephew probed not always gently into the various aspects of love that coloured its characters' lives, and it did so without any of the vast production values and massed personnel that *The Phantom of the Opéra* had used. It also turned out a song that, in hit-parade terms, topped anything from the earlier show: the musical's theme-song "Love Changes Everything" performed better than any Lloyd Webber number since "Don't Cry for Me, Argentina" on the British charts. The show, however, in spite of a fine London run, did not turn out to be the international blockbuster that its predecessor had been. The new, wider audiences that the musical was attracting in the 1980s and the 1990s apparently preferred a diet of chandeliers and hydraulic scenery and romantic glitter. So, after a hugely spectacular remake of *Joseph* had scored a sensation at the London Palladium, Lloyd Webber went back, in his next new show, to the world of the grand and rocambolesque spectacular.

Like *The Phantom of the Opéra*, *Sunset Boulevard* had become a classic as a movie, and – again – one with a singularly grotesque central character. But this grotesque wasn't a creature from the romantic past, she was part of the modern world – or trying to be. Norma Desmond is a silent movie star, one of the greats. Or, rather, she was. And, immured in her Hollywood palazzo, this *grande dame* to crush all *grandes dames* to little bits of stardust is planning a comeback. She hires a young writer to remake the script for her screen reappearance as a teenaged Salomé, and from there on events avalanche desperately downwards to a final reel full of lust, death and madness. Like the other Lloyd Webber shows, the sung-through *Sunset Boulevard* had its eye-tooth numbers, and the star's description of the power of her voiceless acting craft, "With One Look (I Can Break your Heart)" and the young man's cynical look at "Sunset Boulevard" proved the biggest musical moments of the evening.

Sunset Boulevard, with its flamboyantly familiar film story, its burstingly big central character, and the extravagant reproduction of a crazy-age Hollywood mansion that was the heart of its scenic content proved to have all the desired attractions for the audiences that had loved *The Phantom of the Opéra* but to whom the less grand and glamorous *Aspects of Love* had held less appeal, and the show settled down for runs in London and New York that will doubtless – as it makes its way to all those places where major musicals now go – add it to the list of *fin de siècle* mega-musicals.

Fin de siècle

Lloyd Webber's original partner, Tim Rice, also contributed an exciting new work to the musical stage in the late 1980s. He combined with Bjørn Ulvaeus and Benny Andersson – better known as the two male quarters of the Swedish singing-group Abba – to write *Chess*, a sizzling story of Cold War politics and sport set, in the style of the times, to end-to-end music. The show's principal characters were the contestants – one American and one Russian – in a world chess championship that ends up being used by the political people of each country for propaganda and power-plays much more significant than those played out on its chessboards. Caught up in the middle of all this is the Eastern-bloc refugee Florence Vassy, who has become lover and second to the American player but who switches her affections to the Russian and helps him temporarily to defect.

The score to *Chess* held some of the most

Opposite: **Chess**
The American contestant (Murray Head) and his second (Elaine Paige) prepare to attack the world championships.

Above: **Sunset Boulevard**
Broadway saw a real, nowadays film star in the role of the show's olden days film star. Glenn Close is Norma Desmond.

Above: **Miss Saigon**
A moment of spectacle from a show specializing in the visually spectacular.

exciting new stage music of its time, and when the show's pre-production recording came out its two-woman duo "I Know Him So Well" swooped swiftly up the charts, ending that swoop in the number-one spot that no show song had occupied for years. The romantic and dramatic music of the score was its chief glory – the heroine's wondering "Heaven Help my Heart", the Russian's soaring Anthem ("My Land"), the American's ledger-line-ripping tantrum "Pity the Child" and the long-lined duo "You and I" which saw the birth of love between the Russian and Florence – but there were also lighter pieces, as the "Soviet Machine" got drunker and drunker on its march to glory and two bored embassy officials prissily looked over the Russian's application for asylum (Embassy Lament). The show came to its peak in a stormy, concerted "Endgame" in which the Russian – distracted by personal and political problems – fights to retain his championship.

Chess played for three years in London and its songs went round the world (making a notable hit in France), but – in a way that glaringly bucked the modern fashion for breath-for-breath international reproductions of big hit musicals – other mountings of the show deconstructed the text and score of the piece, resulting in a badly weakened show and, in consequence, failure.

The writers of *Les Misérables*, who had

seemed the most likely candidates to help Lloyd Webber and his associates fill the musical stages of the world in the 1990s, followed up their big hit with a worrying *Madama Butterfly* update, set in the Vietnam War and called *Miss Saigon*. It was worrying because, in this show, the ratio of spectacle to content, which had been becoming progressively more lopsided through a series of sometime embarrassing whistle-the-scenery flops on both sides of the Atlantic in the past decade, finally went over the acceptable edge. The abiding memory of *Miss Saigon* is not its uncomfortably remade and worded script or its distressingly bland score, but a helicopter airlifting US Embassy staff from the fall of Saigon. The only thing was, Saigon fell early in Act I, but for "climactic" purposes the helicopter bit was glued into a flashback in Act II. This bit of visuals-first, sense-later was symptomatic of the made-by-numbers nature of a show that, after the thrilling promise of *La Révolution française* and the dazzling confirmation of that piece in *Les Misérables*, was not only a disappointment but a warning. The helicopter of *Miss Saigon* will long remain a symbol of what may be a severe (but, hopefully, not terminal) illness in the musical theatre.

However, like Vietnam, *Miss Saigon* did not fall in a few weeks. On the contrary, this latest large-package product from the *Cats–Les Misérables–Phantom of the Opéra* production house installed itself at London's Theatre Royal, Drury Lane, and at New York's Broadway Theatre, determinedly tacking itself onto the tail-end of the almost motionless group of long-running musicals that now have so many of the biggest houses in the West End and on Broadway occupied in the long term.

But a booking jam there isn't. The multi-year successes of pieces such as *Cats*, *Les Misérables* and *The Phantom of the Opéra* can't be said to have stopped other big new musicals from trying their chance. Even if the brimming houses that they have lived in for so many years had been free, what would have been put into them? Britain has and has had nothing else to export to Broadway, and – in a total contrast to the years after the war – not one truly new Broadway musical has installed itself successfully in the West End since *Barnum* well over a decade back. That doesn't mean, though, that there haven't been some fine shows. On the contrary, the transatlantic musical that came nearest to being a full-blown success in these years was without a doubt the best musical comedy to have made its appearance on the world's stages in many, many years.

City of Angels was a brilliantly funny burlesque of all those Hollywood gumshoe detective movies and their oh-so-repetitive television offspring. It was written by Larry Gelbart – who had been writing TV's *M.A.S.H.* since the days when he gave *A Funny Thing Happened on the Way to the Forum* to Broadway – and it was composed by Cy Coleman. That man again. *City of Angels* was certainly expansively staged, but the staging was only one part of this musical, for it was a show that had its priorities in all the right places. First and foremost it was funny, throat-achingly funny. But it was also not tired-businessman easy. The audience was required to keep its mind agile, to think, to listen to the lines and even to the lyrics to follow the parallel (and sometimes crossing) stories of the show: the effort of a writer to turn his slightly pretentious cop novel into a screenplay, on the one hand, and the bopping-and-bullets story of louche Los Angeles life that that screenplay told, on the other. To make it easier for those with attention problems, the movie scenes were played in black and white, real life in colour. But all the songs – from the yahboo "You're Nothing without Me" to the sultry "With Every Breath I Take" and the cliché-crushing "Tennis Song" – were in full colour.

Yet *City of Angels* did not join the long-run list. Not even on Broadway, where two years (a minor run in these days of ten- and 15-year stints) was its lot. But the show did provoke one interesting and perhaps more depressing than hopeful incident. When the West End production of *City of Angels* was threatened with early closure, the London newspaper critics rose up in a way never seen before to lambast their readers for letting this splendid show die. That was the hopeful part. The depressing part is that even that *cri de coeur* roused only enough folk to keep the show going a handful of months longer. Wit was out. Romance and spectacle were in. And helicopters, it seemed.

Several other shows that scored almost as well or better on Broadway than *City of Angels*

also failed to export profitably. There was *The Mystery of Edwin Drood*, a clever musical comedy version of Dickens's famously unfinished novel, told in the setting of a Victorian music hall. It was written by popular songster Rupert Holmes, and its enjoyable score turned up a mixture of the jolly, the mock melodramatic and the really rather beautiful as illustration to a very lively evening, at the conclusion of which the audience got to vote for their preferred ending. Then there was *Big River*, the work of another singer-songwriter, Roger ("King of the Road", "Little Green Apples") Miller. The umpteenth attempt at turning Mark Twain's Mississippi River tales into musical, it included some lively country pieces for its two young heroes – Huckleberry Finn and Tom Sawyer – and for the folk Huck meets on his raft-ride downriver with runaway slave Joe. *Big River* didn't get a showing in Britain, but it proved a distinct hit in Australia following its 1,005 performances on Broadway.

The last Stephen Sondheim work of the 1980s seemed to have more potential as a really public-winning piece of musical theatre

Below: *City of Angels*
Stine (Martin Smith) has two problems. One of them is keeping his pants on. His wife (Fiona Hendley) prefers he should – when she isn't around.

Above: **Into the Woods**
Frumped-up fairytales. Julia
MacKenzie as the Witch, with
Ian Bartholomew and Imelda
Staunton as the Baker and his
Wife, in London's version of
the show.

Opposite: **Kiss of the
Spiderwoman**
Chita Rivera was the all-
singing, all-dancing creature of
the title.

than anything he had written for a good number of years. *Into the Woods* was a black fairytale burlesque – black, that is, in that it had its happy endings at half-time, and after that everything fell to bits – but it had enough "white" bits as well, and the show stood up as a merry if sardonic entertainment full of such helpfully familiar characters as Cinderella and Jack the Giantkiller, with any subtexts being optional. But although *Into the Woods* (1987) had a 764-night run on Broadway, it flopped in London, and its life elsewhere has been largely in those non-commercial theatres who prize the apparently commercially unviable work of Sondheim above all other music-theatre works.

Sondheim followed up *Into the Woods* with another black piece – a revusical entertainment called *Assassins*, which paraded the up-till-now murderers (and attempted murderers) of America's presidents across the stage in song and sketch – before giving himself to a more attractive side of the darker tones he now seems to favour in *Passion* (1994). *Passion* treated somewhat the same three-cornered subject as *Aspects of Love*, with its hero tossed between his frivolous love affair with a sexy young married woman and the much deeper feelings – ultimately returned – offered by one who is plain, deceived and dying. The return to a real love story with a beginning, an end, and a small cast of characters with oodles of feelings to express allowed Sondheim to spread himself into what was perhaps his most attractive score since his last Continental period piece, *A Little Night Music*. *Passion*, however, failed to take on Broadway, where the latest success to arrive on the Broadway stage is a piece in a very different mode. *Beauty and the Beast* is a stage version of a film. Nothing new about that: screenplays have been being recycled as libretti since silent movie days, and in recent years the fashion for screen-to-stage has been steadily increasing. But *Beauty and the Beast* is a stage version of an animated film, a Disney animated film, with everything that the name of Disney means put right up there on the stage. It's the modern-day equivalent of *Babes in Toyland* or *The Wizard of Oz*, the children's spectacular for all the family, and with credits attached to it –

Little Shop of Horrors' Alan Menken and Howard Ashman, and Tim Rice – that have all the glamour of those on its old-time fellows...

Today and Tomorrow

At the turn of 1994 into 1995, Broadway's stages were offering (in order of longevity) *Cats* (1982), *Les Misérables* (1987), *The Phantom of the Opéra* (1988), *Miss Saigon* (1991), *Blood Brothers* (1993), Kander and Ebb's *The Kiss of the Spider Woman* (1993), *Beauty and the Beast* (1994), and the closing weeks of *Passion* (1994), plus the brand new *Sunset Boulevard* (1994) the old-new Gershwin pot-pourri *Crazy for You* (1992), the late-come stage version of the nostalgia-days recording *Tommy* (1993), and revivals of *Guys and Dolls*, *Damn Yankees*, *Grease*, *Show Boat*, and (but not for long) *Carousel*, scheduled soon to be replaced by *How to Succeed in Business Without Really Trying*.

London played host to *Cats* (1980), *Starlight Express* (1984), *Les Misérables* (1985), *The Phantom of the Opéra* (1986), *Blood Brothers* (1988), *Sunset Boulevard* (1993), the critically crucified but Barry Manilow-penned *Copacabana* (1994), a futureless Japanese vanity production about Hiroshima, *Out of the Blue* (1994), and the umpteenth unsuccessful attempt to be the first-ever off-Broadway show to make money in the West End, *Once on This Island* (1994), as well as a reproduction of *Crazy for You*, several not-really-a-musical shows based on nostalgia-period pop singers, and revivals of *Grease*, *She Loves Me* and a desemitized *Oliver!*.

The mixture was a pretty alluring one – a healthy mélange of the still fairly new to brand new and more than a few fine examples of the old, even if some of those old have – in a worrying whiff of the Hitler years – been politically corrected for their nowadays reappearance. For someone coming to the theatre anew, it was a glorious pageant of musical theatre for the discovering. For those of us who had been around a while, it was mostly a case of repeated pleasures, old and new. But, then, humankind has never been too chary about repeating what it finds pleasant.

Further afield, Australia (though producing virtually nothing original) is confirming itself as the number three bastion of the English-language musical theatre, with productions of the most popular shows of now and then that are every bit as glamorous as those of London and Broadway. Austria and Hungary survive happily on a mixture of translated musicals and a selection of the best from their own tradition, Japan has arrived as an enthusiastic host to modern musicals, whilst Germany has taken a madly-in-love tumble for the shows of Broadway and Britain but is also showing as much enterprise as any other country in the production of new musicals. When they stop being just German imitations of English-language shows and start looking forward rather than back, these German productions may at last result in that country's first contribution to the international musical scene since *Im weissen Rössl*.

That scene seems, for the moment, to be thriving, and it appears that the theatregoers of the foreseeable future won't lack for musical-theatre entertainment, even if some of us more ageing types keep on complaining that musicals these days aren't what they were when we first discovered them. Of course they aren't, and neither should they be. If they were, why, we'd still be listening to pasticcio shows like the ones they turned out in the eighteenth century. Anyway, people have been saying that the musical theatre isn't what it was, and going into press-paragraphs of breathless print predicting its imminent death, at regular intervals since about 1850. And not only is the musical theatre thoroughly alive, a century and a half down the track, but it's attracting more public, all round the world, than ever it did, in spite of conflicting attractions that the musicalwrights of the eighteenth century didn't have to put up with.

So, please Mr Producer, keep those new musicals coming. Because there are lots and lots of us out here waiting for the newest offerings that you've got for us. It doesn't matter what kind they are – romantic, dramatic, funny, big, medium-sized or small (though me, personally, I'd swap all the hydraulics and helicopters in the world for a lively bit of wit and a good, singable tune) – there are some of us out here for every size, shape and style of show you can throw at us. Just good musicals, and lots of them. Lots. Because, otherwise, what are we supposed to do on the other nights of the year?

Around the World

This book has skated through the history of what might be called the mainstream of musical theatre in the Western world. But that doesn't mean to say that the mainstream is the only stream there is. Far from it. In the past century and a half there have been fine musical shows of all kinds produced from New Zealand to Russia, and in a good few other more or less likely countries in between. And some countries have had, for a time, a thriving musical-theatre tradition of their own.

THE ZARZUELA

The most thriving of all was the zarzuela tradition of Spain. During the second half of the nineteenth century and the earliest decades of the twentieth, Spanish theatres overflowed with their own particular kind of musical play: both the little zarzuela "genero chico" and the full-length "genero grande". Some of these latter, in particular, copied the styles and fashions of the French and Italian theatre, but many of the best and most attractive zarzuelas were those that took a small slice of Spanish life as their topic, and decorated it with a small score full of lushly Hispanic music. The subjects and stories might be slight, the songs sometimes incidental to such plot as there was, but the little zarzuela, with its real, unstagey story of life and love in the Madrid or Barcelona suburbs and its score of warm, popular melodies, was one of the most satisfying forms of all musical theatre. It was a form, however, that never succeeded in establishing itself outside Spanish-speaking areas, and the zarzuela and its music remain little known further afield.

Molinos de Viento: Pablo Luna's little 1910 zarzuela was a successful example of an early twentieth-century Spanish musical.

OPERETTA

Italy, too, has produced musical plays regularly over something like a century, although much of the time in styles that simply copied those that were coming from other countries. In the years during and after the war, composers such as Mario Costa, Virgilio Ranzato and Giuseppe Pietri produced some delightful theatre music – though often to libretti that were too copy-catted to be really interesting – and in more recent generations the writing-producing team of Giovannini and Garinei turned out a regular stream of variegated musical entertainments, but Italy has never managed yet to send out a musical to capture the imagination of the rest of the musical-theatre world.

IRON-CURTAINED MUSICALS

Russia has long had a tradition of welcoming all that was good in musical theatre, right back from the days when the top French opéra-bouffe stars and performers such as Britain's Lydia Thompson headed north for the vast wages and wild appreciation they

quit their native land for other parts of Europe or for America seem to have succeeded in the musical theatre.

Once Russia fell under communist rule, music and theatre became subject to the dictates of the state, and the country's acknowledged top musical theatre composer, Isaak Osipovitch Dunajevskij, musical director of the Moscow Railway's Central Cultural Establishment Song and Dance Ensemble, saw several of his pieces – and notably the 1949 *Vol'nyj veter* – become revivable favourites.

The rest of the communist bloc was favoured with the often politico-didactic musicals that Dunajevskij and his colleagues composed (and composed with a thoroughly Continental romanticism that hinted nothing of railways or politics), and other nations were encouraged to follow this example. Even Hungary, the birthplace of so many of the world's finest musical theatre writers and shows, succumbed to heroes in politically correct uniforms with politically correct thoughts and utterances to deliver.

could gather in the rich royal city of St Petersburg. But if the country welcomed the outstanding works of foreign musicians, its own didn't ever manage – and not for want of trying – to produce anything of a similar quality themselves. Only those Russians who

Left: *La Scugnizza:* A 1922 musical that had rich Americans-in-Italy as its central characters, and the shimmy and the foxtrot in its score.

Below left: *Aranycsillag:* The 'silver star' of the title wasn't one to make love under; it was a military decoration.

Below: *Szabad szél:* A Hungarian edition of the music from Russia's *Vol'nyj veter*.

Index

Page references in italic type indicate illustrations, those in bold type featured shows